THE ORIGINS OF THE

FRENCH LABOR MOVEMENT

The Origins of the French Labor Movement 1830–1914

The Socialism of Skilled Workers

Bernard H. Moss

UNIVERSITY OF CALIFORNIA PRESS
Berkeley, Los Angeles, London

University of California Press
Berkeley and Los Angeles, California
University of California Press, Ltd.
London, England
ISBN: 0-520-02982-8
Library of Congress Catalog Card Number: 75-3775
Copyright © 1976 by The Regents of the University of California
Printed in the United States of America

TO THE WORKERS AND STUDENTS OF MAY-JUNE 1968

Contents

Preface

It is a measure of the progress made by social history in recent years that one must be a revisionist to argue the case for institutional history. This is even true for one form of institutional history that was a forerunner of social history, namely labor and socialist history. A new type of social historian has arisen who believes that labor history, the study of organized workers' movements, has exhausted itself and its usefulness, that there is no more work to be done. We are advised to bypass the study of trade unions, socialist parties and ideology, the institutional, political and intellectual history of the working class, in order to discover its real movement at the grassroots, especially as manifested in such direct protest as strikes, riots, and revolts.

Direct action may speak volumes about immediate needs and motivations, but it is usually mute about those social values, strategies, and objectives that as ideology determine the long-term direction and ultimate purpose of the labor movement. Radical historians in quest of a spontaneously revolutionary working class and liberals invested in the myth of a naturally reformist one make curious allies in a common assault against a classic tradition that sees the working class, an economic category, becoming a real historical agent, a conscious class, and hence a subject in history, only through its associational life, only through organization and ideology.

This study seeks to rehabilitate ideology both as a vital force in history and as a serious subject for historical inquiry. Reflecting the general belief in the decline of ideology, Western social scientists have generally downplayed the role of ideology, even in nominally socialist movements. For many years the only alternative to a narrowly pragmatic view of socialism was an equally confining schematic Marxism. Only recently have social scientists rediscovered the importance of ideology and begun to approach it in an open and scientific manner. By reviving the prospects for socialism in an advanced capitalist country, the May-June 1968 Events in France played not a small part in this rediscovery.

To study socialist ideology, one must return to the formal labor movement, those associations where workers come together to determine and pursue common goals. One must return not to repeat past efforts, which were often narrowly institutional and blindly partisan, but to enrich a theoretical perspective that relates ideology and organization to their material and social basis in the mode of production and the working class. The original purpose of social history, at least as set out by the founders of the *Annales,* was not to create a separate and distinct field of inquiry, but to expand the parameters of human history, of history *tout court.* One can no more write a social history of the working class without considering formal labor history than one can write labor history without treating the working class. Political and social history, labor and working class history, in other words, constitute an interrelated whole.

The precise relationship between labor and working class history, particularly between socialist ideology and the working class, is a subtle and complex matter. Ideology does not, as some suppose, arise spontaneously out of the working class, work structures, or economic crises, nor is it merely a direct reflection of them. While there is a long-term structural correspondence between the working class and the socialist ideology it sustains, socialism has its own relatively autonomous internal history to which individual leaders, theories, political institutions, and accidents also contribute. Between class and ideology lie mediating political and cultural structures, intervening variables that may distort the connection between them. France has been a model for the theorist precisely because of the transparency of the connections that can be drawn among class, politics, and ideology in its history. Because French socialism arose directly out of trade organization without the notable intervention of Marxist theoreticians, its federalist structure closely mirrored its social basis among skilled workers.

The underlying ideology of a movement, its core utopia or social vision, may not always correspond exactly with the articulated program or theory of its leaders. In practice the labor movement may reveal tendencies that contradict the official rhetoric of its leaders. The core ideology that united several generations of French socialists was not identical with the program of any one organization or leader. Hence, the historian must always study formal ideology in relation to actual social organization and practice in order to discover underlying structure and purpose.

The French labor movement has never lacked historians, but few went beyond a chronicle of unions, strikes, congresses, and leaders to undertake unifying interpretation and analysis (see Bibliographical Essay). When programs were discussed, historians highlighted republicanism, trade unionism, cooperation, or Proudhonism, and later, anarchism, syndicalism, and diverse forms of socialism without investigating the relationship among these trends and their meaning for organized workers. As a result, labor ideology appeared either hopelessly vague and confused or excessively varied and contradictory. Missing was a concrete analysis of ideology in its historical connection and context, what Marx called the "real movement" of the working class. With such an analysis it was possible to discover a core ideology underlying the many changes and variations in French socialism.

To define this core ideology it was necessary to cut through conventional distinctions between socialism and anarchism and derive an intermediary form, a federalist or trade socialism. As originally manifested in the trade movement for producers' associations or cooperation, this socialism eventually led to the adoption of a revolutionary socialism that in various guises preserved the federalist basis of its origins. Its social base was neither the traditional artisan nor the factory proletarian, but the skilled worker, an intermediary type, who combined a professional trade and working class consciousness. By relating forms of federalist and centralist socialism to their social bases in skilled and industrial workers, this study suggests a broader historical sociology of labor movements.

I wish to express my gratitude to Professor Edward Fox of Cornell University, who first inspired me in the study of French history and taught me the importance of the *longue durée,* to Professor Shepherd Clough of Columbia University, who granted me liberty to pursue a rather diffuse and ambitious project, and to Professor Robert Paxton, also of Columbia, who helped me hammer it into the form of a dissertation. I would also like to thank Collette Chambelland of the Musée Social, Jean Maitron of the Centre d'Histoire du Syndicalisme, Michelle Perrot of the University of Paris, and Hélène Tulard of the Archives de la Préfecture de Police de Paris for their bibliographical assistance. This reappraisal owes a great debt to the work of Rémi Gossez and Jacques Rougerie, who do not always share my conclusions. Among the many persons who generously offered advice and encouragement were Isser Woloch, Lloyd Moote, Richard Rioux, William Weinstein, and Brian Peterson. Special mention must also go to my father, Morris, and wife, Neysa, who also aided in research.

Like all good history, labor history requires a large expenditure of time and money. The initial research for this book was made possible by an eighteen-month grant from the Foreign Area Fellowship Program of the American Council of Learned Societies and Social Science Research Council. The Penrose Fund of the American Philosophical Society and Liberal Arts College of the University of Southern California provided research grants at a later stage.

Echo Park, Los Angeles, California   B. H. M.

1

Introduction

As a sociology, Marxism posits a logical relationship between class and ideology defined in broad historical terms. Because of its separation from ownership of the means of production, the working class is considered to have a propensity for a socialist ideology aiming at social ownership of those means. In contrast, empirical sociology has explored more narrow correlations between social strata and social attitudes or ideologies. Industrial sociology in particular has drawn correlations between various types of workers, defined largely in terms of technology, and their social consciousness or ideology.[1] If sociologists have virtually ignored the historical dimension of class, understood as a property relationship, Marxists for their part have rarely considered sociological differences that may exist within the working class.[2]

The Marxist definition of class contains enough ambiguity to enliven controversy over which sectors of the work force actually belong to the working class. Historically, Marxists have included all production workers in industry and transport, but especially those engaged in large-scale factory production characterized by the extensive use of machinery, division of labor, military discipline, and destruction of skill. The problem with the *Manifesto's* definition of a "modern

1

working class" is that it excludes the majority of workers in the nineteenth century, the real objects of Marx's work and action. This proletariat was composed for the most part of highly skilled workers in small-scale or semiartisanal production where there was little machinery, division of labor, or factory discipline.

Marx and Engels made occasional references to the artisanal character of workers to explain workers' resistance to "scientific socialism," but nowhere did they provide a coherent sociological explanation for this phenomenon.[3] When Marx encountered widespread opposition to his leadership in the First International in the 1860s, he attributed it to the machinations of Bakunin and other sectarians rather than to any sociological determinism. Later Marxists, notably the French leaders Jules Guesde and Paul Lafargue, did observe a connection between what they called "anarchism" and an undeveloped artisanal working class, but they never treated this movement as either truly proletarian or as a particular form of socialism.

The understanding of any fluid social movement requires careful attention to the categories of analysis, especially where, as in the case of labor and socialist movements, the subject tends to generate its own ideological field of categories. In the case of the French labor movement, the conventional distinctions between anarchism and socialism and between artisans and proletarians appeared inadequate to capture the essence of an ideology and social stratum that was intermediate to these categories. Neither traditional artisans nor industrial workers, workers in the labor movement were skilled craftsmen undergoing a process of proletarianization; they displayed characteristics of both artisans and industrial workers, both a professional trade and a proletarian class consciousness.

Through most of the century, these workers were cooperative socialists within the framework of a democratic republican movement. Breaking out of these confines, they later turned to a revolutionary socialism that was neither anarchist nor Marxist, but an intermediary form of trade socialism. Thus, this inquiry into the French labor movement suggested the need for a new set of sociological and ideological categories to understand a general trend in the nineteenth century labor movement and working class—the trade socialism of skilled workers.

During the century, French labor exhibited a variety of ideological trends—trade unionism, cooperation, Proudhonism, Bakuninism, possibilism, Allemanism, and revolutionary syndicalism. Out of this apparent diversity, however, it was possible to discern a single underlying ideological objective in two distinct phases. From its origins after 1830 through the 1870s, the main objective of the labor movement was the creation of producers' associations or cooperatives for the emancipation of trades from the wage system, a cooperative trade socialism. Later, abandoning the cooperative strategy, labor adopted a revolutionary trade socialism that in successive forms of Bakuninism, possibilism, Allemanism, and revolutionary syndicalism aimed at the emancipation of trades through a workers' revolution. In both phases the ultimate goal was a federalist trade socialism in which the means of production would be owned collectively within the framework of a federation of skilled trades.

The original form of trade socialism revolved around the producers' association or cooperative, a social workshop owned and controlled by members of a trade. Arising along with the trade union in many industrializing nations, the producers' association became the main project and goal of the French labor movement. Writing from twentieth century perspectives, historians have failed to see the central importance of producers' associations in the nineteenth century (see Bibliographical Essay). Cooperative historians tended to favor consumer cooperation with its limited objectives and practical outlook to producers' cooperation with its vaster utopian ambition. Labor historians generally believed that producers' cooperation was tangential to the workers' struggle for higher wages and immediate reforms. Republican historians treated it as part of a mild reformist program that would leave the capitalist system intact under a republic. Following Marx, socialist writers condemned it as a utopian and petty bourgeois movement that would only elevate a working class elite to middle class status and divert workers from their revolutionary task. Reflecting ideological differences in the twentieth century, republican, labor, socialist, and cooperative historians forgot that these currents had once been joined around a cooperative project for the emancipation of trades from the wage system.

From the beginning the producers' association was part of a larger socialist strategy for the collectivization of industrial capital and the emancipation of trades from the wage system. Mechanisms were developed to prevent the formation of an emancipated elite in one trade or among the collective trades. Associations were originally designed with expanding funds of collective capital to insure the continual admission of new members without capital and emancipate the entire trade. To give associations an advantage in competition with larger capitalist enterprise, workers looked to the establishment of a democratic and social republic, which would provide leverage in the form of public credit and contracts. Representing the interests of the industrious classes—workers, peasants, and tradesmen—against the privileged bourgeoisie, the republic was expected to supply the credit that was restricted under a regime of privilege. Even without the help of the state, workers could begin to finance themselves by organizing mutual credit and exchange in a federation of trades or universal association. With the help of a social republic and universal association, workers could accumulate capital, outcompete capitalist enterprise, and lay the foundations of a socialist economy administered by a federation of trades.

This cooperative program had its first test in 1848 with the rise to power of social republicans committed to it. The defeat of the social republic did not prevent the emergence of a widespread association movement, the formation of 300 associations from 120 Parisian trades, another 800 in the provinces, and several universal associations of all trades. Napoléon's coup d'état destroyed the movement, which remained moribund during the 1850s. With the liberalization of the Empire in the 1860s came a revival of trade union, association, and republican movements and a return to the cooperative program for socialism with one minor difference. Rather than seeking help from the authoritarian centralized state, workers now looked toward a decentralized communalist republic to serve as the lever of emancipation. As a radically democratic government with a working class constituency, the Paris Commune seemed to offer the ideal political framework for the cooperative program. During its brief existence, the Commune initiated a significant program of assistance, including public credits, contracts, and the expropriation of abandoned workshops for associations. With the advent of the Third Republic in 1879, the government revived the movement with political patronage, legal dispensations, and public contracts.

Thus, the extension of the movement always depended upon the nature of the political regime. Severely restricted under the July Monarchy and Second Empire, the movement was only able to develop during periods of revolutionary mobilization, notably the Second Republic and Paris Commune. Politically, it relied upon the strength and cohesion of republican socialism. In class terms, its success depended upon the mobilization of the working class and its alliance with the petty bourgeoisie and peasants against the bourgeoisie. Even after the Commune, organized workers continued to place their hopes in a democratic and social republic that would emancipate trades from the wage system. When after 1879 the new republic turned out to be neither social nor fully democratic, when it failed to meet the revolutionary conditions of 1848 and 1871, labor militants were compelled to revise their cooperative strategy and replace it with revolutionary socialism.

Workers who had believed that associations could collectivize capital gradually and peacefully within the confines of a middle class republic now asserted that collectivization could only come about through a workers' revolution overthrowing the bourgeois state. This revolutionary socialism or collectivism had first appeared in 1869 among the French leaders of the International, Eugène Varlin, Benoît Malon, and Albert Richard. Influenced by Bakunin, these leaders advocated a workers' revolution to achieve collectivization within a federation of trades and workers' communes, a goal shared by the majority of French cooperative delegates to the International congress of 1869.

It was this revolutionary collectivism, a federalist or trade socialism rather than Marxism, that Guesde reintroduced to Parisian workers after the Commune and that triumphed over cooperation at the third national labor congress of 1879 and in the newly formed Parti Ouvrier. Though this possibilist party engaged in electoral activity, it always insisted on the need for revolutionary action to achieve a socialist economy administered by a federation of trades. When the majority of rank and file or Allemanist militants ousted the electoralist leadership in 1890, they stressed the trade union or *syndicat* and the tactic of the general strike as the instrumentalities of socialism. As a synthesis of several trends within the trade unions, revolutionary syndicalism was essentially a restatement of this trade socialism whereby the trade union would, in the words of the Charter of Amiens, be transformed "from an instrument of resistance into the unit of production and distribution of the future, the basis of social reorganization."

While this federalist socialism was not Marxist, neither was it Proudhonian. During the height of revolutionary syndicalism, a circle of French intellectuals, in opposition to Germanic Marxism, sought to define the French socialist tradition as Proudhonian.[4] While they found no historical filiation between Proudhonism and syndicalism, they established the myth of a Proudhonian labor movement, shared by liberal and Marxist historians alike, which has never been confirmed by historical investigation. In only one period, the early 1860s, did Proudhonism have a definite impact upon labor militants, but this was in the early stages of a movement that soon violated its precepts in theory and practice. The goal of trade socialism, the collective ownership of industry by trade federations, was incompatible with Proudhon's anarchism of small independent producers. If one is to attach trade socialism to the anarchist tradition, then it is surely closer to the "collectivist" anarchism of Bakunin than to the individualistic anarchism of Proudhon.[5]

Proudhonism is notoriously difficult to assess due to its unsystematic, shifting, and essentially contradictory character (see Bibliographical Essay). If Proudhon excoriated capitalist exploitation, particularly in its financial form, he was equally vehement in his denunciation of a collectivist socialism that violated the essential independence and freedom of the individual. With his philosophy of mutualism he sought to find a social equilibrium that respected both individual liberty and equality. Disappointing the faith he placed in the working class, the labor movement consistently disregarded his caveats against strikes, political action, and collective association as coercive means that violated individual liberty.

While echoing the slogans of mutual credit and association, Proudhon always resisted the collectivist tendency of the actual association movement. Whereas he intended his Bank of the People founded in 1848 to be primarily a commercial bank, stimulating exchange among petty producers, labor delegates wished to transform it into an investment bank for the organization of production and consumption around association monopolies in each trade. Although Proudhon later made allowance for very limited associations—voluntary, contractual, competitive, and individualistic—in large industries, he remained unalterably opposed to the principle of association, especially in those semiartisanal trades from which the movement actually sprang.[6] Since Proudhon rejected the cooperative association movement in his own time, he would doubtless have combatted revolutionary syndicalism, which proposed the use of the most coercive revolutionary means to achieve trade association.

The French labor movement arose not among factory workers, the unique product of the industrial revolution, but among skilled craftsmen engaged as wage earners in small-scale capitalist production. Struck with the novelty of factory workers, social observers have neglected an equally important change that occurred during industrialization, the formation of a skilled proletariat. Commonly known as artisans, these skilled wage earners not only outnumbered factory workers, but remained the primary source of capital accumulation through most of the century.[7] Besides creating factory workers, industrialization also multiplied the number of skilled workers needed to supply expanding markets with consumer and luxury goods, to provide housing and public facilities in expanding cities, and to outfit and maintain the new industrial machinery. In fact, the relative concentration of French industry did not really begin until 1900. Since industrial growth was rather slow and regular—about 2 percent annually[8]—it long preserved important enclaves of semiartisanal production. The skilled workers of this sector constituted the active proletariat of the nineteenth century.

As a movement of skilled workers, the labor movement was a distinctly urban phenomenon. Workers of a hundred trades and crafts were integral parts of the preindustrial city with its large consumer and luxury markets. While construction and metal workers continued the itinerant tradition of the tramping artisan, most craftsmen appear to have found more or less permanent settlement in the second half of the century.[9] Migrant workers may have contributed to labor violence and the spread of socialist ideas, but most permanent organization, particularly political organization, generally arose among workers who had developed a network of relationships and a stake in an urban community.[10] The typical leader of the Parti Ouvrier was born in the provinces and had been active for more than twenty years in the

Parisian labor movement.[11] When militants returned to the provinces, they carried with them socialist ideas they had acquired in urban centers.

With its strategic centers in Paris (1.8 million population),[12] Lyons (323,954), and Marseilles (300,131), the labor movement had regional centers in Bordeaux (191,241), Lille (154,749), Toulouse (126,936), Nantes (111,956), Rouen (100,671), and Saint-Etienne (96,620), with minor outposts in smaller cities—Reims, Montpellier, Limoges, Rennes, Besançon, Tours, Grenoble, Dijon, Troyes, Béziers, Angoulême, Cette, and so on. Because of its link with the preindustrial city, especially the capital, the labor movement occupied a strategic position in French politics, out of proportion to its numerical importance, that was manifested in the revolutions of 1830, 1848, and 1871. Reflecting this link also, it was inseparable from the communalist movement, the movement for municipal power and autonomy, that exploded in 1871.

Composed almost exclusively of urban skilled workers, the organized labor movement did not originally represent workers who were not male, urban, and skilled; female workers; semiskilled aids and day laborers; factory, mining, and railroad workers; rural agricultural and village workers with roots in the peasantry; workers in isolated company towns; and unskilled workers from the industrial region of the North.[13] Even within Paris, workers from the relatively small number of industrial plants and factories—sugar refineries, distilleries, wallpaper factories, railroad shops, shipbuilding, glass and pottery, textile, rubber and electrical factories[14]—were absent from the organized movement. Only toward the end of the century would some of these categories organize, usually with the help of skilled workers.

As in other aspects of French life, Paris was the guiding center of this movement. Nineteenth century Paris was not only a capital of sybaritic pleasure and refined taste, of theaters, operas, balls, and elegant restaurants but—it is often forgotten—a major workshop of the world with some

400,000 workers engaged in small-scale manufacture. Not only was the Parisian movement larger and better organized than that in other cities, but, because of its strategic political position, it was able to exercise a commanding moral influence over labor organization in the rest of France. Lyons, Marseilles, and other cities had their regional variations, but the general ideological orientation was set in Paris. With its skilled workers assuming the role of the *sans culottes,* Paris continued to be the revolutionary capital of the world through most of the nineteenth century.

While the factory system took root in outlying areas, Paris remained a major center for quality manufacture, famous for the artistic taste and ingenious invention of its craftsmen. In the face of industrial competition most crafts survived with little technical change. Greatly demanded in an expanding and modernizing city, the construction trades were barely affected by mechanization. Threatened by patterns of mass consumption, the luxury trades—articles of Paris, jewelry, gloves, haute couture, bronze, saddlery, and musical instruments—were still highly prized in world markets. The traditional locksmith found new applications for his hand-craft in the outfitting and maintenance of machinery. Joining the small mechanics' shop of Popincourt with the locomotive factory of Cail, the Parisian mechanic was a vital link between the old craft and modern industry.[15]

In the course of the century, Paris in fact witnessed a relative decentralization of industry as larger textile, chemical, and leather factories relocated in cheaper suburbs and provinces. New techniques and inventions created by Parisian craftsmen were often applied in the provinces where labor, rent, and raw material costs were much lower. As the relative importance of manufacture declined through the century, so did the scale of industry with the loss of large factories and slight increase in the number of independent artisans. In terms of industries there was a virtual disappearance of textiles, relative decline of needle and luxury trades, and growth of metal and construction trades needed to outfit industry and modernize the city.[16]

Trades active in the labor movement were broadly representative of the Parisian working class with greatest participation among those with high rates of literacy and permanent residence in Paris. The largest trades in the Société des Droits de l'Homme, the republican society in which the cooperative program was born, were tailors, jewelers, painters, articles of Paris, shoemakers, and joiners with the largest proportions relative to population among the luxury trades.[17] Under the Second Republic, the trades that participated in the association movement came from all industrial groups except primary metallurgy and chemicals. In relation to other trades, they were close to the average with respect to daily wages, size of enterprise, number of apprentices, and rate of unemployment, but superior with respect to literacy and permanent residence in Paris.[18] The workers who joined Proudhon's bank were also representative—tailors, shoemakers, joiners, typographers, mechanics, cabinetmakers, painters, locksmiths, and carpenters in that order.[19]

The shift from cooperation to revolutionary socialism did not entail any perceptible change in social base. Those trades that affiliated with the International in 1869 were broadly representative of the Parisian working class[20] as were those that joined the Parti Ouvrier in the 1880s—mechanics, tailors, bronze workers, cabinetmakers, jewelers, shoemakers, tinsmiths, piano-makers, painters, and so forth. In the early 1880s more than half of 200 Parisian *syndicats* attended party congresses with nearly a third, generally the largest, becoming active members.[21] During the syndicalist period, nearly all Parisian trades participated in the *bourse du travail*, the municipal hiring hall that was the center of revolutionary activity.[22] The largest trade groups in this period were the construction and metal trades, reflecting their growing importance in the work force.

Several historians have noted the disproportionately large

numbers of metal and construction workers in the revolutionary crowds of 1830, 1848, and 1871, leading them to
distinguish between these radical proletarians and the more
moderate workers of the traditional crafts.[23] The scale of the
construction and metal industries tended to be larger than
that of the luxury, leather, and needle trades, and the metal
industry was the most mechanized. The distinction between
them, however, contains only limited validity. Most Parisian
trades, whether traditional or new, were extremely heterogeneous in structure, containing both small artisanal and
larger factory units. As for the greater propensity of the more
modern workers for violence, this may be more reflective of
their marginality as recent migrants from the provinces rather
than of any greater ideological commitment. In any case,
most of these workers were still semiartisanal in character
and the more traditional types were not absent from their
demonstrations. Organizational activity is a better index of
ideological commitment. In respect to unionization and
political activity, the older trades remained as committed as
the newer ones. While one can perhaps contrast the relative
radicalism of the mechanics, who were the first to adopt
revolutionary socialism, with the moderation of luxury
workers, who were the last, one is struck overall by the
ideological unity of the trades in their passage from cooperative to revolutionary socialism.

Within recent years, questions have arisen regarding the
representativity of formal labor organization and ideology.[24]
The activists in any movement are almost always a minority.
In France labor militants saw themselves quite consciously as
"active minorities" dedicated to the emancipation of all
workers. In fact, as the democratically elected leaders of
unions, which on the average comprised a tenth of the trade,
these militants were no less representative than those of more
moderate British unions. Organizational rates ranged from 40
percent for some luxury trades—bronze, marble, typographical, and musical instrument workers—to less than 10 percent
for tailors, shoemakers, and most construction trades.[25]
Moreover, during periods of mass mobilization—strikes, pro-

fessional elections, and revolutionary situations—the militants became the spokesmen for the majority of skilled workers, including many of the normally unorganized—the apathetic, resigned, fearful, or conservative. Insofar as the socialist labor movement was the only organized and independent expression of the working class, it must be considered as its authentic representative.

These skilled workers have traditionally been characterized as artisans, but this term is vague and misleading in several respects.[26] First, by placing independent artisans, master artisans and skilled wage earners on the same footing, it obscures the class distinction based on the ownership of capital. As applied to the wage earners, the term "artisan" belies their working class status, suggesting that they were incapable of achieving a working class or socialist consciousness. Finally, to place the skilled workers of 1848 and 1871 in the same category as the artisanal workers of 1792 is to overlook the entire process of industrialization, which transformed them into a suffering working class.

Industrialization encompassed more than the introduction of machinery and the factory system. It was a total process involving a series of changes connected by the economic logic of productivity and profit. The impoverishment of the small peasant; rural migration; influx of female and child labor; increased division, speed, and intensity of labor; the growth of mass consumption; and international competition were other aspects of this process. Only exceptionally were traditional crafts completely destroyed by mechanization and the factory system.[27] Rather, they underwent a gradual and partial transformation, which eroded the traditional income, security, and status of skilled craftsmen.

Without destroying the crafts, industrialization threatened them with unemployment, division, speed and intensity of labor, and economic decline at least relative to expanding wealth. The gradual introduction of universal power machines—mechanical presses and saws after 1830, sewing machines after 1860, turret lathes, planing, boring, and milling machines after 1870[28]—downgraded skilled craftsmen. But even without mechanization they encountered competition from rural and foreign migrants as well as lesser skilled and unapprenticed labor, especially women and children, producing cheaper and ready-made goods in domestic piece-work, sweated workshops, subcontracted gangs, prisons, and convents. With the growth of mass consumption, the substitution of standardized merchandise, such as ready-made clothing, for custom-made goods further cheapened the trades. Internationally, competition came from both more industrial nations like Britain and areas of cheaper labor like Germany.[29]

Growing commercial and labor competition caused unemployment, stagnating wages, and intensified labor in most crafts. In addition to cyclical depressions that could idle over half of each trade, workers had to expect long slack seasons of from three to five months, whether due to seasonal demand, as in the needle and luxury trades, or climatic conditions, as in construction, which reduced the annual earnings of even elite workers to a bare minimum.[30] Despite their craft status, skilled workers experienced industrialization as a deterioration, as a transitional process of proletarianization that tended to unite them with new elements of the working class.

Parisian workers appear to have suffered the initial phase of industrialization more drastically and to have derived fewer benefits from later prosperity than their English counterparts.[31] Reaching a rather high plateau under the Empire and early Restoration, they began their relative decline with the onset of industrialization. From 1830 to 1848, a period of industrial growth that enriched the capitalist masters, most trades confronted stagnating wages, declining piece-rates, increased division, speed and intensity of labor, and recurring crises of unemployment. While industrial prices fell, food and rent did not; per capita consumption of wine and meat declined. Parisian workers experienced a real deterioration of living standards in the first half of the century.[32]

The second half was a secular period of improvement with nominal wages doubling in most trades by 1910.[33] But this slow and uneven advance, differing in timing with each trade, was partially offset by the rise of food prices, especially under the Second Empire, and by continuing crises of unemployment. Labor militants evaluated this slight improvement as a real decline. During the depression of the mid-1880s, a majority of trades reported an increase in mechanization, division, speed and intensity of labor, loss of employment, and decline of piece-rates and real wages since the Second Empire.[34] In any case, the small rise in real wages was quickly absorbed by more diversified food consumption, basically of meat and wine, which reached its height in 1880, by higher rents and perhaps such extras as Sunday clothes, family outings, and dowries. At the end of the period, workers still spent more than half their income for food, nearly a quarter for rent, leaving little more than a quarter for clothes, heating, lighting, and other expenses.[35] Despite the rise of real wages, workers usually lacked a surplus for saving in a society that made no provision for the eventualities of unemployment, sickness, disability, or old age.

During the century, the absence of as great wage differentials as apparently existed in Britain militated against the growth of a labor aristocracy interested only in reforms.[36] French economic growth was neither dynamic enough to raise demanded trades into a labor aristocracy nor catastrophic enough to ruin declining ones, but it was regular enough to maintain steady pressure on the economic position of most trades and to form a more homogeneous skilled proletariat.[37] In 1848, 80 percent of Parisian workers earned between three and five francs daily, only 5 percent earned more than five and 14 percent less than three.[38] Only a few trades had a larger elite—piano-makers, engravers, hatters, jewelers, and mechanics—though several trades had a much larger group of depressed workers—embroiderers, buttonmakers, shoemakers, masons, and lace-makers. In 1872, 78 percent earned between five and seven francs, half between five and six, 11 percent less than five and 10 percent more than seven.[39] The best paid workers were in the luxury crafts, jewelry, furniture, and precision instruments, while the lowest were in construction and industrial manufacture—textiles, chemicals, railroads, and food processing—and among women, who earned half as much as male workers. Even these differences tended to level out on an annual basis due to the long slack seasons found among luxury workers. The absence of wide wage differentials may have contributed to the proletarian consciousness of skilled workers.

Another factor that strengthened this consciousness was the working class quarter and city. Despite the identification of some trades with particular quarters—the cabinetmakers of the Faubourg-Saint-Antoine, jewelers of the rue de Temple, bookbinders of Saint-Germain, mechanics of Popincourt, and so on—most trades were distributed rather evenly through the working class quarters, which were all but the central and western *arrondissements.* The only exception was heavy industry, restricted to the periphery, the near suburbs annexed in 1860 and the northern suburbs. Leather and chemical plants had been excluded from the central city because of their dirt and noxious odors. Metallurgical factories sprang up around the railroad depots, leather and slaughter houses around the port of La Villette, but these factories were still integrated into the semiartisanal Parisian workshop and consumer economy. Only the textile, metallurgical, and chemical plants in the suburbs were really part of a national industrial economy.[40]

The working class quarter facilitated the communication of socialist ideas in time and space. There were geographical centers of labor activism. The headquarters, cafés, meeting halls and residences of labor militants were mostly located in the northeast quadrant, particularly where residence is concerned in the area where the 10th, 11th, 19th and 20th *arrondissements* meet.[41] The 10th and 11th nurtured the revolutionary tradition of the faubourgs Saint-Denis, Saint-Martin, Temple, and Saint-Antoine; the 19th and 20th had the highest percentages of workers in Paris, 74 and 75 percent, respectively.[42] In this area the worker lived geographically between the artisanal past of the center and the industrial future of the periphery. Whatever the nature of his work or workplace, the Parisian quarter tended to mold a distinctive working class mentality.[43]

Paradoxically, the proximity to bourgeois quarters, typical of a metropolitan area, may also have strengthened class consciousness. Having once lived among employers, merchants, and tradesmen in the central city, Parisian workers were thrust into the manufacturing quarters of the northeast while their erstwhile neighbors found spacious dwellings in the west. Social proximity to this other Paris raised the general level of culture and material expectations as well as the relative sense of deprivation. Living close to an industrious middle class and within view of a sybaritic bourgeoisie, the worker was constantly confronted with the evidence of his inferiority, both economic and cultural. In a society that placed great value on upbringing, dress, manners, and literary culture, even the elite worker might have difficulty passing the class barrier.[44] With money to spend, he might prefer the fellowship, informality, and swaggering humor of the *"assommoir"* to the constraint of a bourgeois café. Intermarriage between workers and tradespeople was rare.[45] Because of these cultural barriers many elite workers might have well become leaders of their class rather than parvenus in the strange world of the middle class.

Yet, despite these economic and social changes, industrialization never altered the semiartisanal mode of Parisian production or the skilled character of its working class. Mention has already been made of the progressive decentralization of Parisian industry. By 1848, the vast majority of Parisian workers were employed in small and medium-size shops with less than ten and twenty-five employees respectively, and little mechanization. The overall ratio of workers to employers was five to one.[46] The number of large factories with more than a hundred workers and of independent artisans and homeworkers was relatively small. Only 15 percent of all workers were domestic or home workers; only 9 percent were independent artisans. The only trades with a substantial number of independent artisans and homeworkers, more than half of all enterprises, were the shoemakers, tailors, clockmakers, engravers, brush-makers, and articles of Paris. Some of the largest workshops were still in the skilled trades—typographers, construction, and jewelry. Even in the large metallurgical and locomotive factories most work was performed by teams of highly skilled mechanics.[47] A survey in 1864 classified only 5 percent as factory workers.[48] Mechanization was very limited. The average number of steam-driven machines in 1872 was less than one per enterprise, with an average horsepower per machine of eight, appreciably less than that of the suburbs or France as a whole.[49]

Capitalist concentration forged ahead of technical progress. Trades became increasingly dependent upon large capital for its command of raw materials, tools, shops, and markets. Larger workshops in the metal and needle trades required heavy investments in raw materials and equipment. Large capitalists bought up small shops in the same or similar trades, and small shops became auxiliary subcontractors to larger ones, forming vast Parisian manufactories whose divisions consisted of small shops scattered throughout the city.[50] In this process of concentration, workers in small shops often found common cause with their immediate employers or foremen against the larger capitalist contractor or manufacturer. During the first half of the century several strikes and associations were supported by the small masters striving to avoid ruin and absorption by the larger capitalists.

Despite capitalist concentration and relative impoverishment, the Parisian worker did not lose the essential property of his craft acquired through long apprenticeship and experience. As a craftsman, he possessed what sociologists call job autonomy, i.e., control over the process of production and relative freedom from managerial direction of the work place.[51] With this job autonomy, he applied his own personal dexterity and touch to the work, made choices about tools, the sequence and quality of work, and set his own pace and rhythm, fashioning the product as an extension of himself, of his own hand and brain. As a craftsman, he still felt some pride and joy in his work as well as a positive identification with his trade as a status group. Though he may have experienced a sense of economic exploitation, his alienation from the work process was not complete.

Since he still controlled much of the process of production, the skilled worker could readily see himself as the only real producer and his employer as a superfluous parasite, who used his possession of capital to extract the value that the worker produced.[52] Hence, many workers would conclude that they would never obtain the "full product" of their labor until they had come into the collective possession of capital in a trade association. In those trades where skilled labor constituted the major capital and where workers controlled the process of production, they were fully capable of owning and managing their own workshop.[53] As socialists, they were not so much seeking control of the work place, which they still had to some degree, as the end of economic exploitation, the extraction of surplus value by the capitalist. It was precisely because they still possessed some control over the work place that skilled workers felt the capacity to abolish the wage system through their own direct efforts.

This is not to say that workers became socialist spontaneously, but that socialist concepts and projects introduced from the outside appeared to meet their needs and respond to their long-term social situation and interest. Ideology does not arise spontaneously out of a particular work situation or crisis.[54] Nor are the various forms that it takes always to be explained by reference to social or economic processes. Trade socialism provided a solution to the long-term structural crisis of skilled workers rather than to any particular or immediate crisis. While there was correspondence between the long-term social situation of skilled workers and their ideology, this trade socialism went through its own internal development, which had more to do with the political than with the economic or social experience of skilled workers.

Cooperative socialism arose out of the interaction between skilled workers and middle class democrats. It was from the idealistic students of the Société des Droits de l'Homme and other republican societies that workers acquired their egalitarian ethos and socialist concepts, ideological elements that gave purpose and direction to their spontaneous protest and working class consciousness. Through their participation in republican societies and at least three popular revolutions, 1830, 1848, and 1871, they became socialist in their own right. When they switched from a cooperative to a revolutionary socialism, this shift in strategy did not reflect any basic change in economic conditions, the structure of work, or social processes, but responded rather to changes in the political conditions of socialism.

The organizational basis of labor action was the trade society or *syndicat*. Skilled workers first organized their trade on the scale of the city, formulating demands and calling strikes on behalf of the entire local trade. Although a few exceptionally cohesive trades, notably hatters and printers, were from the start able to coordinate their action nationally, most first joined with other local trades for mutual assistance, forming local trade federations that eventually became institutionalized in bourses du travail, municipal hiring halls serving as labor centrals. Generally, such local federations were formed before national trade federations, giving the movement its communalist orientation. Even after the national trade federations were formed in the 1880s and 1890s, the communal bourse continued to serve as the center of labor activity.[55] Based on a traditional trade solidarity, most unions long resisted amalgamation with similar trades to form larger industrial unions or federations.[56]

Like trade unions elsewhere, French *syndicats* defended the immediate material interests of the trade in matters of wages, hours, apprenticeship, and working conditions through the use of strikes and collective bargaining. Even offensive demands for higher wages, lower hours, and the like were presented as measures of resistance in defense of the relative position of the trade in an expanding economy. But political repression and the constant influx of new workers prevented the formation of effective trade unions. Lacking leverage in the labor market, trade societies often appealed to the government to set hours and wages, establish workshops for the unemployed, and prevent the exploitation of labor by employment agencies, subcontractors, prisons, and convents. The failure of effective trade unionism in this period of massive capital accumulation may have advanced the cause of socialism, but it is probably equally true that the belief in socialism distracted workers from building more effective trade unions. Thus, socialism must be seen as both a consequence and a contributing cause of the failure of trade unionism.

After nearly a century of development French unions and trade federations remained remarkably free from central direction and control. Local unions practiced direct democracy, with the frequent rotation and strict accountability of officers and delegates, frequent general assemblies, and the absence of paid officials.[57] Similar democratic procedures were respected in local and trade federations where the important decisions were made by a vote of a federal council and the autonomy of the individual unions was preserved.[58] This practice of direct and federalist democracy was reflected in the design for trade socialism in which the collectivist economy would be managed by local unions and coordinated by local and trade federations.[59]

While trade socialism came to terms with the economic concentration of capital, it never addressed itself to the organizational problems of the emerging industrial system, the technical organization of production in the modern factory and national economy that requires centralized and hierarchical management.[60] The vision of a collectivist society administered democratically by trade federations was essentially the projection of an existing professional situation into a society freed of capitalist and governmental intermediaries. In treating skilled labor as the source of productive value and the organizational basis of society, socialist workers regarded all functions of capitalists and government as parasitic and superfluous, including those functions of planning, direction, and distribution that are essential to any industrial system whether capitalist or socialist.

In the Mannheimian usage, utopia is the social vision of a nonprivileged group that seeks future compensation for its present situation. Marxists distinguish between realistic utopias, which conform to historical trends, and unrealistic ones, which do not. Trade socialism was unrealistic because it ran counter to long-term industrial trends.[61] Rather than a reactionary utopia like Proudhonism, which aimed to restore an economy of petty producers, or a progressive one like Marxism, which anticipates the growth of the industrial system, it was essentially static, seeking the end of human exploitation and the equal distribution of existing wealth, which it deemed sufficient for human happiness.[62] Thus, trade socialism was ultimately utopian because it was the static projection of a superior stratum of the working class whose federalist and professional values were incompatible with the centralist, hierarchical, and technical requirements of the emerging industrial system.

Skilled workers did not suffer the process of industrialization as passive victims but brought to it a set of values and orientations—the autonomy, pride, and solidarity of the trade; organizational experience; and an egalitarian ethos nurtured through popular republicanism—that motivated an active transformative response. Trade socialism arose out of both the worker's strength and weakness, out of his sense of professional value and competence, on the one hand, and his experience of impoverishment and deprivation, on the other, out of his positive professional consciousness and his negative or alienated proletarian consciousness. The skilled worker combined a professional with a proletarian class consciousness.[63] Surviving industrialization with a preindustrial set of values, neither too rich nor too poor, skilled workers could develop a critical awareness of industrial capitalism, distinguishing between its positive and negative features—between potential abundance and actual misery, between the wealth of the few and the deprivation of the many, between the collective form of production and the private mode of appropriation.

This socialism did not arise full-blown from the mind of a bourgeois intellectual, but was primarily the result of workers' organizational experience. Though socialist concepts of class, exploitation, and association were diffused through the republican movement, workers adapted them to suit their situation and experience. Their notions of class did not derive from abstract social theory, but from an empirical generalization of their experience of conflict between workers and employers. For them, the working class was not a unitary theoretical abstraction, but a concrete reality structured and differentiated along trade lines. Similarly, their conception of socialism was not abstract and unitary, but concrete and federalist, a projection of existing workers' organization structured pluralistically along trade lines.

If skilled workers later adopted the fundamental premises of Marxism—labor theory of value, class struggle, even dictatorship of the proletariat—they would resist efforts of Marxist intellectuals to raise their spontaneous "practical socialism" to a level of theory and organization that by anticipating historical development can serve as a guide to labor practice.[64] Because their socialist conceptions were basically empirical, skilled workers could not easily accept a theoretical approach that would allow an enlightened elite to guide a workers' party or rule a workers' state on behalf of the actual working class. Originating in an empirical rather than theoretical approach to social reality, the labor movement of skilled workers remained hostile to the abstract theory, organizational centralism, and authoritarian leadership of Marxism and Social Democracy.

In contrast to the model-type of skilled worker stands that of the unskilled or "semiskilled" factory worker engaged in a fragmented and repetitive task subject to the requirements of an external technical system of labor. In such a technical system as the modern assembly line, the worker loses his job autonomy, his control over the work place and process of production, and becomes a creature of a technical system designed by management. He therefore loses his professional consciousness, his sense of pride, community, and solidarity with other members of the craft. With its extensive use of machinery, division of labor, and technical hierarchy, the modern factory system tends to reduce professional distinctions and barriers among workers, forming a more homogeneous working class than before, one that possesses a stronger sense of collective dependence and discipline and greater acceptance of large-scale organization and the hierarchy of command. Deprived of a professional status that distinguishes them from other workers, factory workers tend to experience a class consciousness that is simpler and less ambiguous than that of skilled workers, an essentially negative proletarian consciousness that expresses an alienated identity and opposition to capitalist exploitation. Because the craft does not give them positive identity, social status, and frame of reference, unskilled workers are more likely to accept a Marxist conception of class, capitalism, and socialism that is theoretical–abstract, global, and unitary.[65]

This difference in social situation and consciousness has had organizational consequences. Lacking the glue of professional solidarity, the unskilled had to organize on the basis of industry-wide unions that included workers of all grades and crafts, all members of the class employed in the industry. As unskilled workers who were easily replaceable, they had to organize their industrial unions on a national as well as a local level. Moreover, because of their alienation from work, their level of organizational participation tended to be lower and more episodic than that of the skilled, alternating between bursts of militancy and long stretches of passivity. Thus, deprived of market or organizational leverage on the local level, they had to rely upon strongly unified or centralist organizations operating on the national level. If during periods of mass mobilization such organizations—industrial unions or working class parties—were democratic, that is truly representative of the class, they would tend to become bureaucratic and authoritarian, acting as a surrogate for the class, when the wave of worker militancy receded. Whether democratic or authoritarian, the organization of unskilled or industrial workers was typically more unitary or centralist, more class-oriented, than that of the skilled. Thus, industrial workers were more amenable to the class theory and centralist organization introduced by Marxists.[66]

French workers first encountered Marxism in the rudimentary form of Guesdism. As rather schematic Marxists, Jules Guesde and Paul Lafargue, Marx's son-in-law, saw socialism arising inevitably from the growth of heavy industry and a concentrated and disciplined industrial working class. In breaking with the possibilist Parti Ouvrier, they denounced its organizational federalism as Proudhonian and its social basis of urban skilled workers as petty bourgeois and set out to construct a centralist party with a single national program and leadership serving the interests of a unitary industrial working class. Consequently, they shifted their efforts from the traditional urban centers of skilled workers to outlying industrial districts of textiles, mining and metallurgy, particularly the textile region of the North.

Coming mostly from conservative peasant backgrounds, the textile workers of the North lacked those urban and craft traditions that had enabled skilled workers to make their own organizational and ideological response to exploitation.[67] Working long hours for low wages in a factory system over which they had little control, the textile workers did not possess the job autonomy, physical freedom, social status and culture of the skilled men. Responding to exploitation with unplanned and irregular outbursts of strikes and violence, they had to await the coming of socialist organization and theory from the outside to organize them for long-range social change. Lacking organizational autonomy, they came to rely upon a political apparatus seeking the conquest of political power for the entire working class.

Remaining marginal to the trade union movement, Marxism only made a decisive impact upon organized labor during the industrial unionization that occurred in the 1930s under the Popular Front. Having attributed the growth of opportunism to the influence of a skilled labor aristocracy, the Communist International stressed the organization of mass production workers, who were potentially more unitary, disciplined, and revolutionary than skilled workers. Benefiting from the unification of the national labor confederation and the advent of the Blum government, the Communists led the mass strike and unionization movements among production workers in metallurgy, especially automobiles, chemicals, electrical industry, and so on. These industrial workers proved more receptive to a Marxist theory and organization that appealed to the working class as a mass and engaged in a unified economic and political struggle for a change in the national system of power and wealth. By organizing centralist industrial unions and working class party, the Communists succeeded in industrializing the French labor movement.[68]

Such a typological description of French labor suggests a broader historical sociology of labor movements that have gone through similar phases and patterns of organization and ideology. On the basis of their job autonomy, professional consciousness, and political culture, skilled workers were nearly everywhere able to form their own local unions for defense against exploitation. Coordinating their action with workers in other local trades, they first formed local federations and later national trade federations that respected the autonomy of the local trade. Because these federations developed historically from the ground up on the basis of local subgroups, they tended to remain free from centralized bureaucratic control.[69] British trade unions, for instance, began as strongly democratic local groups although they later formed more centralized organizations in order to control market conditions on a national level.[70]

Ideologically, many movements went through a similar phase of trade socialism. The comparatively reformist tendencies of craft unions in the twentieth century have obscured their socialist origins. In many industrializing countries, including the United States and Britain, the trade union movement began with a cooperative project for the emancipation of trades from the wage system.[71] Later, unions passed from this cooperative program to a revolutionary strategy for the collectivization of capital in a federation of trades. This revolutionary collectivism predominated in the Latin countries—Spain, France, Italy and French-speaking Belgium and Switzerland—and formed the basis of the so-called Bakuninist opposition to Marx's leadership of the First International.[72] In the period of the Second International, this revolutionary collectivism reappeared in the same countries in the form of revolutionary syndicalism.

Why did not the same ideological pattern apply to Germany and nations influenced by German Social Democracy? The social basis of Social Democracy, highly skilled workers, was certainly the same. The answer seems to lie in the political origins of the German trade unions. Whereas in France the first socialist party, the Parti Ouvrier, grew out of the trade unions, in Germany the process was reversed. The Social Democratic Party was created before most of the trade unions. Strongly influenced by the Lassallean tradition, which was very political and centralist, German socialists organized trade unions on a more centralist and amalgamated basis than that of the French *syndicats*. While there is some evidence of a German revolutionary syndicalism based on local trades, the main thrust of the German trade unions within Social Democracy was reformist and antirevolutionary. Certainly, in the postwar crisis, the craft unions offered a rather solid body of resistance to a revolutionary movement supported largely by unskilled industrial workers.[73]

This latter pattern has prevailed in the twentieth century.

Industrial workers have constituted the main social basis of modern Communist parties, at least wherever such parties have developed mass organization.[74] To explain the comparative moderation of skilled workers in the twentieth century, Marxists have suggested the theory of labor aristocracy. Because skilled workers are economically privileged, this theory says, deriving greater benefits from the expansion of industrial capitalism or imperialism than industrial workers, they are more susceptible to middle class values and ideology.[75] To the economic privilege stressed by Marxists this study adds the professional privilege discussed here. But if this pattern of greater moderation among skilled workers holds true today, then why was it different in the nineteenth century, as this study also argues?

In the nineteenth century, as we have seen, skilled workers formed the mass of a working class that was being ground into a proletariat, suffering real deprivation—probably a greater relative deprivation than the factory worker—in a period of capital accumulation. It was not until the growth of heavy industry and assembly line production in the twentieth century that skilled workers became in fact a privileged minority relative to the mass of industrial workers. Having already formed their own trade organization, originally for socialist objectives, they could now use it for reformist purposes, carving out protected monopolistic positions in the labor market. Protecting themselves from outside competition, skilled workers were thus able to secure greater benefits from the expansion of industrial capitalism and imperialism. Thus, the growth of industrial capitalism finally destroyed the trade socialism of skilled workers, which constituted an important stage in the history of socialism and the working class.

Having presented a social analysis of trade socialism, this study must now proceed with historical narrative in order to demonstrate that it was indeed the dominant ideology of French labor in the nineteenth century. To do so requires a reexamination of several familiar social doctrines and movements—cooperation, Proudhonism, possibilism and syndical-ism—as well as a review of some larger issues in French history. The functions and purposes of social doctrines vary with time and circumstance. Doctrines must be understood not as abstractions in historical isolation, but in context, in time and place, as part of the larger historical process. Thus, a doctrine or ideology that was reformist or utopian in ultimate effect may have served a socialist purpose in its own time and place.

Chapter 2 covers the formative period from the July Monarchy through the early Third Republic during which the labor movement was attached to republicanism and the utopia of association. The association movement has tradi-tionally been given only secondary consideration as the effort of elite workers to raise themselves to middle class status. While this was indeed the ultimate function of the move-ment, its original purpose and function were radically different. Associationism was originally part of a larger republican and labor movement seeking collectivization of the means of production. It was the formative socialism of skilled workers, the movement that gave them a socialist consciousness. As part of the republican movement, it contained a real threat to capitalist property relations that was met by the bourgeoisie with political repression and support for authoritarian regimes. A specter indeed haunted the French bourgeoisie of the nineteenth century, the specter not of Marxism but of radical republicanism and cooperation.

Chapter 3 discusses the change from cooperative to revolutionary socialism or collectivism. Collectivism was not Marxism but the federalist trade socialism that had grown out of the cooperative labor movement and First International. Only the strategy changed; the goal of trade socialism remained the same. Denying that collectivization could be achieved peacefully within a middle class republic, the revolutionaries asserted this change could only come about through a revolution against the bourgeois state. Since the social basis of the movement remained the same, the explanation for this change must be sought elsewhere, primarily in the new political conditions that obtained after 1879—the consolidation of the Opportunist Third Republic under stable social conditions, the reconciliation of the bourgeoisie to democracy and of middle class democracy to the bourgeoisie. By removing juridical barriers to revolutionary activity and disappointing the hopes of social transformation, the rise of the republicans precipitated the formation of a separate workers' party with a revolutionary program.

Chapter 4 treats the formation of the new Parti Ouvrier, the first French socialist party, and interprets the significance of its organizational disputes and divisions. The conflict between Guesdist centralists and Broussist federalists was related to the question of the proper social basis of a socialist movement. In rejecting Guesdist or Marxist socialism, skilled workers were expressing hostility to a form of socialism that jeopardized their job autonomy, trade organization and federalist tradition. They did not, however, share the Broussist faith in obtaining significant reforms under capitalism. When the leader Paul Brousse negotiated electoral alliances with Radicals, they expelled him and as Allemanists returned the party to a more revolutionary trade unionist orientation.

Chapter 5 then explains the emergence of syndicalism as the culmination of trade socialism. Syndicalism is habitually treated as a rather unique movement with a theory and practice all its own. Deriving its ideology from the Parti Ouvrier, syndicalism was merely the expression of revolutionary collectivism in a trade union setting. Rebelling against socialist "politicians," trade unions emerged from under their tutelage to pursue socialism in their own independent movement. With the general strike they found their own instrument for the collectivization of capital in a federation of trades. In syndicalism the ideology of trade socialism found its final expression.

2

The Utopia
of Association

The French labor movement was born under a judicial regime
based on the protection of private property and strict
economic liberalism. The French Revolution liberated workers from the trammels of the guild system and exposed them
to the rigors of individual competition in a free market. When
workers during the Revolution did unite in combinations or
strikes to challenge the exclusive power of capital, the
Constituent Assembly passed the Le Chapelier Law, which
prohibited either workers or employers from assembling to
deliberate upon their common interests. The laws against
workers' combinations were strengthened by Napoléon, who
introduced legal discriminations in favor of employers,
including a maximum penalty of five years imprisonment for
striking workers. As a result of Napoleonic legislation,
workers enjoyed fewer rights and suffered greater legal
discrimination than even a strict liberalism might indicate.[1]
Several forms of worker associations did survive this
repressive legislation. With roots in the late Middle Ages, the
compagnonnages were secret societies of journeymen that
provided shelter, placement, and training for itinerant craftsmen, particularly carpenters and other construction workers
on their customary tour de France.[2] As traditional sectarian
associations, with their own special rites, hierarchy and

costumes, they were generally tolerated by Restoration governments though they occasionally led strikes and kept alive the spirit of worker solidarity. Similarly tolerated and even encouraged were the mutual aid or friendly societies, which offered sickness, old age, and occasionally unemployment insurance.[3] In 1823 Paris had 160 societies of which 132 were from individual trades; by 1848 there were 230. Representing individual trades, these societies became the bases for trade unions, serving as legal covers for strike committees and strike funds. Occurring with greater frequency since the Empire, strikes were violently suppressed with their leaders receiving stiff fines and long prison terms.[4] However, it took the Revolution of 1830 to generalize workers' protest and encourage the formation of permanent organization on a national scale.

COOPERATIVE ORIGINS UNDER THE JULY MONARCHY

Associationism was born during the wave of strikes and organized protests provoked by the Revolution of 1830. Arising in the midst of an industrial depression, the revolution aroused new expectations and unleashed new forms of labor action from petitions and demonstrations to strikes, associations, and even insurrection.[5] As a result of the depression, craftsmen faced massive unemployment and depressed wages caused by widespread bankruptcies and technical innovations, such as mechanical presses, saws, cutters, and sewing machines, and the substitution of ready-made clothes and hats for custom-made.[6] As the victors of the *trois glorieuses,* workers assembled in trades to formulate demands for higher wages, shorter hours, public works, and restrictions on mechanization. Leading the movement, Parisian printers demanded a ban on the mechanical presses that were threatening the protected status and security of the trade. Expectations were rudely dashed when the government declared that public intervention in industrial disputes was "contrary to the laws that have established the principles of the liberty of industry"[7] and proceeded to disperse and suppress all further demonstrations and strikes.

In the midst of the agitation there appeared a workers' newspaper that went beyond the trade unionist demands voiced by the assembled trades. For the printers who published *l'Artisan, journal de la classe ouvrière*,[8] these demands expressed a deeper protest against the working class condition, which was to be exploited by a capitalist master for his profit. Holding the potential for liberating workers from the burdens of physical labor, machinery was only harmful so long as the masters used it to increase their exploitation. Viewing workers as the only productive class, the source of all wealth, they suggested cooperative association as the way to end capitalist exploitation. To benefit from machinery, they advised workers to become their own masters of machinery by pooling their savings and establishing a cooperative association.

With this rudimentary analysis of exploitation and the association project, *l'Artisan* laid the basis for trade socialism. Surprisingly, the immediate source and impact of *l'Artisan* remain obscure. Certainly, disciples of Robert Owen, Charles Fourier, and Henri de Saint-Simon, notably Philippe Buchez, had circulated concepts of exploitation and association, but none of their programs corresponds with this practical suggestion for association.[9] Though these printers were doubtless aware of republican and Saint-Simonian ideas, there is nothing in their simple language, awkward expressions, or professed antagonism to middle class journalists to suggest outside collaboration. In the absence of other evidence, one should accept their word that the new consciousness was primarily the result of their experience since the revolution threw the working class into the political and social spotlight.

At the same time, the emergence of the working class as an independent force and perhaps contact with *l'Artisan* had persuaded Buchez that skilled workers could form their own associations. Buchez distinguished between the "gifted" skilled workers and factory workers, "cogs in a machine," who required outside direction and control. In those industries where skilled labor constituted the major capital and where workers controlled the process of production, they could operate their own workshops without·the help of a capitalist master. In the course of discussions with Parisian workers, he proposed a new formula for the emancipation of entire trades from the wage system. He suggested the establishment of public credit banks to supply the initial capital and the formation of a collective, indivisible, "inalienable" capital from reinvested earnings to allow the continual admission of new members without capital. Buchez thus pointed toward the collectivization of all skilled trades in cooperative associations.[10]

Doubtless influenced by Buchez, republican leaders Godefroy Cavaignac of the society Amis du Peuple and Armand Marrast, editor of *La Tribune,* also advocated the formation of associations and public credit banks as means of transferring the instruments of labor to the working class. During the round of general strikes that erupted in the autumn of 1833, several Parisian trades, including tailors, box-makers, chairmakers, and glove-makers, opened their own associations or, as they were termed, "national workshops." Formed for the purpose of employing striking workers and applying competitive pressure on employers, these associations came to be seen as a definitive method of trade emancipation. Printers and shoemakers planned to establish huge workshops for the emancipation of their trades, and the shoemakers initiated the formation of a national workers' federation to supply credit to associations.[11]

La Tribune and the republican Société des Droits de l'Homme saw them as the beginning of a new organization of labor that could only come to fruition under a republic. After the strikes and associations were crushed by wholesale arrests and prosecutions, the Société des Droits de l'Homme urged labor leaders to draw political lessons from the defeat. Appealing to them to join in the political struggle, it promised that "the essential duty of the republic will be to furnish the proletarians with the means of forming themselves into cooperative associations and exploiting their industry themselves."[12] The alliance of skilled workers with republicans was thus founded upon a cooperative strategy for workers' ownership of industry.[13]

Similar developments occurred in the provinces where striking trades planned associations in Lyons, Marseilles, Bordeaux, Nantes, Tours, Montpellier, Rennes, and other towns.[14] Through the exchange of statistics, statutes, and brochures, Parisian tailors and shoemakers coordinated the offensive of 1833-34 on a truly national scale. The tailors' network of correspondence survived police repression for several years after the suppression of the April 1834 insurrection in Paris and Lyons. In Marseilles, associations were started by striking hatters, turners, shoemakers, and stonecutters, the latter after troops replaced the strikers. In Lyons, the silk weavers planned a central commercial house for each branch of the industry.[15] Designed to eliminate the parasitic role of the merchant manufacturers, who reaped the profits, these commercial houses were to be truly collective associations in which the master weavers would contribute their looms to a common fund of capital and share wages and earnings equally with their aids. The government systematically eliminated all associations resulting from collective effort, permitting only a few isolated experiments that had no connection with the larger trade or republican movements.[16] Everywhere this trade association movement had been supported by republican societies and newspapers as the beginning of a new organization of labor that would triumph under a republic.

Through a process that has remained obscure, the main assumptions of this program were disseminated throughout the republican party even before Louis Blanc published his *Organisation du travail* in August 1840.[17] Already in May 1840, François Arago had spoken in the Chamber of Deputies of the need for a new organization of labor. During the republican electoral campaign of that year, the call for workers' associations to "end the exploitation of man by man" resounded in banquet halls all over France.[18]

The most influential publicists of this program were Blanc
and the workers who published the Buchezian monthly
l'Atelier. Too much perhaps has been made of the differences
between their respective programs. Both looked to the
republic to provide the credit and contracts needed to
overcome capitalist competition, accumulate capital, and
emancipate workers from the wage system. When *l'Atelier*
first criticized Blanc in 1841, it was a matter of degree rather
than substance. Where Blanc had stressed the state's initiative, *l'Atelier* advised workers to rely more on their own
efforts and sacrifice. Where Blanc insisted on the establishment of an association monopoly in each trade, *l'Atelier*, like
Buchez, wished to preserve limited competition among
multiple associations as an incentive for technical innovation.
Nevertheless, it continued to share the basic assumptions of
the program whereby the republic would assist trades toward
the collectivization of industrial capital in associations.[19]

At the same time, doctrinaire socialists and communists,
disciples of Saint-Simon, Fourier, Gracchus Babeuf and
Etienne Cabet, had found vehicles for the realization of
association in the labor and republican movements. As
adapted to suit the needs of the labor movement, their
utopian blueprints—the universal hierarchical association of
the Saint-Simonians, the passionate community of the
Fourierists, and the communist state of the Icarians and
Babouvians—became transmuted into the democratic trade
association. Socialists and communists rallied to producers'
association as a practical and transitional form of utopia.
Several members of these schools, notably the Saint-
Simonians Jules and Pierre Vinçard, embraced the cooperative program on the working class newspaper *l'Union*. In
1845, several Fourierists, Saint-Simonians, and communists
joined labor and republican leaders on the Compagnie des
Industries Unies, a universal association formed to establish
cooperative production in each trade. Beginning with an
industry of vital necessity, they planned to extend operations

until all trades were included in a national circuit of collective production and exchange.[20]

During the 1840s, the cooperative program became the main social policy of the entire republican movement, not merely its explicitly collectivist wing.[21] While the radicals of *La Réforme* generally shared Blanc's collectivist approach, the moderates of *Le National* preferred the slightly more liberal version of *l'Atelier*. In 1846, both sides met to decide how to assist in the formation of associations. While Blanc and the labor leaders favored establishing a single association in each trade, the moderates, including the banker Michel Goudchaux, Alexandre Marie, Hippolyte Carnot, Louis Garnier-Pagès, Armand Marrast, and the *Atelièristes,* wanted them to be multiple and competitive. Yet, even the moderate majority, with its more liberal gradualist approach, advocated association as the regime of the future; in the final analysis most republicans, both radicals and moderates, were cooperative socialists.[22]

Republican socialism reveals the idealistic and contradictory character of the democratic movement that makes it impossible to characterize it simply, as did Marx,[23] as either bourgeois or petty bourgeois. By tradition and class interest most republican leaders were inclined toward a liberal democracy of small property owners—independent peasants, shopkeepers, and petty capitalists. The Saint-Simonians had contributed much to the republican analysis of the social conflicts in French history. Viewing the landed and financial aristocracy as the privileged class, the republicans did not see any basic conflict between petty capitalists and their workers. They did not see these capitalists as independent exploiters of labor, accumulators of profit, and owners of capital, who were continuously rising into the bourgeoisie. By extracting the wealth of the people in the form of rent and interest, the proprietary ruling class exploited both workers and small capitalists, causing material suffering and industrial disorder. Since petty capitalists also suffered from exploitation, they would have a common interest with workers in the expansion of credit and association. Thus, a middle class democracy could be expected to help workers establish their own cooperative workshops.[24]

Cooperative socialism was the republican response to working class protest that appeared after the July Revolution. Industrial strife persuaded idealistic young democrats of the need to improve workers' conditions and relieve their suffering. In the working class they found determined and dedicated followers who were willing to sacrifice their lives for the cause of equality. Enrolling workers in the revolutionary sections of the Société des Droits de l'Homme, they instructed them in Robespierrist principles that subordinated property rights to the social requirements of security, harmony, and equality. Despite a tradition that favored capitalist property, class conciliation, and middle class democracy, radical republicans formed revolutionary societies that were essentially working class in composition and popularized a cooperative program that would tend to undermine capitalism and the middle class. The application of egalitarian principles to industrial society led them beyond their middle class interest toward an authentically socialist program.[25]

Republicanism was a loosely organized and socially diverse movement, including both middle class newspapers and electoral circles and working class societies—Babouvian, Icarian, and Blanquist. It is not possible to divide the movement between moderates who cared only for political democracy and radicals who wanted a social democracy.[26] In the program of both radicals and moderates political and social forms of democracy were entwined. The program expressed the social alliance of petty bourgeois businessmen and professionals, who were starved for credit and influence under the July Monarchy, with the disenfranchised and exploited working class. Only a small faction around Blanc was explicitly collectivist. But aside from a few liberal or "Girondist" republicans, who faded into the dynastic opposition, most republicans embraced the cooperative program without always being aware of its collectivist implications.[27] Whether formal collectivists or not, they still supported a program and social alliance that were potentially subversive of the bourgeois social order.

Why did the cooperative program appeal to skilled workers? To what social situation and condition did it respond? The cooperative movement has been seen variously as a revolt against industrialization—against machinery, factory discipline, and managerial authority—an effort of an elite to raise themselves to middle class status, and as a return to the corporatism of the guild system.[28] These interpretations rest on the assumption that cooperators were traditional artisans with a social situation and outlook quite distinct from that of factory workers. Doubtless, they were superior to the factory workers with respect to social status, job autonomy, trade solidarity, and political and material culture, but to treat them as traditional artisans is to overlook the process of industrialization that had transformed them into a skilled proletariat.

The primary thrust of associationism was economic, a revolt against the capitalist exploitation and competition that had reduced craftsmen to a suffering working class. During a formative period of relative deprivation and misery, they acquired a socialist outlook that endured even through better times. From 1830 to 1848, a period of great economic growth, the wages of most Parisian trades remained constant, with few rising or falling.[29] The lowest point in this relative deterioration was reached in 1847. Thus, when Marx in the *Manifesto* wrote of the increasing misery of the working class, he was not in the case of Parisian workers merely theorizing.

During this period most trades were confronted with the influx of cheaper labor and more efficient methods of production. The wood and furniture trades suffered from an influx of provincial and foreign, especially German, workers. Lacking employment, many cabinetmakers were forced to

make furniture in their own flats, later hawking it on their
backs along the boulevards, a practice called *la trôle* that
further depressed both prices and wages. By 1840 clothing
merchants had discovered a mass market for ready-made
clothing, replacing custom tailors with women and children
working at home or in sweated workshops. The construction
industry was swelled with large numbers of sweating subcontractors; they hired gangs of unapprenticed and inexperi-
enced workers, who did not own their own tools, at
substandard wages. The luxury trade industry faced competition from imitation and standardized products as well as
foreign manufacturers stealing Parisian models. Whether
partially mechanized or not, most trades experienced a
greater division, speed, and intensity of labor. This growing
competition and exploitation prompted workers to seek a
solution in the cooperative association.[30]

Against this competition and exploitation, the strike
weapon proved unavailing. Prefects often showed sympathy
for workers in labor disputes, but they never hesitated to use
the full force of the law when they found workers' demands
to be excessive or politically dangerous. During the Parisian
strikes of 1830, 1833, and 1840, involving as many as
100,000 workers, the government dispatched troops and
arrested hundreds of strikers to quell the disturbances.
Striking effectively during periods of economic recovery,
workers often lost their new advantages during the subsequent downturn. With their craft cohesion, high wages and
educational standards, the printers were one of the few
Parisian trades to maintain an illegal trade union and engage
in regular collective bargaining. Few trades were so exceptionally endowed to overcome both legal and economic
obstacles to trade unionism.[31]

Where strikes proved ineffective, the association appeared
as the only practical remedy to the workers' material
suffering, the only way to guarantee steady employment,
decent wages, and the full product of labor. Cooperators
could show that the introduction of machinery, influx of
cheap labor, and legal repression made trade union action

impracticable. Rather than oppose machinery and technical
innovation, they advised workers to reap their benefits
through the collective ownership of industrial capital. Unlike
strikes, commercial societies were legally protected by the
code. With partial reform blocked, workers reached out for
the solution that would end forever the exploitation of man
by man.

ASSOCIATION UNDER THE SECOND REPUBLIC

The Revolution of 1848 stirred tremendous hopes for the
emancipation of labor through association. For labor spokesman Pierre Vinçard, "the 24th of February was but the
political prologue to a serious drama whose conclusion is the
complete and radical emancipation of the producers."[32] The
workers who overthrew the monarchy in the streets wanted a
democratic and social republic that would favor associations
with credit and contracts. Not only the formal socialists
Blanc and Albert, the mechanic who was named minister, but
even the moderate republicans—Goudchaux, Marie, Marrast,
Garnier-Pagès, Carnot, and General Eugène Cavaignac—
seemed willing to cooperate. By officially recognizing that
workers should form associations in order to enjoy the fruits
of their labor and establishing a commission for workers at
the Luxembourg Palace, the provisional government encouraged the association movement that emerged from the newly
organized trades.[33]

The revolution produced a mass mobilization of workers
and a veritable Parisian general strike in which workers
refused to resume production under old conditions. More
than two hundred trades met and dispatched delegates to the
Luxembourg Labor Commission. As workers assembled in
halls and wineshops to elect delegates, they drafted petitions
for higher wages, shorter hours, and an end to subcontracting
and discussed projects for trade associations. Trade defense
and associationism were complementary aspects of the same
movement. Immediate improvements would give workers
more energy and resources with which to build associations,
while associations would increase pressure on employers for

greater concessions. Trade unionism and associationism were thus aspects of a single coalition against the capitalist masters.[34]

The new government acceded to the most pressing demands, creating national workshops for the unemployed, outlawing sweating subcontractors, limiting hours to ten in Paris and eleven in the provinces, replacing private employment agencies with public ones administered by the trades, prohibiting commercial production in prisons and convents, and admitting worker delegates to the wage conciliation boards known as the *Prud'hommes*. At the Luxembourg, the commission presided over wage negotiations in which workers wrested major concessions from employers and listened to various programs for association. Before it disbanded, it approved Blanc's program for a ministry of progress that would nationalize major industry and use the operating revenues to finance a general association movement of all trades. While workers awaited the formation of a ministry of progress, a few associations were begun with the aid of the commission, notably the tailors' association, which employed more than 2,000 at the Clichy prison for the manufacture of National Guard uniforms.[35]

Despite the triumph of reaction—the defeat of Luxembourg candidates in the April election, the rejection of the ministry of progress, and the dissolution of the commission in May—the Luxembourg labor delegates continued the commission's work on their own, coordinating strikes and political action and organizing their own universal association, the Société des Corporations Réunies, seeking the "end of the exploitation of man by man through the immediate association of producers by the creation of associated workshops."[36] Beginning with contributions from 50,000 workers, they planned to establish a social workshop in a vital industry, gradually expanding production to other trades until all were included in a complete circuit of collective production and exchange. Led mostly by workers from the national workshops with the participation of some

Luxembourg delegates, the June insurrection ended this first project for universal association.

Although the repression following the June Days temporarily halted political and strike activity, it hardly interrupted the association movement. Under the state of siege during which rights of assembly were suppressed, workers sought refuge in associations that were protected by the commercial code. Holding out association as a positive alternative to violence, moderate republicans in the assembly approved a three million franc credit for associations and granted them concessions on public works projects. Initially inspired by the socialism of *l'Atelier,* the official commission denied requests for loans from monopolistic trade associations, granting them only to small competitive associations—thirty-two in Paris and twenty-nine in the provinces—that agreed to establish funds of inalienable capital and to admit auxiliary wage earners to eventual membership. The Cavaignac government was sincerely committed to this admittedly modest cooperative experiment. By November, however, opposition to associationism had surfaced both in the assembly and the commission, where the *Atelièristes* were forced to resign. Only with the demise of Cavaignac and moderate republicanism, however, did official policy turn to neglect and outright hostility.[37]

In a more radical direction, the Luxembourg delegates took advantage of the favorable associationist climate to develop their own independent movement. In lieu of a ministry of progress, they continued the formation of a universal association to expand and coordinate the movement. At first they launched the Chambre du Travail in order to organize mutual credit and exchange among the newly created associations. When this failed, they agreed to collaborate with Proudhon in his Bank of the People. Proudhon's bank was originally intended to provide commercial credit at low interest rates to small entrepreneurs as a means of stimulating exchange and competition, but the Luxembourg delegates saw an opportunity to use its credit facilities to

organize association monopolies in each trade. In return for
their cooperation, they obliged Proudhon to annex to the
bank syndicates of production and consumption that would
"centralize the function of production and consumption" in
order to "constitute the free and democratic *corporation* as
the absolute and definitive regime of the workers."[38] Within
six weeks more than 20,000 workers, from a cross section of
trades,[39] and forty-nine associations had joined. Operations
had not yet begun when Proudhon was arrested and
imprisoned for slandering the government. When, fearing the
collectivist influence of the Luxembourg delegates, he liqui-
dated the bank, they continued the project as the Mutualité
des Travailleurs under the patronage of Blanc and the
"democratic socialist party."[40]

After several other abortive efforts, association delegates
finally agreed upon statutes for a Union des Associations in
November 1849. Initiated by the socialist feminist Jeanne
Deroin, the Union proposed to organize mutual credit and
exchange among associations until all trades had acquired
their own means of production. With 104 member associations, the Union was preparing to issue its own labor bonds
for this purpose when the government, fearing the resurgence
of republican socialism, invaded its headquarters in May
1850, arrested its leaders, and dissolved the organization.[41]

Other projects for universal association followed, including
the Corporations Nouvelles, a central committee of Parisian
trades organized by the typographers on the eve of Napoléon's coup d'état.[42] Similar universal associations were tried in
provincial cities, especially Lyons, where several rival associations set up cooperatives in the food industry.[43] As in Paris,
these associations were continuously harrassed by the police.
Bound to republicanism, the association movement shared its
fate under the dictatorship of Louis Napoléon.

Under the Second Republic, nearly 300 socialist associations with perhaps 50,000 members from 120 trades were
created in Paris, with an additional 800 projects underway in
the provinces.[44] Open to all members of the trade willing to
make a nominal investment, they were designed with an

expanding fund of inalienable capital to ensure the eventual emancipation of the entire trade. Patterned on either Buchezian or Luxembourg models, their statutes proclaimed a socialist aim "to free workers through the extinction of the wage system" and "to return to the producers the entire product of their labor."[45] Through association the bronze workers sought

> the elimination of the intermediary parasite and usury capital through the socialization of the instruments of labor, ... the emancipation of workers through the abolition of the employer class, ... [and] the realization of harmony in work, the republic in the shop and justice in the distribution of social burdens and advantages.[46]

Established with insufficient capital, associations could only grow on the basis of severe wage deductions and the reinvestment of all earnings. In fact, the only tangible advantage of membership in this period of persistent crisis was the assurance of steady employment. Displaying the carpenters' level as the sign of equality, associations usually found their first customers among other socialist workers and associations. Several exchanged products using printed labor bonds as currency. True to Luxembourg principles, the vast majority of trades had only one association. In those small trades where associations proliferated, notably the barbers and cooks, who served as channels of communication for the movement, efforts were made to centralize credit and supplies. Nearly all associations contained provisions for an inalienable fund to be used for the extension of the association movement as a whole.[47]

Without the help of a democratic and social republic, organized working class, and universal association, the movement was bound to fail. For most associations life was hard and short. Lacking credit and customers, many were also beset with administrative problems and disputes. Elected managers did not always possess the requisite managerial and commercial skills. Internal disputes over managerial authority and the distribution of earnings often led to the dismissal of managers and the exclusion or resignation of members. Of the subsidized associations for which we have records, most remained marginal operations, comprising fewer members in 1851 than when they began; fewer than half survived the four years. Of forty-nine trades that started associations in 1849, only twenty-six still had them in 1851. Since new ones were constantly being created, however, there were still 200 in that year.[48]

What kind of trades participated in the movement? Did they, as the traditional argument would suggest, represent only the more independent, well-paid, or artisanal workers? One cannot determine whether or not the workers who formed associations were elite in their trades, but one can say something about the kinds of trades that participated. Participating trades were as diverse as the Parisian working class itself—from food, construction, furniture, clothing, leather, metal work, printing, and luxury trades, indeed from all industrial groups except chemicals. As for the specific characteristics of participating trades, one can compare them statistically with the average Parisian worker with respect to size of enterprise, daily wage, number of apprentices, rate of unemployment, literacy, and nature of residence.[49]

As regards daily wages, associated trades very much represented the Parisian average with few poor workers and very few well-paid workers.[50] They were average with respect to unemployment as well, which reached an average of 54 percent in 1848.[51] Where the traditional view would suggest greater participation among the smaller artisanal trades with many apprentices, independent artisans, and domestic workers, the precise opposite is the case.[52] Instead, associated trades tended to come from the more concentrated industries, which admittedly were not very concentrated. In only two respects did associated trades constitute an elite—rates of literacy and permanent residence in Paris.[53] These then were Parisian workers with a high level of education and political consciousness, who had undergone the process of proletarianization, to which the association movement was an active transformative response.

Thus, the Parisian association movement represented the aspirations of an authentic proletariat for trade socialism, the collective ownership of industrial capital by a federation of skilled trades. With the help of the organized working class, a social republic, and universal association, associations could be expected to outcompete capitalist enterprise, accumulate capital, and eventually emancipate all trades from the wage system. Since skilled trades represented the vast majority of French workers and still constituted the primary source of capital accumulation,[54] this program would eventually encompass the socialization of all industrial means of production.

Past historians, notably Marx,[55] saw this as petty bourgeois socialism, an essentially utopian, middle class movement. If this were true, however, it was not because of its social base, which was primarily working class, nor its objective, which was certainly some form of collectivization, but because of its belief that the objective could be attained peacefully within the framework of an essentially middle-class republic, that is, in Marxist terms, without the prior seizure of state power by the proletariat.

Yet, if middle class republicans, transcending their narrow class interest, were sincere about the association program, and little indicated that they were not, then what was so unrealistic about this belief? After the June Days, elements of the petty bourgeoisie and peasantry had joined workers in a social democratic alliance against the bourgeoisie.[56] With demands for easier credit, tax reform, land for the landless, and workers' association, republican socialism reached beyond working class centers into small towns and rural areas of independent peasants and tradesmen. In 1849 many moderate republicans also joined this alliance. While the leadership of republican societies remained middle class, the dominant social element was working class.[57] If not in itself socialist, a social republic could have served as a transition to a working class regime. Threatening capitalist institutions, its specter frightened the bourgeoisie into the arms of the cesarian democrat, Louis Napoléon. What was most utopian about republican socialism was that the bourgeoisie did not allow it to continue. Why? Perhaps because it contained the seeds for the development of a working class regime and socialism.

COOPERATIVE REVIVAL UNDER THE SECOND EMPIRE

Historians have usually drawn a sharp contrast between the socialist associations of 1848 and the more practical and reformist cooperatives of the Second Empire. Certainly, under the repressive conditions of the 1850s, surviving associations lost much of their original socialist inspiration. Reflecting upon the failure of 1848 and their own tenuous liberty under the Empire, a new generation of labor activists in the 1860s initially professed a practical reformist outlook that found an ideological expression in Proudhonism. Yet, as labor, association, and republican movements revived under the liberal Empire, these activists returned in practice to the cooperative strategy for socialism.

Napoléon's coup d'état of December 1851 destroyed the association movement of the Second Republic. During the antisocialist repression that followed, police arrested thousands of labor and association leaders, dissolved some associations, and frightened others into dissolution. The official council on associations was disbanded, and those remaining were compelled to conform to the restrictive provisions of the commercial code. As a result of this legal and political repression, only fourteen remained from the days of the Republic in 1863.[58]

Without the external support of the labor and republican movements, few could survive in a normal business environment. Those that survived did so by abandoning the socialist principles of 1848 and adopting normal commercial practices, hiring professional managers and employing auxiliary wage earners at free market conditions. After many years of hard work and sacrifice, charter members had accumulated a large equity, which they were reluctant to share with newcomers from the trade. Rather than admit new members, they raised the value of shares and hired auxiliary wage earners. All seventeen in 1863 had declined from their peak membership; fifteen employed auxiliaries on a permanent basis, and twelve had raised the value of shares rather substantially.[59]

Perhaps the most successful commercial transformation was that of the masons. Founded in 1848 with fifty-franc shares and dreams of emancipating all construction workers, this association reorganized itself in 1852, raising the value of shares to 1,000 then 3,000 francs and inviting capitalist participation. Rather than admit new members, it expanded operations by hiring as many as 1,600 auxiliaries. So much of a capitalist enterprise had it become that during the 1866 masons' strike, the manager Antoine Cohadon sided with the employers. Instead of serving the interests of the trade, it enabled an elite of fifty masons to accumulate enough capital to become individual entrepreneurs in their turn.[60]

Associationism always contained a certain ambiguity that made it appealing to liberals and socialists alike. So long as it remained partial and limited in its effects, it attracted the interest of bourgeois reformers, who saw it as a way of creating new property owners and thus consolidating the social order. Appearing to have lost its socialist character, the movement was originally patronized in the 1860s by a wide variety of bourgeois reformers—republicans, Orleanists, and imperialists. While republicans sponsored the first cooperative bank, the Crédit au Travail, the Orleanists had their own Caisse d'Escompte for cooperatives. Even the Emperor set up a special fund and introduced a new commercial law that facilitated their formation.[61]

The original sponsor of the revival was the Crédit au Travail, a cooperative bank founded by Jean-Pierre Beluze, Cabet's son-in-law, with the support of association managers and republicans. This new generation of cooperators preferred a more practical gradualist approach to the "vague and ambitious" utopias of 1848. In its model statutes the Crédit au Travail jettisoned the 1848 clauses requiring a fund of inalienable capital and barring auxiliary labor. It advocated the formation of small competitive associations by a capable elite that could later expand through their own efforts without governmental assistance. It also fostered the creation of consumer cooperatives on the model of the Rochdale weavers in England, which many viewed as a method of accumulating capital for producers' cooperatives.

Reformers from diverse ideological backgrounds— Fourierists, Icarians, *Ateliéristes,* antisocialist Proudhonians like Gustave Chaudey and Charles Beslay, and socialist republicans like Elie Réclus and Alfred Talandier—found common cause in this "practical socialism." Despite its emphasis on competition and self-help, the Crédit au Travail envisaged association as an instrument of social transformation and the universal regime of the future. Through its legal advice and loan assistance, its monthly bulletin *l'Association*—later suppressed and republished under the more innocuous title *La Coopération*—and annual cooperative almanacs, and provincial branches in Lyons, Lille and other cities, the Crédit au Travail became the center of the association movement.[62]

The resurgence of trade organization would eventually restore a more pronounced socialist character to the association movement. The initial impetus for this organization came from the Emperor himself, acting through his cousin Jérôme and Armand Lévy to create a working class clientele as compensation for the loss of conservative Catholics and protectionists under the liberal Empire. In a series of subsidized pamphlets published in 1861, workers in Jérôme's entourage acclaimed the Emperor's liberalism and appealed for the toleration of trade organization. As if in response, the Emperor in 1862 pardoned imprisoned leaders of a printers' strike and sponsored trade delegations to the London Exposition of 1862.

With official authorization the Workers' Commission, composed of presidents of mutual aid societies and led by the bronze sculptor Henri Tolain, conducted elections in which a majority of Parisian workers, 200,000, from fifty trades, selected 200 delegates along with 140 provincial delegates to London. They returned from their visit full of admiration for English labor institutions and demanded the formation of trade societies and the right to strike. Four delegations, including the tailors and bronze workers, still considered "the common possession of the instruments of labor" in association as the only definitive solution to the social problem.[63]

Far from winning friends, Napoléon's overtures only spurred greater militancy. In the legislative elections of 1863 and 1864, Tolain and other trade delegates sponsored labor candidates to campaign for freedom of association and combination.[64] In defense of their action, which threatened to divide the republican opposition, they issued the Manifesto of the Sixty, the first declaration of the French labor movement. Repudiating violence, they advocated the use of "free institutions"—"liberty, credit and solidarity"—to "facilitate the transition between the old society based on the wage system and the future society ... based on common law."[65] The only specific institutions they mentioned were mixed commissions for collective bargaining and mutual credit societies, small cooperative banks that had been formed by artisans and workers for consumer and commercial credit.

The theoretical idiom of this new generation was Proudhonism. As an anticapitalist philosophy that was also antisocialist, it was well suited for the pioneers of a movement that at least initially had to remain free from overt socialist or even republican connections to be tolerated. The authors of the manifesto were not themselves influenced by Proudhon. But with their emphasis on mutual credit and free institutions, they inspired Proudhon to write his last work, *De la Capacité politique des classes ouvrières,* in which he recognized the working class as the leading reformist class with its own mutualist idea for the transformation of capitalism.[66]

Proudhonism first appeared among French members of the

International Workingmen's Association, founded in London
in 1864 as a result of the contacts established between
French and English skilled workers in 1862.[67] Its first
Parisian bureau, set up by Tolain, Ernest Fribourg, and
Charles Limousin on the rue Gravilliers, served mainly as a
study circle in which various proposals for cooperative and
universal association were discussed.[68] While open to workers
of all tendencies, this first bureau drafted an explicitly
Proudhonian program that was approved by all French
delegates to the first congress of the International at Geneva
in 1866.[69] In addition to public education, female labor, and
political action, they condemned strikes and the collectivist
associations of 1848 in favor of a form of cooperation that
respected individual liberty and initiative. Yet, already in
1866 there was a discrepancy between this ideological
manifesto and practices that violated both the letter and
spirit of Proudhonism. As trade organization developed
further, it became increasingly clear that Proudhonism was an
ideological mask for a movement that actually supported
strikes and political action and sought in association the
collective emancipation of trades.

Despite his obeisance to association and mutual credit,
Proudhon remained profoundly antagonistic to the collectivist tendency of the association movement. In 1848 he had
set up his credit bank to stimulate competition and exchange
among small producers in contrast to the Luxembourg
delegates, who wanted to fund trade monopolies that would
destroy free enterprise and competition. Although, in response to economic concentration, Proudhon later made
some allowance for open contractual associations in large
industries, he remained unalterably opposed to collective
association, especially in those skilled trades from which the
movement actually sprang.[70]

Once again Napoléon opened the floodgates of the labor
movement. A law of May 25, 1864, abrogated the ban on
strikes while still punishing threats of violence and interference with the "liberty of work." The ensuing strike move-

ments produced the first representative trade societies since 1851.[71] Most commonly known as *sociétés de prévoyance et de solidarité,* these societies sought both immediate improvements for wage earners and trade emancipation through association. During several strikes in Paris, Lyons, Marseilles, and other cities, workers set up temporary workshops and drafted plans for more permanent ones. After a successful strike in 1867, a leader of the Parisian bronze workers announced that part of their gain would go toward their emancipation—"association in work after association in struggle."[72] Under the influence of the International, most construction trades rejected strike action in favor of saving for association in a regular type of commercial society, the *société civile d'épargne et de crédit mutuel.* [73]

The final form adopted by most trade societies was the *chambre syndicale* or *syndicat.* [74] Meaning literally an assembly of syndics and originally applied to employers' associations, the term had been appropriated by workers' societies to give them parity in negotiations with employers. Labor delegates to the 1867 Paris Exposition recommended the formation of a *chambre syndicale* for workers in each trade and petitioned the government for its toleration. A ministerial report approved by Napoléon in March 1868 granted workers' *syndicats* the same toleration previously enjoyed by employers' associations, requiring them, however, to register with the police and allow police surveillance. Serving the same function as the *sociétés de prévoyance,* the *syndicat* combined immediate trade defense in matters of wage rates, hours, apprenticeship, mutual insurance, and the like, with projects for association, "the only means of salvation for the workers."[75]

Thus, associationism renewed its ties to trade organization. The trade societies of the 1860s—*société de crédit mutuel, société de prévoyance,* and *syndicat*—all combined trade unionism with projects for association. In 1865 an estimated fifty Parisian trades were accumulating funds for association. By 1868 there were 53 producers' associations in Paris and

53 in the provinces, including 19 at Lyons. Most grew out of
trade organization and strikes. Trade societies encouraged
associations to lower the prices of shares and expand
membership into the trade. Starting with 3,000-franc shares,
the Parisian tailors reduced shares to 100 francs and admitted
more than 200 new members during a strike in 1868. Despite
the absence of socialist clauses in their statutes, most
associations aimed toward the eventual emancipation of
entire trades.[76]

Once the trades started to federate, they began to take
over the coordination of the association movement from the
Crédit au Travail. At the workers' assembly inaugurated at
the 1867 Paris Exposition, delegates from 120 Parisian trades
approved a socialist program of association. Criticizing the
Crédit au Travail for its high interest rates, they recommended associations that would "go beyond" the wage
system, "absorb" private enterprise, and "eliminate the *rente*
paid the idle rich"[77] and proposed the formation of a
federation of trade societies with a mutual credit fund, "a
general fund of association, a fund of humanity belonging to
all."[78]

Under the leadership of the Internationalist bookbinder
Eugène Varlin, such a federation was eventually begun in
1869 by forty societies from a cross section of Parisian
trades. In addition to offering mutual strike assistance on the
basis of loans secured by members' dues, this federation of
workers' societies proposed to employ "those means deemed
proper by the workers of all trades to make them owners of
all machinery and credit them so that they can free
themselves from the despotism of the employers and the
demands of capital . . . ."[79] During a protracted strike of
tawers in 1869, the federation tried to collect 40,000 francs
to emancipate the entire trade from the wage system. Led by
Internationalists, similar workers' federations were set up in
Lyons with 30 societies and 20,000 workers, Marseilles with
20 societies and 4,000, and Rouen with an unknown number
of societies and 1,100 workers. Linking strike and association

movements under the aegis of the International, these federations pursued a cooperative strategy for socialism that was the very opposite of Proudhonism.[80]

The socialist implications of this strategy were drawn in the arena of the International where skilled workers from several countries discussed their common experience. By the late 1860s, the original mutualism of French International- ists, largely verbal to begin with, had been radicalized by the experience of political and economic struggle. Drawn into the 1867 bronze strike for the right to organize, the Parisian bureau had begun to organize support for strikes on an international scale. At the same time it joined republicans in several political demonstrations. At the International's con- gress of Lausanne in 1867, French delegates revised their opposition to strikes and political action, recognizing the importance of republican liberties for the growth of trade organization.[81]

Criticizing the commercial tendencies of existing associa- tions, this congress urged trade societies to establish associa- tions as a means of socialist transformation. At the next congress held in Brussels in 1868, several French delegates joined the Belgian César de Paepe in extending the principle of collective property to agriculture, the last preserve of individualism for most mutualists. Though a mutualist minority continued to oppose the collectivization of agricul- ture in 1869, all French delegates approved a report calling for the collectivization of industry in a federation of trades and workers' communes. Divided on the agricultural ques- tion, they were all trade socialists.[82]

The experience of political and economic struggle under the Empire and exposure to new ideas served to radicalize the mutualism of French Internationalists. Their participation in strikes and republican demonstrations ended the official toleration of the society. In 1868, the Parisian bureau was twice condemned and dissolved along with several provincial sections.[83] Taking advantage of the liberalization of the law on public assembly and press in 1868, Parisian militants were exposed to revolutionary Blanquist and communist ideas for the first time since 1851. During a series of public assemblies on the social question held in working-class quarters, one orator, Alfred Briosne, expressed the general consensus when he called for the collectivization of all but the most artisanal trades.[84] By 1869, leadership of the French International had fallen into the hands of militants who considered themselves revolutionary collectivists.

Beginning to reorganize the sections into "a great socialist party," these new leaders—Varlin and Benoît Malon in Paris, Albert Richard in Lyons, and André Bastelica in Marseilles— abandoned association for a revolutionary program of class struggle. Richard and Bastelica had enrolled in Bakunin's Social Democratic Alliance, which advocated that a workers' revolution overthrow the bourgeois state to achieve the collectivization of the means of production in a federation of industrial and agricultural associations. Varlin and Malon, the imprisoned leaders of the Parisian bureau, perhaps also under the influence of Bakunin, also disavowed the cooperative strategy for a revolutionary one. Only after the Commune, however, would the ideas of these revolutionary collectivists triumph in the French International and labor movement.[85]

COOPERATIVE SOCIALISM UNDER THE COMMUNE

The Paris Commune has usually been treated as a primarily political republican movement, resulting from exceptional wartime circumstances and an exacerbated patriotism, divided politically between a Jacobin majority and mutualist minority, and vague and confused in its social purpose. Marxist historians criticized its deficiencies as a socialist phenomenon, liberals its excesses as a republican one (see Bibliographical Essay). Both concluded that the Commune was not socialist because they were looking for the wrong kind of socialism—Marxism rather than the cooperative socialism of the labor movement. The standard assessment thus overlooked the continuity of the Commune with 1848 and its underlying cooperative project for trade socialism.

Labor and association movements developed in conjunction with "irreconcilable" republicans who constituted the Radical Party. In publishing the first Radical newspaper, *Le Réveil,* in 1868, Charles Delescluze wished to build an alliance of left republicans and socialists with social reform as its end. The first Radical candidacy of Léon Gambetta in 1869 was sponsored by a committee of socialist workers in Belleville. Accepting a mandate from this committee, Gambetta demanded political and civil liberty, direct election of municipal and government officials, free public education, separation of church and state, and the abolition of standing armies but made only vague references to economic reforms and the "abolition of privileges and monopolies." If Radicals like Gambetta stressed political reforms, however, it was not because they opposed social reform but because they believed that radical democracy was a necessary precondition for radical social change.[86]

The major difference from 1848 was that Radicals now looked to a communalist rather than centralist republic as the lever for social change. The experience of cesarian democracy under the Empire had taught them to distrust the bureaucratic and authoritarian state and to seek reform within the urban commune, the stronghold of Radicalism and the working class. As in 1848, many Radicals still sought the solution to the social problem in producers' association. After the bankruptcy of the Crédit au Travail in 1868, republicans continued their support through the Commission Consultative, which counted 40,000 Parisian workers in 80 cooperative societies in 1869.[87] The major Radical dailies, *La Marseillaise* of Henri Rochefort and *Le Rappel* of Victor Hugo, actively promoted associations. Within the framework of municipal governments, Radicals could once again be counted upon to assist with public credits and contracts.

Only a few Radicals—Blanc, Alfred Talandier, Alfred Naquet, Elie Réclus, and others—were self-declared collectivists. Many supported associationism as a form of "practical socialism" without defending the collectivist ideal.[88] Since they had to appeal to a socially heterogeneous constituency consisting of urban workers, tradesmen, provincial business-men, and professionals, they appreciated the ambiguity of a formula that was attractive to liberals and socialists alike. Yet, whatever their original intention, they could be led by circumstances and their working class allies to support, as under the Paris Commune, a socialist cooperative program.

After 1869 the International grew in alliance with Radical-ism. Over the opposition of Richard and Emile Aubry, Malon led the majority of Internationalists into the republican movement, hoping thereby to obtain greater liberty, build the organization, and push the entire movement in a socialist direction. After hesitating between abstention and a labor candidacy, Internationalists rallied to the Radicals Gambetta, Rochefort, and Jean-Baptiste Bancel, adding a series of economic demands, including the collectivization of banks and public utilities, to their programs. They collaborated closely with Rochefort, the first "socialist" deputy, on *La Marseillaise* and joined in several mass street demonstrations against the Empire, notably at the funeral of Victor Noir, the journalist killed by Napoléon's cousin, which nearly erupted into a premature uprising. [89]

While fighting the Empire, they continued to build their organization, encouraging the formation of unions, associa-tions, and workers' federations and collecting funds, for strikers. In response to their gestures of solidarity, trade societies from all over France voted their adhesion to the association in a mostly symbolic act. The only place where the International was seriously organized was in Paris where neighborhood sections combined with trade society members to form the Parisian Federation, which shared common headquarters, rue de la Corderie, leadership, and policies with the older workers' federation. If we exclude the members of the workers' federations, who were not strictly affiliates, the total membership of the International in France probably never exceeded 40,000. [90] For the most part, the International was still oriented toward the republican alliance and the cooperative strategy for socialism. The new revolutionary leadership had little time to propagate their ideas before government prosecution sent them to jail in June and the Franco-Prussian War ended the activity of the International.[91]

Having opposed the dynastic war, Internationalists rallied to the defense of the new French Republic on September 4, 1871, forming local vigilance committees and the Central Committee of the Arrondissements to strengthen its democratic and social character. Struggling against both Prussians and moderate republicans, they demanded the immediate election of municipal governments or communes, the arming of the people, and controls on prices and rents. Disillusioned with the economic liberalism, military timidity, and tergiversation of the government, they participated in a series of abortive uprisings in Paris, Lyons, Marseilles, and Brest, notably the Parisian insurrections of October 31 and January 22.[92] For the legislative elections of February 8, following the armistice, they proposed a list of revolutionary candidates, demanding: "the political accession of the workers; overthrow of the governmental oligarchy and industrial feudalism; [and] organization of a Republic which will achieve political liberty through social equality by giving the workers the instruments of labor."[93]

The election of a monarchist National Assembly on February 8 dashed all hopes of achieving a social republic through parliamentary means. As the Assembly ratified the humiliating peace agreement and dismantled the social institutions of the Republic, the Central Committee of the Parisian National Guard was formed to defend its arms and the Republic. When Thiers on March 18 attempted to seize the cannon of the guard, he set off a spontaneous communalist revolution. Arising in working class quarters and the largely working class guard, this insurrection contained the seeds of radical social change.[94] Hesitating at first to support a revolution that was not of its own making, the Parisian International rallied with a manifesto on March 23:

> The independence of the Commune is the gage of a contract whose clauses, freely debated, will put an end to the antagonism of classes and will assure social equality. We have demanded the emancipation of the workers, and the communal delegation is its guarantee, for it should provide the citizen with the means of defending his rights, of effectively controlling the acts of his representatives entrusted with the administration of his interests and of determining the progressive application of social reforms.[95]

Communal autonomy was favored not as an abstract political principle, but as the political regime most favorable to "the organization of credit, exchange and association in order to assure the worker the full value of his labor."

Although survival was the primordial concern of the newly elected Commune, it was prepared to enact those reforms leading to workers' emancipation from the wage system. If only twenty-five members were manual workers, a majority of the journalists, tradesmen, and intellectuals came from working class districts, which had been mobilized in vigilance committees, clubs, unions, and sections of the International.[96] If only twenty-three were members of the International, a majority of Radicals and Blanquists had during their campaigns promised "the continuous and assiduous search for the best means to provide the producer with capital, the instruments of labor, markets and credit in order to end forever wage labor and horrible pauperism. . . ."[97] In the official Declaration of the Commune to the French People, drafted jointly by Radicals and mutualists, the entire assembly claimed the "right to enact those economic and administrative reforms that the population demands; to create institutions to promote . . . education, production, exchange and credit; to universalize power and property according to the necessities of the moment, the wishes of all those concerned and the lessons of experience."[98] Though the Radical majority and mutualist minority differed over governmental forms, they were in basic agreement over the necessity for revolutionary defense and the ultimate goal of labor emancipation.[99]

Through the Commission on Labor and Exchange controlled by Internationalists, the Commune began to enact those reforms leading to emancipation. The key measure toward this end was the decree of April 16 that provided for the seizure of abandoned workshops and their exploitation by associations of former employees under the supervision of the unions.[100] New associations created by unions received guarantees of public credit and contracts. Several trades, notably mechanics and iron founders, seized private shops and operated them as associations. The mechanics gave their delegates to the commission the following mandate: "Eliminate the exploitation of man by man, the last form of slavery, organize work through *associations solidaires* with collective and inalienable capital."[101]

When the Commune awarded uniform contracts to a sweating subcontractor, the tailors petitioned for a collective contract for all 30,000 in their trade. Reporting favorably on the petition, Léon Frankel, Internationalist head of the commission, asserted: "We must not forget that the revolution of March 18 was made exclusively by the working class. If we who believe in social equality do nothing for this class, I see no reason for the Commune."[102] A decree of May 12 authorized the award of public contracts to associations under preferential conditions to be determined jointly with the unions. In response to a similar petition from the Union des Femmes, the central women's organization, the Commune agreed to open workshops for unemployed women under the supervision of the International and newly organized female unions. Finally, the commission of unions on the April 16 decree received several projects from workers for universal association, including one under the aegis of the International that would eliminate capitalists in the various trades gradually without "in the least disturbing the egotistical and absurd laws that regulate us."[103]

While the association movement had little chance to develop under the embattled Commune, it constituted, as Marx alone noted,[104] its authentically socialist project. As in 1848, workers assumed they could overcome capitalist enterprise with the aid of public credit and contracts without otherwise violating the rule of the free market. Over the workers of 1848 they possessed the advantage of the Commune, a radically democratic government with an active working class constituency that was even willing to confiscate some private capital for their associations. Marx believed that the success of the association movement depended on the workers' possession of state power. The same cooperative socialism that he denounced as petty bourgeois in the context of the Second Republic he would recognize as truly proletarian under the Paris Commune because he saw it as a workers' government in transition to a dictatorship of the proletariat.[105]

EARLY THIRD REPUBLIC: THE FINAL CONSECRATION

The defeat of the Commune was a severe setback for the labor movement that had formed under the Empire. As supporters of the Commune, workers bore the brunt of the repression that brought death, deportation, and exile to tens of thousands—a temporary loss of 100,000 workers in 1872 and permanent loss of 30,000—including many leaders of unions and the International, and the dissolution of all labor organization. More than 20,000 died in defense of Paris. Of the nearly 40,000 arrested and held under primitive conditions, the vast majority were skilled workers, with the largest numbers coming from the metal and construction trades. By 1875 military courts had condemned 10,000 to death, deportation, and prison. The professions with the largest numbers convicted were locksmiths, masons, joiners, shoemakers, house painters, typographers, stonemasons, cabinetmakers, and jewelers. Thousands of others escaped the terror to exile. So grave was the immediate labor shortage that some employers appealed to the government for amnesty.[106]

Under the state of siege that lasted until 1876, the government exercised arbitrary authority over rights of assembly, association, and the press, dissolving assemblies and unions and suspending newspapers at its discretion.[107] Until full amnesty was granted in 1880 workers could still be arrested for deeds committed under the Commune. Prudence and moderation were requisite for survival. Having blamed the International for the insurrection, conservatives passed the Dufaure Bill, which imposed stiff penalties for persons joining or assisting any "international association . . . that seeks to incite work stoppages, [or] to abolish property rights, the family, [or] religion."[108] In addition, the government proscribed all labor assemblies or federations as attempts to revive the dreaded International.

While barring trade federations, the government did tolerate the reorganization of unions that began in 1872. Under the state of siege, they had to obtain prior authorization for meetings, which were closely guarded by the police. Profiting from the labor shortage caused by the repression, several trades struck successfully in 1872 for higher wages. By October, forty-five societies had been reorganized. Efforts were resumed to create associations. To insure their socialist orientation, as a check against the elitist tendencies that had appeared under the Empire, several were organized under the direct supervision of the unions.[109]

Radical journalists and politicians encouraged this revival and defended workers' civil and political liberties, including full amnesty for the Communards and the right to strike and organize. They also lent their support to the surviving association movement, which returned the compliments.[110] The central figure in this Radical-labor alliance was Joseph Barberet. As the labor editor of the popular daily *Le Rappel*, Barberet opposed strikes and promoted the formation of syndical associations, owned and controlled by the unions, as well as the universal or trade federation, aiding what he called the "spontaneous" movement for the "gradual abolition of the wage system."[111]

Barberet was a rather mysterious figure; he had worked with Rochefort on *La Marseillaise* and with Paschal Grousset, delegate for foreign affairs under the Commune. Remaining immune from prosecution for the crime that sent Grousset to deportation, he was subject to persistent speculation about his relations with the police. In 1879 he was fired from *Le Rappel* after a former policeman testified that he had received immunity in return for services rendered the Préfecture. In the climate of fear and suspicion following the Commune, the police had infiltrated the labor and Radical community, recruiting some of the leading figures to its intelligence network. Whatever the nature of Barberet's connection, he appears to have served the cooperative labor movement with sincere dedication even after his ascent to the Ministry of Interior in 1880.[112]

His chief collaborators in the early 1870s were Julien Dupire and Charles Chabert. A former editor of a labor newspaper under the Commune, secretary of the tailors' union and cooperative, and labor columnist for several republican newspapers, Dupire became the first cooperative leader to convert to revolutionary socialism. Police used a youthful indiscretion to force him to report on labor activities, a duty which he performed quite reliably until his exposure in 1879.[113] Despite suspicions that he may have acted as a provocateur, he, too, appears to have been devoted to the cause of worker emancipation.

Chabert was a prize-winning metal engraver whose life exemplified the history of the Parisian proletariat. Born in 1818 on the Ile Saint-Louis, he had known 1830, 1848, 1851, and 1871. He had been imprisoned for the June insurrection and deported for resistance to Napoléon's coup d'état. During the 1860s he was active in his union and in the International. Later, he was a leader of his neighborhood vigilance committee and municipal candidate under the siege and Commune. His political experience, oratorical talent, and relative moderation made him the ideal leader of the post-Commune movement.[114]

From 1872 to 1875 the police thwarted several attempts by this group to form a general trade and mutual credit federation. Having assembled the trade delegates, however, Barberet was able to sponsor labor candidates for the 1873 *Prud'hommes* elections, to promote collective bargaining, and send 105 labor delegates to the Universal Exposition at Vienna. Out of this delegation came the idea for an independent labor newspaper and labor candidacy. Radical politicians and editors used promises of financial aid to associations and support for amnesty to curtail these projects of labor independence.[115]

During the legislative elections of 1876, which resulted in republican victories, several labor candidates appeared in the shadows of Radical candidates, promising to withdraw for them on the second round. The growing tendency of Radicals like Gambetta to compromise on their program, particularly the demand for amnesty, a tendency that Rochefort labeled "opportunism," impelled labor militants to approve the principle of separate labor candidacies. Running against an Opportunist in an April by-election, Chabert was nearly elected on a program of social reform. Out of this campaign came the project for a new Radical daily with a distinctly socialist tinge. With Chabert and Louis Pauliat as its labor editors *La Tribune, organe républicain des questions démocratiques et sociales,* set out to organize the first national labor congress in France. In reaction to Gambetta's opportunism, a new labor party was beginning to emerge from under the protective wings of Radicalism.[116]

By 1876 the labor movement had nearly returned to its prewar strength with 86 *syndicats* and 14 other trade societies comprising over 20,000 workers in Paris and perhaps 80 other societies in the provinces. As previously, the largest and most representative unions were in the highly skilled trades—bronze workers, typographers, plumbers, jewelers, mechanics, and so on.[117] Because of government repression and stiff employer resistance in this period, few strikes were successful and none originated in the unions. Thus, labor delegates at Vienna had condemned strikes as a "primitive form" of association and recommended the syndical association as the way to abolish gradually the wage system.[118]

The republican legislative victory in February 1876 set the stage for the first national labor congress held in Paris in October. As the final report put it, "From the moment that the republican form of government was assured, it was indispensable for the working class, which had marched until then together with the republican bourgeoisie, to affirm its own interests and to seek the means by which it could transform its economic condition."[119] The congress was convoked by the new socialist Radical daily *La Tribune* with the help of Radical politicians and press. An organizing committee headed by Chabert set strict rules for the assembly, admitting only bona fide worker delegates, selecting speeches, barring debates, and fixing a "practical" agenda. Amid rumors of dissolution, delegates were told to "conform to all the prescriptions of the law, even the most petty"; to avoid politics, systems, and ideologies; and to "observe a great prudence of language." Nearly 300 delegates and alternates came from 98 Parisian societies—68 unions, 11 consumer cooperatives, 6 producers' associations, and 9 mutual aid societies. They were joined by 105 delegates from 37 provincial towns, notably Lyons, Bordeaux, Grenoble, Saint-Etienne, Dijon, Nantes, and Lille, representing mechanics, tailors, joiners, painters, shoemakers, and other skilled trades. With the exclusion of both middle class and revolutionary representatives, this was a congress of the cooperative labor movement.[120]

Delegates demanded complete liberty of association and recommended the *syndicat* as the "organizing committee" for association that alone could obtain the "full fruit" of labor for the worker. While many delegates also saw the unions as instruments of trade defense, they felt that their economic weakness and the hostility of employers precluded effective trade unionism. Criticizing existing associations,

Parisian delegates insisted on the need for truly collectivist syndical associations. Considering the weakness of unions in the provinces, several delegates presented projects for universal associations of all trades. On the agricultural question, delegates extended their cooperative program to the countryside, calling for the purchase of land and machinery by peasant associations.[121]

The final cooperative resolution drafted by Dupire evaluated various kinds of cooperatives on the basis of socialist desiderata:

> What strikes us particularly in the social institutions that govern us is the antagonism of interest that exists between each member of society; it is this general battle of life, this struggle of every day and every moment in which only the most clever, intelligent, strong and deceitful triumph. In this situation the eternal principles of justice and equity are continuously violated in the name of order, society and even of law. All this is obviously the result of the continued application of the principles of individualism that govern us in the operation of existing institutions instead of the fecund principle of solidarity that we all profess but do not practice.[122]

The only "radical means to liberate labor and eliminate poverty," he said, was the syndical association constituting a collective and inalienable capital:

> Social capital ... should not be appropriated either by individuals or groups of individuals, but should, by virtue of the principles of solidarity so resolutely asserted nowadays, be the impersonal, indivisible, and inalienable property of the mass of workers, considered either by trades, or by department, city, canton or commune.[123]

While adopting the traditional cooperative program, the congress did take the first hesitant steps toward the creation of a labor party. Speaker after speaker denounced the exploitation and political monopoly of the bourgeoisie. The

most popular speaker was Victor Prost, a clockmaker from
Dijon:

> Citizens, our bourgeoisie is no longer in the path of progress. It
> is petrified in place like the wife of Lot; it holds all the political
> and administrative offices and thanks to its capital controls the
> entire economy in which, as you know, the worker, who has only
> his labor and professional skill, does not count, the same labor
> and talent that are the honor and wealth of the country without
> which the bourgeoisie would not have a scrap of bread to eat or
> clothes to cover its back. . . . The bourgeoisie has completely lost
> all the ties that once attached it to the people; it now constitutes
> a separate class in society with distinct interests that are not at all
> those of the worker.[124]

Even those bourgeois Radicals who proclaimed their love of
the people were ignorant of the workers' needs and aspirations. Only labor candidates drawn from the ranks and
responsible to them could effectively represent workers in
parliament. In a final report, the congress approved Chabert's
project for a labor newspaper and recommended the presen-
tation of labor candidates with mandates not "to force the
state to take charge of our affairs, but to eliminate the
numerous barriers strewn in our path and give us the political
liberties that are necessary for the improvement of our
condition."[125]

The second national labor congress, held in February 1878
in Lyons, after the preceding May 16 crisis, confirmed this
basic orientation: "The *syndicats* must not forget that the
wage system is but a transitory stage between serfdom and an
unnamed state; they must do their utmost to establish
general societies of consumption, credit and production
under their close surveillance, the absence of which has
caused past failures."[126] The congress of Lyons also reaffirmed its support for Chabert's labor newspaper and the
labor candidacy as the basis for a *"parti socialiste
ouvrier."*[127] Thus, while reaffirming cooperative strategy,
these congresses already prefigured the break of the labor
movement from Radicalism and the formation of a labor
socialist party.

The only trade that executed the cooperative program was the tailors. With fifty-franc shares collected from union dues, they formed an association with a "collective, indivisible and inalienable capital" for the emancipation of all Parisian tailors. Rather than pay interest or dividends, the Union Syndicale reinvested its earnings, hoping to accumulate one million francs, the sum estimated to employ all tailors. It functioned until 1880 when it was calculated that 200 million francs—2,000 per tailor—would be needed for the entire trade.[128]

The association movement fell short of expectations in the 1870s. Though nearly every *syndicat* had plans for association, few were actually begun. A survey in 1880 found that only seventeen had been started between 1872 and 1878. Fear of a monarchical restoration and the end of the inflationary spiral of the 1860s put a damper on the movement. Several succumbed to the industrial crisis of 1877 and 1878, which ruined many luxury trades with international competition. Still, cooperators could look forward to the definitive triumph of the Republic to begin their projects under more favorable circumstances.[129]

Thus, until the advent of the Third Republic, the French labor movement remained tied to a cooperative program for socialism. Whether formulated explicitly by Buchez or Blanc or in the actual practice of trade societies, this program assumed that associations could accumulate capital, outcompete, and eventually absorb private enterprise peacefully and gradually with the aid of a democratic republic. Representing the popular classes, middle and working classes together, such a republic would provide the decisive leverage needed to overcome capitalism and expropriate the bourgeoisie. This form of socialism, seeking workers' ownership of the means of production, was generated within a broader democratic movement and ideology. It was thus based upon faith in the socialist determination of middle class republicans and the basic harmony of interest between the working and broad middle classes.

If, in the end, such a faith proved to be utopian, it was not obvious to workers through most of the century. From 1830 through 1880, under the Second Republic and Paris Commune, radical republicanism had been a revolutionary movement struggling against the bourgeois state with an active working class constituency and cooperative socialist program. Workers had little reason to question this program until it was put to the test of political power, until republicans were forced to choose between socialism and capitalism, between the workers and the bourgeoisie. Blocked by Napoléon and Thiers, the social experiments of 1848 and 1871 had done little to destroy workers' faith in republican socialism.

Already in the 1870s, however, the growth of an Opportunist Radicalism, exemplified by Gambetta, championing the middle class *couches nouvelles* and economic liberalism, impelled militants to begin the formation of a separate labor party. As Radicals attempted to reconcile the broad reaches of peasants and middle class to the republic, they were forced to abandon their revolutionary and utopian pretensions.[130] But the real discovery of bourgeois Radicalism did not come until republicans failed the test of political power and an alternative was found in revolutionary socialism. The advent of the Third Republic in 1879, after fifty years of struggle, and the return of revolutionary socialism provided that test, that alternative, and that discovery.

3

From Cooperation
to Revolution

From its origins under the July Monarchy through the Second and early Third Republics, the French labor movement remained attached to republicanism and the utopia of association. Beginning in 1876, Jules Guesde returned from exile to propagate revolutionary collectivism, the revolutionary trade socialism that had grown out of the First International. Suddenly, in 1879 at the third national labor congress in Marseilles, delegates decided to abandon republicanism and form a separate labor party seeking collectivization of the means of production. Leading Parisian unions joined the new Parti Ouvrier and adopted its revolutionary program. In 1886 a national trade union congress endorsed a similar program, confirming the Parisian trend on a national scale. The vehicle of socialism thus shifted from the producers' cooperative to the revolutionary labor party.

Like the cooperators, the Parti Ouvrier also sought the collectivization of the means of production in a federation of trades. Like them, it appealed almost exclusively to urban skilled workers. But whereas the cooperators had believed that socialism could be attained peacefully within the confines of a middle class republic, the party asserted that this change could only come about through a revolution overthrowing the middle class state. In the new program,

former cooperators found not only an explicit statement of
their socialist goal, but a strategy that, far from depending
upon the good will of middle class reformists, appealed
directly to their experience of class antagonism and to the
revolutionary tradition acquired in the struggle for the
Republic.

Two types of explanation have traditionally been advanced
for the ideological change of 1879. In arguing their case, the
revolutionaries frequently cited the failure of cooperation
and one historian has seen the "manifest failure" of
associations in the 1870s to open the way for the revolutionaries.[1] Whatever the state of cooperation in the 1870s, it
does not seem to have dampened enthusiasm for the idea at
the national labor congresses of 1878 or even 1879. The
belated resurgence of the movement in 1879 seems to
indicate that it was very much alive and that most trade
unions had merely been awaiting the triumph of the Republic
to begin their projects under favorable circumstances. In any
event, there had always been a great disparity between
promise and performance in the association movement and
the relative lack of success in the late 1870s does little to
explain the volte-face of 1880.

More generally, it has been suggested that the growth of
heavy industry condemned the association movement.[2]
Associations might have been viable in artisanal trades in
which skilled labor constituted the major capital and workers
controlled the process of production, but they had little
relevance to heavy industry, which required enormous
outlays of capital and central managerial authority. In the
revolutionary mobilization of 1848 and 1871, Parisian
mechanics had operated large metallurgical factories as
associations[3] but, generally, unskilled workers lacked the
capacity to purchase and organize their own productive
apparatus. While industrialization would have certainly condemned associationism as a viable socialist strategy in the
long run, the change did not occur in the long run, but in the
particular circumstances of 1880. Though there had been

considerable industrial growth in the 1870s, it represented a recovery from the ravages of the Franco-Prussian war and did not alter the predominance of traditional production.[4] From all available indices it appears that artisanal production continued to predominate through 1900. In any event, large-scale industrialization did not affect Parisian industry, which experienced decentralization, or alter the social basis of its labor movement.[5] The shift to revolutionary collectivism did not involve a significant influx of more industrial workers, and the Parti Ouvrier continued to reflect the concerns and outlook of skilled workers.

Though the growth of heavy industry and failure of cooperation provided solid arguments against the traditional strategy, the decisive reason for the change appears to lie in the realm of politics. When revolutionaries returned to the trade unions in 1879, the debate turned not on the feasibility of associations, but on the relationship of workers to the new Republic, Radicalism, and the reformist middle class. Predicated upon the rapid accumulation of capital, the success of the association strategy depended upon the mobilization of the working class and active assistance of the social Republic and reformist middle class. In 1848 and even in 1871, a significant portion of the middle class had aligned itself with the workers and supported their association movement. The advent of the Third Republic in 1879 brought not a repetition of 1848 and 1871, but the consolidation of political democracy under relatively stable social and economic conditions, the accession of middle class *couches nouvelles* to political power, and the reconciliation of the bourgeoisie to liberal democracy. The consolidation of the Republic after 1879, by ending restrictions on revolutionary activity and disappointing hopes of socialist transformation, determined the break with the cooperative program.

INTERNATIONALIST ORIGINS OF COLLECTIVISM

Rather than an abstract doctrine elaborated by a single theoretician, collectivism was an ideology that had grown out of the discussions and experience of the First International. The International had been founded in 1864 as a "central medium of communication and co-operation among workers of different countries seeking . . . mutual aid, progress and the complete emancipation of the working class."[6] It was founded by French, English, and German workers who shared sentiments of class solidarity and concern for social justice rather than any single conception of socialism. Through mutual discussion and experience, it became a crucible in which the practices of English trade unionism, French cooperation, and German communism were fused into a common labor program. As seen previously, the exchange of ideas and the experience of political and economic struggle had radically transformed the original Proudhonism of French, Swiss, and Belgian members. As German representative on the executive general council, Karl Marx had provided the association with statutes, principles, and programs that expressed the general consensus, the real movement of the international labor movement.[7]

By 1869, the several currents of the skilled labor movement that had gone into the International reached a general ideological consensus known as collectivism. Introduced by de Paepe, the term originated with Baron Hippolyte de Colins, the Belgian socialist who advocated the collectivization of landed property through the gradual abolition of inheritance. Within the International, it was applied to all those who were willing to extend the principle of collectivization beyond industry, where it was admitted by all, to agriculture as well. Although the term was later appropriated by state socialists, it originally designated a federalist socialism in which the means of production would be owned and controlled by workers directly in a federation of trades, associations, and communes. Although, with the exception of a few French Proudhonists, there was general agreement on collectivism, the International before the Commune had never really discussed, let alone resolved, the ways and means of collectivism, whether it could be achieved through cooperative, electoral, or revolutionary means.

If a majority of French Internationalists in 1871 were still cooperative socialists, most others had already converted to revolutionary collectivism. The main inspiration for this change had come from the fiery Russian Bakunin. Combining his passion for conspiracy and insurrection with the collectivist principles of the International, Bakunin founded the Social Democratic Alliance in 1869 to serve as a revolutionary vanguard.[8] Under its influence the new leaders of the French International—Richard, Bastelica, Varlin and Malon— had abandoned cooperation for revolutionary collectivism. Richard, Bastelica, and Varlin were among those "intimates" whom Bakunin trusted to form a "collective dictatorship of revolutionaries" to lead the spontaneous workers' revolution to a successful collectivist conclusion.[9] These collectivists viewed the trade union or *syndicat* as the main instrument of revolution and unit of production in a socialist federation of trades and workers' communes.[10] Thus, they pursued trade socialism by revolutionary rather than cooperative means.

The prewar leader who had best articulated the strategy of revolutionary collectivism was Varlin. Born of peasant stock and apprenticed to a Parisian bookbinder at an early age, Varlin played an important part in nearly all phases of the labor movement under the Empire. Founder and leader of the bookbinders' society, he was perhaps the most radical of the mutualists who established the first Parisian bureau of the International. After he had broken with the cooperators in 1868, he worked tirelessly to organize strikes and trade unions as schools for the collective revolutionary action that alone could abolish the wage system. As against state socialism with its centralist and hierarchical organization, Varlin advocated an "antiauthoritarian communism" or collectivism in which the means of production would be owned and controlled by the workers themselves in their trade unions, which would be transformed by the revolution from organs of resistance into producers' associations. In contrast to the pure syndicalists, who believed in the sufficiency of trade union representation, Varlin saw the continuing need for some form of communal or political apparatus to serve the needs of men as citizens as well as producers.[11]

While eliminating revolutionaries like Varlin from the trade unions, the repression of the Commune further radicalized those Internationalists who remained in the underground or escaped the terror in exile. The suppression of the Commune heightened skepticism about the possibilities of peaceful change, especially electoral action, which the ban on the International excluded altogether. Meanwhile, the revolutionaries in the International, Marx in London and the Swiss Jurassians, offered moral and material aid to the Communard refugees, the latter helping them escape and settle in Switzerland. When the French refused to join a small Bakuninist circle in Geneva, a larger Section de Propagande et d'Action Révolutionnaire was formed to welcome them. In this way were the French refugees drawn into an alliance with the Jurassian Federation in its dispute with Marx and the executive general council of the International.[12]

For five years as the "anonymous spokesman" of the general council, Marx had guided the International, respecting democratic norms and trusting in mutual discussion and the lessons of experience to lead workers toward socialist conclusions.[13] The entry of his old friend and rival Bakunin into the association and Bakunin's rapid success in winning friends in Italy, Spain, France, Belgium, and the Swiss Jura seemed to threaten both his leadership and the gradual evolution toward socialism. Holding Bakunin responsible for the authentic manifestations of federalism in the labor movement, Marx decided to use his authority on the council to root out Bakunin's intrigues and influence.[14]

The conflict broke out over the question of electoral activity in the French Swiss Federation of the International where Bakunin had acquired a following among foreign—and thus ineligible—construction workers in Geneva and among Jurassian clockmakers led by James Guillaume. When the native skilled workers of Geneva entered into an electoral alliance with Radicals, the Genevan Bakuninists and Jurassians adopted a position of electoral abstention, preferring to concentrate on purely economic or trade union activity. When the Genevan Bakuninists were refused admission to the French Swiss Federation in April 1870, the organization split into two. Speaking for the council, Marx settled the dispute in favor of the electoralist Genevans, reminding the Jurassians that the statutes recognized political action as a means of economic struggle and advising them to form their own federation.

The failure of the Commune and the Europe-wide repression that followed had persuaded many Internationalists of the need for greater political unity in the association. Thus, in 1871 Marx and Engels seized the opportunity to eliminate Bakunin's antipolitical influence and to accelerate the transformation of the International from a strictly trade organization into a political party seeking the conquest of state power. Exercising dictatorial authority, they postponed the regular general congress and convened a secret London conference with their own followers. This conference ratified their action in the Swiss dispute, extended their power to combat the Bakuninists, notably dissolving the French Section de Propagande in Geneva, and passed a resolution that, as rewritten by them, asserted that "the proletariat can only act as a class by forming itself into a distinct political party opposed to the old parties formed by the propertied classes."[15]

By making these unilateral decisions Marx swung most of the French exiles into the Jurassian camp. While endorsed in the statutes and declarations of the general council, the use of political action had never been formally approved by French Internationalists from whose version of the statutes the political means clause had been deliberately omitted.[16] Accidental mistranslations in the French version also tended to reduce the council's power. Thus, the action of the council appeared to violate basic principles of the International, federalist democracy, ideological pluralism, and the subordination of the political to the economic struggle. Following the London conference, the French Section de Propagande, including such leaders as Malon, Gustave Lefrançais, and Jules Guesde, took up the Jurassian cause, making their weekly *La Révolution sociale* the official organ of the Jurassian Federation.[17]

The French and Jurassians formed a federalist organization in which the federal committee served merely as a bureau for correspondence, statistics, and information and issued a circular to other federations of the International. This *Sonvillier Circular* accused the general council of trying to create "a hierarchical and authoritarian organization of disciplined sections" and demanded a return to "its normal function ... of a simple bureau of correspondence and statistics."[18] Despite Marx's desperate efforts to retain their loyalty, the *Circular* received a favorable response from French, Spanish, and Italian members. By treating all these federalists, including Malon and other French militants, as Bakuninists, Marx threw all the major federations into opposition.[19]

With an artificial majority assembled at The Hague congress of the International in September 1872, Marx expelled the leading Bakuninists, expanded the authority of the general council, and had the association recognize the need for a working class political party seeking the conquest of state power. Knowing that his victory was essentially pyrrhic, Marx then had the council transferred to New York where it would be immune from the federalist majority on the continent. In the "antiauthoritarian" congress of Saint-Imier that immediately followed The Hague, delegates from Italy, Spain, France, and the Jura repudiated its decisions and approved a series of revolutionary collectivist resolutions that received the endorsement of the clandestine French sections. After all the organized federations had repudiated The Hague, the Jurassians convened a general congress in Geneva in 1873 to continue the International without the general council. Agreeing to disagree on the question that had caused the split, the use of political action, the International thus survived as an "antiauthoritarian" federalist organization.[20]

Though this "antiauthoritarian" International actually possessed greater ideological diversity than its predecessor, including both English trade unionists and German state socialists, its core federations, Jurassian, Italian, Spanish, French, and Belgian, were revolutionary collectivist. Like its predecessor, it was chiefly representative of urban skilled workers.[21] As the pivotal federation, the Jurassians were very flexible regarding appropriate revolutionary tactics. Considering conditions in the Jura unpropitious for either immediate insurrectionary or electoral action, they concentrated on trade organization, but they were willing to concede the usefulness of violent propaganda in Italy or electoral action in Germany or Belgium. As regards the federalist form of socialism, they were willing to grant the degree of centralism in a federation of trades that was dictated by economic concentration and arose from the free choice of federated groups rather than from the imposition of a central authority. Treating these questions as matters of tactics and circumstance rather than principle, the Jurassians maintained revolutionary unity between more "anarchistic" and more political collectivists.[22]

In 1872, Marx had labeled the entire collectivist opposition as "anarchist" but it is inappropriate to speak of a separate anarchist movement before 1880. The anarchist collectivists were those who, like the Italians, advocated the use of direct revolutionary propaganda. Following Bakunin's advice, the Italian Federation carried out a series of abortive uprisings in 1874 and again in 1877 at San Lupo in order to rouse the slumbering peasants to revolution.[23] In addition to practicing this "propaganda of the deed," the Italians also adopted the communist ideal. For the collectivist formula of reward "to each according to his work," they substituted the communist "to each according to his needs," considering "the collective ownership of the products of labor as the necessary complement of the collectivist program, the cooperation of all for the satisfaction of the needs of each being the only rule of production and consumption that corresponds to the principle of solidarity."[24]

At the other end of the collectivist spectrum were the political collectivists led by the Belgian de Paepe. Though a federalist trade socialist, de Paepe saw the national state or collectivity as the repository for social capital and as the administrator of those public services like the railroads that had a national scope and function.[25] Originally an electoral abstentionist, he gradually came to accept both electoral and reformist campaigns as the result of changes in the Belgian socialist movement, the growth of independent trade unions in Brussels and a Social Democratic Party in Flanders. Working to reconcile collectivists with state socialists, he helped bring both sides together at the Universal Socialist Congress of Ghent in 1877. With the exception of the Spanish and Italian "anarchists," nearly all factions at this congress agreed that "the proletariat, organized into a distinct party opposed to those formed by the possessing classes, must employ all political means that further the social emancipation of all its members,"[26] thus vindicating Marx's position five years too late. Isolating the anarchists, this congress registered the triumph of a political collectivism in the International movement.[27]

Originally divided between anarchist and political collectivists, French Internationalists also drifted in the latter direction. The anarchist faction was headed by Paul Brousse. A medical student at Montpellier, expelled from a local section because of Jurassian sympathies, Brousse had escaped to Spain, where he set up a clandestine revolutionary committee for the South, and later to Berne where he organized a section of the Jurassian Federation. In 1876, together with Prince Peter Kropotkin, Brousse subscribed to the communist anarchism of the Italians and defended "propaganda of the deed" as a powerful method of awakening a dormant revolutionary consciousness. In 1877, he founded a clandestine anarchist newspaper *l'Avant-garde* and a French Federation of the International whose first secret congress endorsed insurrectionary action. Reflecting upon the isolation and impotence of the anarchists, Brousse began to revise his position in 1878 when he recommended the electoral conquest of municipal government as a way of precipitating general revolution, a basic tactic of French labor in the 1880s. Expelled from Switzerland and then from Belgium, he finally landed in London where he too began to work for the reconciliation of all collectivists within a broad socialist party.[28]

A majority of French Internationalists were political collectivists. Led by Lefrançais and Arthur Arnould, the Genevan Section de Propagande had broken with the Jurassians in 1874 over the question of electoral action and the administrative state.[29] During this time Malon, the proletarian deputy, theoretician, and historian of the French movement, collaborated with anti-Bakuninist Italians in Milan and Palermo, attacking "propaganda of the deed" and urging a return to both trade and electoral activity.[30] Like de Paepe, his "intellectual older brother," Malon began to stress immediate reforms and a reconciliation of socialist tendencies in his bimonthly *Le Socialisme progressif* published in 1878.[31] From exile in Zurich and Lugano he worked for the creation of a broad socialist party stretching from anarchists on the left to social Radicals on the right.

The actual creation of the party was more the accomplishment of Malon's friend Guesde. A Radical journalist from Montpellier, condemned to prison for supporting the Commune, Guesde had escaped to exile in Switzerland.[32] Repelled by the authoritarian tactics of Marx's Genevan allies, he became a founder of the Section de Propagande and a leader in the struggle against Marx, learning about revolution-

ary collectivism only in the process. Like Malon, he also
emigrated to Italy where he worked with anti-Bakuninists in
Rome and Milan. As a result of his readings of the French
materialists and Russian mutualist Nikolai Chernyshevsky,
Guesde in 1874 undertook to write an *Essai de catéchisme
socialiste*.[33] From rather abstract premises about the social
nature of man, he derived the obligation to provide each
individual with the education and capital he needed to
achieve his and society's maximum development. As a
collectivist, Guesde advocated a federalist socialism administered by a federation of trade groups without re-creating a
centralized state with its distinction between rulers and ruled.

Thus, it was as a federalist socialist rather than Marxist
that Guesde returned to France in 1876 to create a socialist
party. Having accepted the necessity for electoral action, he
immediately supported the principle of the labor candidacy
and joined the struggle for the Republic. As a political
journalist and collectivist, he soon attracted the attention of
Marx and German socialists, becoming the first leader with
contacts in both the anarchist and Marxist camps. As the
"flaming sword" of the party, Guesde spearheaded the
conversion of French labor to revolutionary collectivism.

THE RETURN OF REVOLUTIONARY COLLECTIVISM

Following Guesdist orthodoxy, the standard history of
French socialism credits Guesde with converting a reformist
and Proudhonian labor movement to Marxist socialism.[34] The
importance of Guesde notwithstanding, this judgment is
deficient in several respects. First, as we have seen, revolutionary socialism was introduced not to a reformist or
Proudhonian movement, but to one already committed to a
form of socialism. Second, the form of socialism that Guesde
first introduced was not centralist or Marxist but the
federalist trade socialism he had learned in the First
International, which was itself largely the product of the
trade cooperative movement. Like its predecessor, this
socialism chiefly appealed to skilled workers. Thus, it hardly

differed from that of anarchists and other federalists who also played their part. Finally, when after 1880 Guesde did undertake a new departure, the creation of a unitary and centralist Marxist party appealing to industrial workers, he was repudiated by a labor movement that remained true to its trade origins.

The program that Guesde revived in the weekly *l'Egalité* was basically an extension of the collectivism of the "antiauthoritarian" International with but faint hints of Marxism. Arising out of trade organization, this socialism envisaged a workers' revolution collectivizing land and capital in a federation of trades and communes. *L'Egalité* defined collectivism as the negation of authority and the state:

> Every effort should be made to bring about the disappearance of the central power before the free federation of liberated communes. In the commune the municipal council is sufficient to administer—they will govern no more—the single recognized domain: Economy. The role of the Federation is to prevent the return of inequality among the communes themselves.[35]

In Guesde's collectivist design, borrowed from Malon and de Paepe, social capital administered by the commune would be leased to "free associations of producers" in return for social rent.[36] After the deduction of social rent for education and social insurance, workers organized into trade groups could then enjoy the "full product of their labor." Both Malon and Brousse treated Guesde as an anarchist in 1878. In regard to intermediary forms of struggle, namely reforms, Guesde was even more of an anarchist than Malon.[37] Holding to the rigid Lassallean iron law according to which the wages of all workers tend toward the subsistence level of the unskilled, Guesde denied the efficacy of intermediary reforms and urged socialists to prepare only for the inevitable revolution.[38]

Where Guesde differed from the anarchists, with whom he collaborated until 1880, was on the question of electoral

action versus insurrectionary violence as the most effective
means of propaganda. Guesde condemned the San Lupo
uprising and praised the labor candidacy as a means of trade
organization that could alone transform the wage system.[39]
The revolution was predicated upon the prior organization of
workers in unions and "the consciousness of their right to
capital aroused ... by an active and continuous propaganda."[40] The function of the socialist party that Guesde
wanted to create was to arouse this consciousness, using the
revolutionary candidacy as a "means of propaganda and
agitation" to articulate workers' aspirations and enable them
to judge the moment for revolutionary action.[41] Although
Guesde never excluded a peaceful electoral revolution, he
anticipated a spontaneous workers' insurrection resulting
"not from the conspiracy of a few, but from the nature of
things, the complications and difficulties that the present
economic regime inevitably produces."[42]

What was originally Marxist about Guesde was less his
actual theoretical knowledge than his pedagogical conception
of party leadership. Upon returning to France, he distinguished himself from other Internationalists by insisting that
the workers themselves could never find the proper remedies
for their suffering but needed the advice and counsel of
socialist intellectuals like himself.[43] Because of the restrictions on the unions the revival of revolutionary collectivism
had to come from without, from a circle of middle class
intellectuals. Guesde found his first disciples among a circle
of journalists and students who met regularly at the Café
Soufflot to discuss social questions. In this circle Guesde met
his future collaborators Gabriel Deville, John Labusquière,
Victor Marouck, and Emile Massard as well as Karl Hirsch, an
emissary of German Social Democracy. With little knowledge
of Marxist theory, several of the students had, as members of
a section in Toulouse, sided with Marx and admired him as a
political leader. Through this circle Guesde himself was
introduced to Marx and Marxism.[44]

As the first French collectivist leader to recognize the importance of political leadership and electoral action, Guesde attracted the attention of Marx and German Social Democracy.[45] The socialist philanthropist Karl Hochberg contributed money, and Marx and Engels sent articles and advice to *l'Egalité*. Nevertheless, they were embarrassed by Guesde's ignorance of Marxist theory. Hirsch had to apologize to Marx for Guesde's anarchist notions. So great was the difference between French revolutionary élan and German sobriety that when Guesde urged the Germans to take up arms against the antisocialist laws, they regarded it as a police provocation. In the end, what drew Marx to Guesde was not his ideas, which were more anarchist than Marxist, but their common understanding that leadership for the new party "must come from above, from those who 'know more'."[46]

The target of the first series of *l'Egalité* was the cooperative socialists in the labor movement. "Outside of revolution," it asserted, "all the cooperative societies built upon all the unions will not be powerful enough to give them [the workers] possession of the capital they lack."[47] Cooperative and revolutionary socialists shared the same goal. Had not the Commune in its April 16 decree recognized the workers' right to capital? Where they differed was on means. Associations might be viable in traditional crafts where they could only delay the process of concentration, but they could never accumulate the enormous sums needed by the industrial proletariat of mines and factories. In contrast to the cooperators, *l'Egalité* publicized strikes and organized assistance, defending the strike weapon as the only defense against exploitation and as a school for socialism.[48]

The impact of the first *l'Egalité,* which appeared weekly from November 1877 until it was fined for publishing unpatriotic articles in July 1878, was rather circumscribed. Lacking variety and written anonymously by Guesde and his circle, it was more a socialist catechism than a workers' newspaper.[49] In the first series, only fourteen notices from trade societies, including five from the mechanics, appeared. Still, through the newspaper Guesde recruited a small number of labor activists—the tailor Dupire, the mechanic Albert Amand, the *employés* Alexandre Paulard, Jules Vaidy, and Gaston Picourt—who would introduce revolutionary ideas into the unions.[50]

Anarchists also worked with Guesde on *l'Egalité*. Arriving in Paris to form a section of Brousse's federation at the end of 1877, the Italian Andrea Costa saw the futility of insurrectionary activity and suggested using Republican liberties, including the electoral system, to promote revolution. Advised by the federation to seek out "partis voisins," Costa befriended Guesde, who welcomed the anarchists as allies. Alerted to the public revival of revolutionary propaganda, highlighted by a March 18 commemorative banquet for the Commune, the police arrested Costa and raided the homes of all known revolutionaries. With evidence collected in these raids, Costa and a French anarchist were condemned to two years in prison for participation in the International, incidentally allowing Guesde to assume uncontested leadership of the revolutionaries.[51]

The revolutionaries made their first public appearance at the second national labor congress in Lyons in 1878 where the recent republican victories encouraged a new freedom of expression. All the Parisian collectivists had joined together to send Dupire to be their common representative at Lyons.[52] Influenced by the Colinist socialists, Dupire had left the tailors' cooperative association for Guesde's *l'Egalité*.[53] At Lyons, he was joined by several other revolutionaries, including Ballivet, a Lyons mechanic and secret representative of Brousse's federation.[54] Reviewing the historical record of failure, Dupire attacked cooperative associations as a device used by the bourgeoisie to divert workers from their revolutionary task: "We will obtain the true emancipation of labor in the future by the overthrow of these vicious institutions [the state and private property] for which will be substituted the free federation of workers' groups."[55]

Dupire's speech, made outside the regular agenda, prompted similar collectivist declarations from former cooperative socialists like Chabert, who announced his conversion to collectivism. The airing of revolutionary ideas disturbed public opinion and impelled the government to intervene. The organizers of the congress were summoned and instructed to curb further "disorders." Warning that deviations from the agenda would not be tolerated, they barred Dupire from the podium, refused to respond to a collectivist address from Andalusia, and deleted the demand for complete amnesty from the final resolutions. Drawing collectivist implications from the cooperative program, Dupire's rather moderate collectivist resolution received only fifteen votes, a small number resulting no doubt from the threat of government intervention.[56]

Revolutionaries anticipated victory at the international labor congress scheduled during the 1878 Paris Exposition, an event which was supposed to mark the triumph of a conservative Republic. Two different labor congresses were actually planned. Parisian unions had been mandated by the congress of Lyons to convene an international trade union congress that would bar outside socialists, while Parisian revolutionaries prepared a strictly collectivist congress in conformity with a resolution from the Universal Socialist Congress at Ghent.[57] Following the arrests of the Internationalists, Guesde persuaded the revolutionaries to merge with the unions. The revolutionaries entered the assembly of trade union delegates as worker representatives, taking over the publicity committee and nearly obtaining approval by forty to fifty votes for their collectivist agenda.[58]

Yet, even without a collectivist agenda, the projected congress presaged a dangerous resurrection of the International to a government pledged to preserve calm until the

senatorial elections of 1879. Frightened by recent assassina-
tion attempts against the Kaiser, the German government
may have applied diplomatic pressure. On July 31, the
Dufaure government banned the congress and ordered the
delegates to disperse. While the cooperators counseled com-
pliance, Guesde declared his intention to proceed. Guesde's
defiance and the disappointment of foreign and provincial
delegates, who had already arrived, eventually shamed the
cooperators into convening the congress as a private meeting
where, on September 5, its leading organizers were arrested
for forming an illegal association.[59]

In the trial held in October the prosecution distinguished
between the formal guilt of the cooperators, the true
workers, and Guesde's "violent group," who were the "men
and substance of the International." In a collective defense,[60]
Guesde argued that the government had violated the natural
rights of working men and that its real aim was to punish
them for their opinions and "prevent a congress that the
ruling class would consider as the beginning of a revolution in
the working class."[61] Finding all defendants guilty, the judge
signaled out Guesde and his disciples for the stiff penalties,
including six months' imprisonment for Guesde.[62]

Once again, government intervention had prevented the
radicalization of the labor movement. Despite their public
disavowal of Guesde, many labor leaders had already been
touched by the revolutionaries. Disappointed with the slow
progress of associations and the opportunism of Radicals,
many already foresaw a break with Radicalism and an open
declaration of war on the bourgeoisie. At the end of 1878,
police informants found collectivism spreading outward from
a nucleus of fifty revolutionaries "like an oil spot," affecting
one-third of the 15,000 Parisian trade unionists.[63] The
congresses of 1878 had demonstrated how contagious revolutionary collectivism could be to a cooperative movement
already committed to socialism. Only a repressive government now seemed to stand in the way of a revolutionary
victory, which had to await the consolidation of the Republic
in 1879.

COLLECTIVIST VICTORY AT MARSEILLES

The final consolidation of the republican regime in 1879 created the necessary political condition for the radicalization of the labor movement. So long as the Republic was endangered and republican liberties insecure, labor was tied to Radicalism. Yet, while considering republican liberties as indispensable for their movement, workers were no longer convinced that they were sufficient for socialism. Since 1876 the growing tendency of Radicals like Gambetta to compromise with the bourgeoisie, especially on the issue of amnesty to Communards, prompted workers to initiate the formation of a labor party representing working class interests in parliament. Only once republican liberties were secure, however, could they afford to make the definitive break with Radicalism. The election of a republican Senate on January 5, followed by a republican President and president of the Chamber, initiated an opening to the Left that precipitated the formation of the first French labor party at Marseilles in October.[64]

The decision to form a separate labor party opened a wedge for the revolutionaries in the labor movement. With the support of Parisian unions, Chabert's project for an independent labor newspaper was finally launched in November 1878. At first welcoming the political changes of 1879, *Le Prolétaire* quickly passed into opposition, denouncing the "bourgeois oligarchy" and Radicalism on such issues as amnesty for Communards, civil liberties, the labor candidacy, and strike support.[65] As a bellwether of ideological currents in the trade unions, it revealed the penetration of revolutionary ideas. Thirty five of its founders, three of its officers, two and later three of its original five editors were revolutionary collectivists.[66]

The strongest revolutionary voice was that of Prudent Dervillers, a former leader with Dupire of the tailors' cooperative. Citing Marx, Guesde, Lassalle, and Malon, Dervillers presented an analysis of the wage system and surplus value in terms more Marxist than Guesde himself.[67]

Reflecting the progress of the revolutionaries, the members
of *Le Prolétaire* voted in September to submit a collectivist
program stressing transitional reforms such as association,
education, and the abolition of inheritance to the next labor
congress.[68] In *Le Prolétaire*, collectivism took on a reformist
dimension that was missing in Guesde's program. As the
organ of the trade unions, it supported struggles for higher
wages, lower hours, public education and women's rights as
ways to strengthen the revolutionary cause.

The Guesdists were also active. They were prominent in
the campaign for amnesty, helping to organize a socialist
amnesty committee with committees in working class quarters and launching the candidacy of the imprisoned revolutionary Auguste Blanqui, which triumphed at Bordeaux in
April, resulting in his release.[69] To aid the rising number of
strikers, which in 1879 was three times the average from
1874 to 1878, the Guesdists formed a socialist strike
committee seeking to draw workers into the "revolutionary
socialist party."[70] While in prison, Guesde drafted a platform
for the new party, a revolutionary address that was eventually signed by 541 people, mostly skilled workers—tailors,
shoemakers, locksmiths, mechanics, joiners, and the like—
from nineteen cities, including Paris, Grenoble, Saint-Etienne,
Vienne, Marseilles, Béziers, and Troyes.[71]

This revolutionary address represented a transition from
collectivism to Marxism. Here Guesde advocated the nationalization of capital "to be placed at the free disposition of
producers' groups," abandoning political but not economic
federalism. While warning peasants, artisans, and shopkeepers
of their imminent destruction in dogmatic Marxist fashion,
he promised them a large degree of autonomy under
socialism:

> The Revolution ... that we call upon you to make strikes only
> the idle classes, only the landed, industrial and commercial
> feudality that has replaced the ancient feudality of birth and
> sword. It safeguards all legitimate interests, that is the interest of

all those who work and produce under whatever title or form. That is why it will take place sooner or later, because it is the Revolution of Justice.[72]

Still relying on abstract reasoning, Guesde failed to draw the logical connection between economic concentration, the polarization of classes, and the necessity for a dictatorship of the proletariat establishing a centralized economy.

The new doctrine was beginning to penetrate the trade unions. In May the Parisian mechanics, perhaps the most industrial of the trades, became the first to endorse Guesde's program. After several weeks of debate, Parisian union delegates approved a collectivist agenda for the Marseilles congress. When the majority accepted a subsidy from the Radical Municipal Council, the revolutionary unions formed an independent delegation. Composed of twenty-four leading unions, this delegation dispatched two Guesdist workers, wallet-maker Gustave Fauché and jeweler Eugène Fournière, to Marseilles. In deference to the collectivist trend, even the ten cooperative Parisian delegates called themselves "peaceful collectivists," agreeing on the ends if not the means.[73]

The formation of the independent delegation was a political decision, reflecting the determination to break with Radicalism. The unions in this group came from a broad and representative range of trades, from more industrial mechanics, tawers, and locksmiths to more artisanal tailors, tinsmiths, cabinetmakers and artificial florists. These revolutionary trades were not structurally different from more moderate ones. The shift did not apparently reflect any change in social base, any influx of unskilled or industrial workers, or any significant crisis or industrialization of the trades. Indeed, if scale is any indication, the revolutionary trades had become less industrial since mid-century.[74] Because of new political conditions, the cooperative leaders and unions of the 1870s became the revolutionaries of the 1880s.

The third national labor congress at Marseilles has usually been viewed as the scene of Guesdist triumph.[75] An

important step was taken at Marseilles, but the shift to
revolutionary collectivism took place over several years in
two essential stages, neither of which was a specifically
Guesdist triumph. At Marseilles, union delegates undertook
the formation of a socialist labor party, the Parti Ouvrier,
based on collectivism without endorsing either a revolutionary or Guesdist program. Only during the first few years of
the Opportunist Republic would French labor generally
abandon cooperation for a revolutionary program. A third
stage, the acceptance of a centralist Guesdist or Marxist
socialism, an entirely new departure, was never reached by
the skilled trades unions.

In most ways, Marseilles was a continuation of previous
labor congresses, which had approved the formation of a
labor party and collectivization. As previously, it was broadly
representative of organized skilled workers, especially needle,
metal, and construction trades, with a strong regional
preponderance—more than 40 percent from Marseilles and
two-thirds from the Southeast. From the debates it appears
that committed revolutionaries constituted only a small
minority—perhaps no more than 17—of the 130 delegates,
most of whom were cooperative socialists. Only 11 had
signed Guesde's program. Coming from Marseilles, Paris,
Lyons, Saint-Etienne, Grenoble, Toulouse, and Béziers, these
revolutionaries represented a variety of trades which were not
perceptibly different in industrial structure from the more
moderate ones.[76]

Nevertheless, by coordinating their action, the revolutionaries were able to dominate the proceedings. In Marseilles,
leadership of the organizing committee had fallen to the
jeweler Jean Lombard and other members of a study circle
which had been converted to collectivism by Malon, who
continued to advise them, even writing Lombard's opening
address.[77] In a large music hall decorated with the mottoes of
the International, Lombard announced that the aim of the
congress was the creation of a labor party to prepare the
overthrow of the bourgeois state. Strictly speaking, only two

delegates, Fauché and Fournière, were Guesdists. The speeches of the organizers reflected the reformist collectivism of Malon. Several delegates from the South, notably the shoemaker Jean Grave, manifested more violent anarchistic tendencies. Greetings were received from Communard exiles and foreign revolutionaries urging a clean break with Radicalism. As a result of their daily caucuses, the revolutionaries were able to dominate the debates and secure control of the resolutions committees.[78]

Contrary to the trend of the debates in which a majority had defended associations, the congress approved a resolution asserting that "they were not a powerful enough means to emancipate the proletariat."[79] In resolutions on property and the wage system, the congress voted for the "nationalization of capital, mines, railroads, etc., thereafter to be placed directly in the hands of those who exploit them, the workers themselves," organized by trade.[80] Though there is no record of a vote, an amendment favoring individual ownership of land was defeated by fifty to twenty-six. Fewer than half of the delegates signed a revolutionary declaration calling for collectivization "by all possible means." From this one may conclude that a majority of delegates at Marseilles were still cooperative or at least "peaceful collectivists."[81]

Significantly, the only principled opposition came not from cooperators, but from Isidore Finance, perennial spokesman for the Proletarian Positivists, a small sect that advocated reformist trade unionism, and two Gambettist delegates dispatched from Clermont Ferrand whose protest against "the violent revolutionary demonstrations that occurred" was eventually signed by twenty-one others.[82] The final resolution creating a Parti Ouvrier was a victory for moderation and the broad principles of collectivism. The Guesdists had wanted to establish a revolutionary socialist party, an ideological party of socialists organized outside of the trade unions. Instead, the congress founded the Fédération du Parti des Travailleurs Socialistes de France, a socialist labor party composed of unions, ideological groups, and cooperatives and divided into six autonomous regional federations.[83] One of the major purposes of this party was to represent workers in parliamentary assemblies. This was a collectivist rather than a Guesdist victory.

Nevertheless, following the congress, Guesdists, anarchists, and reformist revolutionaries seized the initiative in organizing local and regional federations of the party. In May, twenty-two Parisian groups, mostly unions, approved statutes for the Union Fédérative du Centre, a federation of unions and neighborhood workers' clubs led by members of both *l'Egalité* and *Le Prolétaire*. By June membership had risen to forty, including twenty-eight leading unions—jewelers, shoemakers, tailors, carpenters, painters, locksmiths, mechanics, cabinetmakers, piano-makers, tawers, and so on—with the active support of others.[84] According to one informant, all but the food and luxury trade unions were now revolutionary. The first regional congress of the Union Fédérative du Centre in July adopted a minimum electoral program submitted anonymously by Marx and Guesde, which declared that "collective appropriation [of capital] can only result from the revolutionary action of the producing class," adding that "social Revolution by force remains the only definitive solution possible."[85]

Elsewhere, however, anarchists and cooperators repudiated this minimum program.[86] The first regional party congress of the South rejected the program thirteen to eight, refusing all electoral and reformist action in favor of violent propaganda of the deed. Similarly, the regional party congress of the East held at Lyons opposed electoral action, allowing at most the participation of ineligible candidates as a means of agitation. The regional congresses of the West at Bordeaux and the North at Lille were still firmly controlled by cooperative socialists, who favored associations and gradual reforms within a republican framework. Reflecting these regional differences, the fourth national labor congress held at Le Havre in November 1880 separated into two distinct congresses, a majority of cooperators mainly from small provincial towns and Parisian luxury trades, including goldsmiths, furriers, saddlers, and the like, and a strong minority of revolutionaries from the larger cities and more common Parisian trades, such as shoemakers, tailors, mechanics, masons, and locksmiths.[87] The struggle for control of the labor movement had reached a climax. After fifty years of predominance, cooperative socialism was making its last stand.

COOPERATIVE SOCIALISM: THE LAST STAND

If revolutionary collectivism triumphed in Paris in 1880, it took a long time for it to penetrate the provinces and make an impact on the national political scene. Republicanism and cooperative socialism continued to hold sway among provincial labor leaders through the mid-1880s and among working class voters even later. The change occurred in direct proportion to the disappointment experienced with the new Republic, its failure to pass a significant program of social reforms and to deal with the economic depression of the mid-1880s. In this situation, cooperative socialism suffered not so much on its own account, for the number of associations was still growing, as from its identification with Opportunism and the bourgeois Republic. Cooperators began to see in revolutionary collectivism not only an explicit statement of their own goals, but a strategy of class struggle that, far from depending upon the goodwill of Opportunist republicans, appealed directly to their sense of class antagonism and to the revolutionary tradition acquired in the struggle for the Republic. Predicated upon the Republic and reformist middle class as the lever of emancipation, the cooperative strategy could not survive the first years of a Republic that was neither social nor fully democratic.

Resistance to the revolutionaries in the unions was organized by Gambetta and the republican government, which in 1880 appointed Barberet, former leader of the cooperative movement, to head the first Bureau of Trade Societies. Dispensing official and unofficial aid to republican

labor leaders, Barberet and Gambetta helped organize a
separate republican labor federation, the Union des Chambres
Syndicales. With a promise to respect property and vested
interests, the Union supported Opportunist candidates in the
1881 elections and sought gradual reforms within a republican framework: legalization of unions, formation of mixed
arbitration boards, ten-hour day, state pensions, and aid to
associations. In 1882 the Union began publication of its own
newspaper, *Le Moniteur des syndicats,* which was openly
sympathetic to the government and Minister of Interior René
Waldeck-Rousseau, by whom it was doubtless subsidized.
Again, with the help of Barberet and Waldeck-Rousseau, the
Union founded in 1884 a republican federation of associations, the Chambre Consultative, to promote and coordinate
the movement.[88]

The collectivist victory at Marseilles had impressed Gambetta and other republicans with the need to redeem pledges
made to workers during fifty years of struggle for the
Republic. The new governments encouraged the association
movement with political patronage and public contracts.
Parisian officials awarded contracts on preferential terms and
administered the legacy of Benjamin Rampal, who left 1.4
million francs in low-interest loans to Parisian associations.
Unofficially, Barberet helped obtain loans for associations
that were connected with the Union. When Waldeck-
Rousseau became minister in 1882, he and Barberet conducted an inquiry to facilitate access to public contracts.
Acting on their recommendations, the Floquet government in
1888 revived an 1848 decree granting preferential treatment
on equal bids and a dispensation from posting bond. Finally,
in 1893, republicans in the Chamber of Deputies voted a
small annual subsidy for the association movement.[89]

Spurred by the advent of the Republic and economic
upturn, the association movement experienced a strong
resurgence in 1879 that exceeded that of the Second Empire
in scope. Between 1881 and 1884, forty new associations
were established, making a Parisian total of seventy-one with

4,500 working members in 1885. Nearly all organized trades, including many that had already joined the revolutionary Parti Ouvrier, participated in this movement. Most associations arose out of strikes and trade organization; several were founded directly by their unions for trade emancipation. By the 1890s this resurgence reached the provinces where eighty-eight existed in 1895.[90]

Despite its organizational weakness, never exceeding more than fifty member unions nationally, the republican Union proved to be an effective lobbyist. On its behest, republican legislators filed bills for the legalization of unions, workers' pensions, and state assistance for associations. In 1880 Barberet persuaded the government to file the first bill for the legalization of unions, which required police registration and barred union federations. When Gambetta came to power in 1882, he introduced a more liberal version that permitted federations and granted unions the right to own and transfer property. When the conservative Senate balked, the Union obtained the personal intervention of Waldeck-Rousseau, who persuaded the last hold-outs and thus quite erroneously became known as the father of trade union liberties in France.[91]

But this minor reform and the resurgence of associations were not enough to convince workers of the socialist intentions of the Opportunists. Despite their concern for associations, the Opportunists failed to provide those competitive advantages that could make them into instruments of socialist transformation. Fearing the rise of revolutionary socialism and the criticism of the industrialists, Waldeck-Rousseau had to abandon several reformist schemes, including one for a national credit bank for associations.[92] Republicans thus failed to offer the decisive aid that, by creating a truly dynamic association movement, might threaten the growth and prosperity of capitalist enterprise. Despite relative growth, an official survey conducted in the 1890s showed that most associations were small, weak, and under-capitalized, representing traditional crafts, especially

construction, and a tiny elite of the French working class.[93]
While accommodating the bourgeoisie to the institutions of
democracy, the republicans had disappointed workers in their
long held dreams of emancipation under a democratic and
social republic.

The demise of cooperative socialism in the labor movement can be measured by its strength at labor congresses
from 1880 to 1886. For the 1880 Le Havre congress,
Barberet worked closely with the organizer Emile Lyonnais,
an Opportunist municipal councillor, to defeat the revolutionaries, recruiting republican delegates and raising money
for their expenses. Eliminating the theoretical issues of
property and the wage system from the agenda, Lyonnais
announced that the aim of the congress was "to consolidate
the Republic" and obtain "immediately realizable reforms."
Since many revolutionary groups kept their membership
below twenty in order to remain within the law, Lyonnais
altered the rules to exclude workers' circles with less than
twenty-five members. Lyonnais's machinations caused the
other federations to consider changing the location, but in
the end they decided to do battle with republicans at Le
Havre.[94]

When Lyonnais barred the revolutionaries from the congress, it split into two separate congresses, a majority of
sixty-four republicans and a minority of fifty-eight revolutionaries. The republicans passed motions on reforms—hours
legislation, abolition of night work, factory inspection, and
the admission of associations to public contracts—and on the
gradual abolition of the wage system through easy credit and
the "cooperative organization of workshops."[95] With concessions to the anarchists, the revolutionary congress approved
the minimum program on a trial basis, agreeing that "if this
does not succeed, it will retain only exclusively revolutionary
action."[96]

The Le Havre proceedings formalized the division between
revolutionaries and cooperators in the labor movement. If
republicans were a majority in 1880, it was an artificial

majority recruited by government officials. Though cooperators still wanted the gradual abolition of the wage system, the
socialist dynamic in their movement had passed into the
revolutionary camp. Having been authentic socialists during
the struggle for the Republic, cooperators became defenders
of class conciliation and vested interests under the Republic,
visibly identified with the Opportunists and established
order.

Forced to choose between this "official socialism" and
revolutionary collectivism, most unions eventually chose the
latter. Several Parisian unions—mechanics, shoemakers,
tawers, pianomakers, tinsmiths, and so on—immediately
abandoned their association project, while others—cabinetmakers, jewelers, carpenters, joiners, and masons—used their
associations to provide extra employment during strikes and
slow-downs.[97] Originally divided between cooperators and
revolutionaries, several unions—coopers, wheelwrights,
bronze workers, painters, and plumbers—did not join the
Parti Ouvrier until the mid-1880s. Despite governmental
assistance, the separate labor congresses organized by the
republican Union in 1881 and 1882 were complete fiascos.
Only twenty-nine delegates, mostly from elite Parisian
trades—saddlers, gilders, jewel setters, printers, and so forth—
came to the Paris congress of 1881; only twenty-seven, nearly
all from Bordeaux, to the Bordeaux congress of 1882. Rather
than support the Opportunist Union some Radical leaders
even joined the Parti Ouvrier.[98]

In the early 1880s almost one-third of the 200 Parisian
unions, generally the largest and most important, joined the
Parti Ouvrier with nearly half of the 200 attending regional
congresses where they endorsed the revolutionary collectivist
program. Luxury trades appear to have held out longer than
others, but most of them later affiliated, too. Except for a
few highly specialized trades—furriers, articles of Paris,
painter-decorators, phototypers, and so on—which remained
with the republican Union, nearly all sectors of the skilled
working class were present in the Parti Ouvrier. In the 1880s,

it was the authentic ideological expression of the Parisian labor movement.[99]

The final national test of strength between the republican Union and revolutionary collectivism took place during an independent trade union congress held in Lyons in October 1886 in the depth of an industrial depression and aftermath of the violent Decazeville miners' strike. The Opportunist response to a cyclical depression that idled 10 percent of the work force was liberal inaction. An independent union of silk weavers that had just broken with the Opportunists convened the congress with a view toward uniting all revolutionary socialists. Seeing a chance to reverse the revolutionary trend, the Opportunist government provided financial assistance and contributed to the success of the congress. With mandates from 248 unions—about one-quarter of all existing unions—representing 155,000 skilled workers and 120,000 miners, 110 delegates came to Lyons—46 from Lyons, 22 from Paris and 42 from diverse provincial centers. Most of the provincial delegates were still nominal republicans. Twenty-one were Opportunists, 18 were Radicals, and 28 called themselves Radical-Socialists after a group of Radical deputies who had just declared themselves in favor of collectivization through parliamentary means. This congress was doubtless the most representative trade union assembly that had ever been held in France.[100]

In the course of lengthy debates, delegates discussed the Waldeck-Rousseau law on trade unions, Opportunist legislation on the *Prud'hommes* and an official labor advisory board, the eight-hour day, relations between capital and labor and the formation of an independent trade union federation. Fourteen delegates from luxury and specialized trades belonging to the Union defended the Opportunist position. Speaking for the last time at a national labor congress, several cooperative delegates introduced plans for state aid to associations that were reminiscent of 1848. The proceedings, however, were dominated by revolutionary delegates from

Paris and Lyons, who denounced the Opportunist legislation as police traps and called for unrelenting class struggle to achieve socialism. At the end, all but a dozen Opportunist delegates endorsed the revolutionary program for collectivization of the means of production.[101]

Marking the definitive triumph of revolutionary collectivism in the labor movement, this congress reflected the profound disillusionment with the Opportunist Republic that soon contributed to the rise of the antiparliamentary General Boulanger.[102] While continuing to expand, the association movement lost its connection with the trade unions. By 1895, only half of the associations had a trade orientation.[103] Originally a creation of the trade unions, associations would henceforth become part of a separate and rival cooperative movement. Though many cooperators continued to view associations as a means of trade emancipation, the leaders of the movement gradually adjusted their sights to a more limited goal, the creation of a small cooperative sector within a dominant capitalist economy.[104] While emancipating a small semiartisanal elite, the association movement gradually abandoned the hope of emancipating all trades and transforming the capitalist system. From a socialist project during much of the nineteenth century, it became a reformist one in the twentieth.

The functions and purposes of social movements vary with times and circumstances. The association movement must be evaluated not in the abstract, but in its historical context, in time and place. The same movement that Marx, perhaps erroneously, condemned as petty bourgeois under the Second Republic, he praised as working class under the Paris Commune. The same movement that was reformist under the Second Empire and socialist under the Commune turned out to be reformist under the Third Republic. The difference in each case depended upon the mobilization of the working class and disposition of the middle class and republican movement. Straddling working and middle classes, with an egalitarian ideal that stood above classes, the republican movement contained two souls, socialist and capitalist, struggling in one breast. So long as it played a revolutionary role, fighting against the privileged bourgeoisie, it had to appeal to the working class with a socialist program. But once ensconced in power under the relatively stable conditions of the Third Republic, it had to relinquish this program in order to accommodate the bourgeoisie. In the end, most middle class republicans preferred capitalism. Disabused of their faith in the democratic and social Republic, most worker militants turned to the revolutionary movement that inherited the mantle of trade socialism.

4

Formation
of the
Parti Ouvrier

In the 1880s, organized labor shifted from a cooperative
program to revolutionary collectivism without adopting a
specifically Guesdist or Marxist approach to socialism. While
endorsing such Marxian principles as class struggle and the
revolutionary overthrow of the bourgeoisie, it failed to
accept the centralist implications of Marxism. Cooperative
socialism thus conditioned not only the rapid conversion to
revolutionary socialism, but also its federalist form. In the
newly formed Parti Ouvrier, French socialism preserved the
federalist trade character of its origins: the social basis among
urban skilled workers; the strategy of self-emancipation that
respected workers' trade democracy and rejected abstract
theory and political leadership as guides to practice; and the
utopia of a federalist socialism administered by a federation
of trades and communes.

The formation of the Parti Ouvrier was a step beyond
trade organization because it created a political intermediary
between workers and their emancipation. In the new party,
workers added electoral, parliamentary, and other political
functions to their economic activity. The organizational basis
of the labor movement was extended beyond the trade union
to include workers associated geographically in local clubs
and electoral circles. Within the political party, theoretical

leaders, some middle class in origin, came to the fore. They tried to lead the workers in new directions, both more centralist and more reformist. Yet, these leaders failed to move the party beyond the bounds of trade socialism.

GUESDE AND THE EMERGENCE OF FRENCH MARXISM

The first challenge to trade socialism came from Jules Guesde. The Parti Ouvrier had been founded at Marseilles on broad collectivist principles. Although Guesde had contributed to this victory, he had failed to find support for his increasingly Marxist conceptions. After 1880, under the direct influence of Marx and Lafargue, Guesde began to develop some of the practical implications of Marxism in opposition to Malon and Brousse, the other party leaders. Repudiating the federalist tradition of skilled workers as petty bourgeois, Guesde sought to provide leadership for a centralist party with a single revolutionary program directed at the unskilled industrial working class. In organizing the party and formulating its policies, the two sides clashed over a number of issues: organizational centralism versus federalism, theoretical leadership versus workers' democracy, and the role of reformist struggles in a revolutionary party. Each of these issues was implicitly related to the question of social base: which stratum of the working class had the greater interest in socialism? To which should the party direct its appeal? Guesde believed that the industrial working class, the truly revolutionary class, would be more amenable than the skilled to a centralist revolutionary socialism. The skilled workers of the Parti Ouvrier therefore rejected Guesdist Marxism and adopted a possibilist program that more nearly reflected the ideology of trade socialism.

From the start Guesde had assigned to socialist intellectuals like himself the task of guiding and teaching the workers' movement. In correspondence with Marx and Lafargue in 1879, he found that they shared his pedagogical conception of leadership. Lafargue had also sounded out Blanqui as "the man to form the party of the proletariat."[1] In a letter to

Guesde in 1879, Marx expressed confidence in his leadership. Guesde replied that he had always admired Marx as a theoretician even during the conflict in the International. Like him, he had always opposed "anarchist insurrections." Like him, he believed that the creation of a socialist party, a "conscious army," was essential and that "for some time the initiative must come from above, from those who 'know more.' "[2]

Guesde was well-suited to offer that leadership. Possessed of a sharp intelligence with great powers of analysis and synthesis, Guesde was a master propagandist. In writing or speaking, his discourse was composed with inexorable logic salted with irony and sarcasm. Tall, pale, and emaciated, with a prophetic beard, black hair tossed behind his head, and piercing eyes behind wire-rim glasses, he was the very image of an apostle arousing the conscience and stirring the devotion of his followers. Chronically ill and often unemployed, Guesde had to rely upon the contributions of his followers to provide for himself and his family. Demanding an obedience and sacrifice that soon antagonized many of his original disciples, he acquired a reputation for his pedagogical, almost evangelical, style of leadership—"Torquemada in pince-nez" one critic called him. If lacking in intellectual depth and originality, he was nevertheless the "man to create the party."[3]

This pedagogical conception was seen in Guesde's reaction to the 1879 congress of Marseilles. The delegates there did not and, as workers, could not understand the theoretical or "scientific" side of collectivism. They had embraced collectivism as an emancipatory ideal, a way to end capitalist exploitation, rather than as a positive system for economic growth and social development, a way to increase individual and social productivity—a theme Guesde had stressed from his earliest writings. Guesde thus dimly perceived that skilled workers at least were more interested in preserving their own trade autonomy than in industrial growth and development. Since workers needed outside instruction, he proposed the creation of a separate socialist party, outside of the Parti Ouvrier, devoted to ideological study that would gradually raise the workers to the level of "scientific socialism."[4]

With knowledge acquired in talks with his father-in-law, Lafargue added a Marxist dimension to the second series of *l'Egalité* in 1880. In a series of articles he laid down the fundamentals of historical materialism. Linking class struggle to technological development, Lafargue foresaw socialism arising from the growth of heavy industry and a disciplined and concentrated industrial proletariat.[5] Vastly exaggerating the degree of concentration in French industry, he predicted an imminent revolution that would be ignited by economic or political crisis. If socialism was to arise from the industrial working class, it would be necessary to abandon skilled workers with their federalist traditions. Guesdists began to treat them as a petty bourgeois element, infected with the spirit of individualism and Proudhonism, whose elite status and federalist ideology were condemned by industrial development.[6] To bring socialism to the industrial working class, Guesde was instructed to create a centralist socialist party with a single national program representing its unitary class interest.

Le Prolétaire had already endorsed a collectivist electoral program for the party, but Guesde wanted a more "scientific" statement of socialism. Writing from Zurich, Malon had been urging Guesde and Lafargue to collaborate with him on an electoral program based on historical materialism. Suddenly in May, without consulting Malon, Guesde traveled to London where he requested the assistance of Marx and Engels on the party program.[7] Marx himself dictated the preamble, which defined socialism dialectically as the product both of economic concentration and the voluntaristic action of the proletariat. Industrial capitalism engendered the "material and intellectual elements" of socialism, which could only be actualized through the "revolutionary action of the productive class—or proletariat—organized into a distinct political party."[8] Though the Marxists did not exclude a peaceful electoral revolution, a parliamentary road to socialism, in countries with liberal traditions like England, in most Continental countries they anticipated a violent revolution on the model of 1789, 1848, and 1871.[9]

The minimum electoral program was designed solely as a "means of organization and struggle." It consisted of a series of minimum demands that Guesde drew from labor and Radical movements: civil liberty, arming of the people, religious separation, communal autonomy, eight-hour day, weekly day of rest, abolition of child labor, minimum wage law, equal wages for equal work, free public education and child maintenance, employer responsibility for industrial accidents, an end to employer interference with workers' treasuries, worker consultation on shop regulations, the return of all alienated public property, including banks, railroads and mines, to the nation and their exploitation by their own workers, the abolition of indirect taxes, and imposition of a progressive tax on incomes of more than 3,000 francs and all estates of more than 20,000 francs.

Discounting the possibility of obtaining these reforms from the bourgeoisie, Guesde regarded them not as a practical program of struggle, but simply as a means of agitation, as bait with which to lure the workers away from Radicalism. Since in his view these reforms were—with the exception of a minimum wage—compatible with the capitalist system, their rejection would free the proletariat "of its last reformist illusions and convince it of the impossibility of avoiding a workers' '89."[10]

Because of widespread hostility to Marx, a legacy of the conflict in the International, and to intellectuals in general, Guesde enlisted the help of Malon to present the program as his own handiwork. Having agreed to it in advance, Malon declared himself satisfied with the result.[11] Pending the addition of a historical and philosophical manifesto and of some other immediate reforms, Malon presented the program as the collective product of several French labor leaders. Opposition was aroused in several quarters. Refusing to engage in electoral action, at least with eligible candidates, the anarchists resigned from *l'Egalité* and formed their own separate group.[12] Members of *Le Prolétaire* found the program too minimal and "scientific" in tone. Nevertheless, it soon won the endorsement of several party groups and was approved in July at the first regional congress of the Union Fédérative du Centre, basically Paris and its region, and in November 1880, with certain reservations, by the fourth national labor congress, the first congress of the newly formed party at Le Havre.[13]

Beyond their basic ideological agreement, there were significant differences between Malon and Guesde in their approach to the new program and to party organization. While in exile Malon had studied German, translated works by Ferdinand Lassalle and Albert Schäffle, written a comprehensive, if discursive, history of socialism, and made friends with the rather reformist Social Democrats Karl Hochberg and Eduard Bernstein. In certain respects Malon was more of a Marxist than Guesde. The temperamental differences between the "lethargic" meditative Malon and the "violent" Guesde had political extensions.[14]

Malon was a reformist revolutionary. Doubting the imminence of revolution, he wished to build party organization through the struggle for reforms. Reforms like the reduction of working hours and the control of city government would raise the workers' consciousness and prepare them for the revolution. The control of city government would give them administrative experience and enable them to enact reforms in the area of taxation, trade, education, and commerce, especially with communal shops that would "lay the basis of communal property and prepare the grand socialist federation of communes. . . ." Moreover, added Malon, "though we can hardly count on it, who knows if thereby we could not accomplish the revolution without the spilling of blood? "[15] Consequently, Malon unlike Guesde wanted to open the party up to social Radicals, who still had the allegiance of the working class, thus creating a broad-based party stretching from anarchists on the left to Radicals on the right.

These differences had not disturbed Malon until he learned from Brousse, who was then in London, of Guesde's visit with Lafargue and Marx. Having been rebuffed by the Marxist circle, another legacy of the dispute in the International, Malon was piqued to learn that Guesde had entered it in 1880.[16] As a democratic federalist, he immediately warned Guesde against Lafargue's "Marxist" tendency toward "absolutism," his pretension to dictate to the party.[17] The first quarrel involved Malon's relationship with Radicalism. At Guesde's insistence he turned down the job as labor editor of the Radical daily *l'Intransigeant.* After the second *l'Egalité* folded in July 1880, Malon started a daily party newspaper in Lyons with Radical support. On *l'Emancipation* Malon tried to limit the participation of the Guesdists, disclaimed their minimum program, and promoted a reformist municipal program drafted by Brousse.[18]

In his quarrel with Guesde over reformism, Malon found an ally in Brousse, the other member of the Internationalist triumvirate who had been excluded from the London talks. In London, Brousse had founded in March 1880 *Le Travail,* an international socialist monthly open to all socialist "schools." While maintaining ties with the Jurassian anarchists, he was also interested in building a broad-based socialist party. Upon his return to France in July, he was able to observe the extreme weakness of the anarchists. Abandoning plans to form an insurrectionary Parisian committee, he joined the Montmartre circle of the Parti Ouvrier and organized a central committee of the 18th *arrondissement.* For the municipal elections of 1880, he drafted an elaborate program of reforms that was adopted by the party's Union Fédérative du Centre. He nevertheless continued to correspond with the Jurassians through 1882, indicating how little he had abandoned anarchism.[19]

Like Malon and de Paepe, Brousse based his argument for a

federalist or communal socialism on the fact of uneven economic development.[20] Since different industries operated on different scales, e.g., municipal gas works and local trades, national railroads and communications, international shipping and oceanography, and since the degree of capital concentration varied with each locality, socialism could only accommodate these differences within a federalist or communal framework. By controlling city governments under capitalism, workers could begin to create communal property with a vast number of immediate reforms: democratization of police, army, and the courts; municipal ownership of public utilities, local transportation, and commerce in basic commodities; public education and child maintenance; and a progressive income and confiscatory inheritance tax. On this platform, the Parti Ouvrier presented labor candidates, including eight shoemakers and seven mechanics, in fifteen *arrondissements,* receiving less than 5 percent of the total Parisian vote after a campaign of intensive revolutionary propaganda.[21]

Brousse joined with the editors of *Le Prolétaire,* Dervillers, Paulard, Harry, and Aimé Lavy, to offer a rival collective leadership to Guesde. In their new leadership circle called Le Travail, they too subscribed to the basic assumptions and tenets of Marxian socialism: the tendency toward economic concentration and the polarization of classes, the formation of the proletariat into a political party, the conquest of political power by all possible means, and the establishment of a "revolutionary class dictatorship" to expropriate the bourgeoisie. Where they opposed Guesde was on the question of party organization. As federalists, they wanted to organize the party on an administrative basis without erecting an authoritarian "governmental leadership in its midst."[22]

Meanwhile, Guesde had been acting as party spokesman in public meetings and on the Radical daily *Le Citoyen* where he held an editorial position. Believing it time to organize a more unitary centralist party, Lafargue encouraged him to assume the role of party leader, to revive the weekly *l'Egalité,* and run for public office.[23] The two sides clashed over the 1881 legislative elections, first over a projected Radical electoral alliance, and then over Guesde's candidacy at Roubaix, which was made in violation of a public pledge and the principle of the labor candidacy.[24] Despite an active campaign of electoral meetings, the Parti Ouvrier garnered only five percent of the votes in Paris, and 40,000 elsewhere, including 493 out of 10,868 votes at Roubaix for Guesde, who had once predicted a million votes at the party's first national election. Rather than waste their votes on obscure revolutionaries, workers preferred to support the more effective Radicals, especially since they had borrowed a good part of the socialists' reformist program.[25]

This electoral debacle led to recriminations between the Guesdists and Broussists over party organization. The Guesdists blamed the defeat on the absence of strong leadership and organization, in short, on anarchist influence in the party. They proposed the formation of a national council, an executive body with discretionary powers over elections, propaganda, strikes, and international representation. While conceding the need for better organization and moral leadership, Brousse, in a barely veiled metaphorical attack, claimed that Guesde was threatening party democracy with his own personal dictatorship. He recommended instead the formation of a federalist national committee, elected by regional federations, subject to recall, and charged with mere administrative functions. Malon concurred that such an organization was preferable because of regional differences, e.g., between the industrial East and North and the artisanal South, West, and Center, and because of the prevailing federalist ideology.[26]

The vast majority of Parisian groups and militants rejected Guesde's pretension to lead the party. Malon left Guesde on the daily *Le Citoyen* and joined Brousse, who contributed his inheritance to *Le Prolétaire.*[27] Repelled by Guesde's demands for obedience, several of his disciples, Vaidy, Labusquière, Fournière, and Marouck, also joined the Broussists. Raising himself above the party as legislative candidate and independent propagandist, Guesde had violated collective discipline. While few shared the Broussist faith in reformism, most preferred a democratic to an authoritarian leadership.[28]

Dominated by Parisians, the second congress of the party at Reims in November 1881 settled organizational issues in favor of the Broussists. Insisting on the need for a more flexible program to accommodate local differences, the Broussists took advantage of their numbers to attack the minimum program, which they blamed for the recent defeat. In reply, Guesde argued that a single national program was needed to unite the working class and that any flexibility would allow the infiltration of reformist ideas. On Brousse's motion the congress voted to consider allowing local groups to append their own local demands to a revolutionary communist preamble.[29]

The Broussists wished to open the party to all workers, cooperative or revolutionary, who sought the abolition of the wage system, and to encourage the struggle for immediate reform.[30] According to Malon, reforms obtained through collective struggle strengthened workers materially and morally, tempering them for the inevitable revolutionary confrontation that would arise from the resistance of the bourgeoisie. Answering accusations that he had abandoned his anarchist principles, Brousse asserted that he wanted to apply communism to reality, "to make some of our demands immediate in some way in order to finally make them possible . . . , to draw from every situation all that it contains . . . and realize the greatest sum of communism possible."[31] Hence, the Broussists became known as possibilists.

The Broussists introduced their new electoral program in the December 1881 legislative campaign of the mechanic Jules Joffrin in Montmartre. The program contained an updated communist version of Marx's preamble for the International along with a modified list of minimum demands. Guesde immediately attacked it as being contrary to party rules, which allowed stronger but not weaker versions of the minimum program. The preamble of the International, he asserted, was a petty bourgeois document, which had been designed to please the Proudhonians in the labor movement. In his defense, Joffrin pointed out that his program contained both a revolutionary and a communist declaration, making it stronger than the minimum program. Arbitrating the dispute, the newly formed national committee, organized along Broussist lines, agreed with Joffrin. Running as an avowed Communard and revolutionary, Joffrin had not in fact weakened the revolutionary program.[32]

In December 1881, Guesde revived *l'Egalité* in order to create a more centralist party. Party centralism was required because of the historical conditions of struggle, growing economic concentration and centralization of the bourgeois state. Declaring itself "openly and scientifically centralist," *l'Egalité* repudiated the federalist heritage of the French labor movement. Claiming that all federalism was bourgeois, Lafargue even withdrew the socialist imprimatur from the Paris Commune whose federalist errors he attributed to the undeveloped state of industry at the time. Admitting the fact of uneven economic development, the Guesdists were willing to abandon the "petty bourgeois" urban skilled workers to Radicals and Proudhonians and to concentrate their propaganda on the industrial proletariat, which was already experiencing the collective form of production in the large mechanized factory. The Guesdists thus drew opposite conclusions from the Broussists from the fact of uneven development, choosing to organize the more modern sector of the working class.[33]

Industrial workers were also less reformist and potentially more revolutionary than skilled workers. According to Guesde's Lassallean iron law, the wages of industrial workers could not be permanently raised above the subsistence level. The municipal reforms suggested by Brousse would be neutralized either by the influx of new unskilled workers seeking the benefits or by the flight of private industry to regions of lower taxation. When Joffrin, the first elected

municipal representative of the party, filed a bill for the
construction of municipal housing and limitation of real
estate speculation in Paris, Guesde contended that the
bourgeois state would never allow public housing to drive out
the private entrepreneur. In opposition, he circulated a
petition for national rent control as a measure of propaganda
to demonstrate the ill-will of the bourgeoisie, fearing in fact
that a successful struggle would deprive the party of its raison
d'être. He, too, drafted a municipal program, but only as a
means of agitation for the purpose of provoking a national
workers' revolution.[34]

With the question of organizational centralism in the
background, the immediate issue before the party was
Guesde's authoritarian leadership, notably his attempt to
impose his program on the party, a trait which Brousse called
Marxist.[35] The term had originally been applied by the
Jurassians to Marx's coterie, especially Lafargue.[36] Reintro-
ducing the term into the political lexicon, Brousse drew a
parallel between Guesde's conduct and previous Marxist
attempts to impose a certain tactic—electoral action—on the
International. Admitting the anarchist error on this point,
Brousse did not quarrel with the basic tenets of Marxian
socialism:

> Marxism does not consist in being a partisan of Marx's ideas. If
> that were so, many of his present adversaries, particularly the
> author of these lines, would in large measure be Marxists. Marxism
> lies not in the system that seeks to spread Marxist doctrine, but in
> that which seeks to impose it in all its details.[37]

The Marxists' error lay in their attempts to decide local
tactics for socialists everywhere, their "unacceptable pretension to encompass the entire socialist movement in the limits
of their minds,"[38] and their willingness to use unscrupulous
means, including the violation of party democracy, to that
end. In contrast to Marxist politics, which Brousse considered
old-fashioned, authoritarian, and utopian, he advocated an

"experimental politics," which by respecting federalist democracy would allow correct tactics to emerge experientially
through a constant process of debate and discussion.

The basic issue that emerged in this discussion was the
relationship between socialist theory and practice. Where the
Marxists stressed theory as a guide to practice, the Broussists
saw theory as a process arising from practice. Whereas the
"authoritarian" Marxists were trying to impose correct
tactics on the labor movement from the outside, the
Broussists were willing to allow the movement to work out
correct tactics on the basis of its own experience. As
intellectuals with a completed theory, Marxists were often
tempted to sacrifice the lessons of experience to the dictates
of theory while the Broussists, by virtue of their closer
connection to the actual labor movement, were inclined to
make the opposite mistake. The misapprehension between
Marxists and Broussists was thus rooted in the social and
historical origins of the two movements.

The Marxists had not always adopted this authoritarian
posture. Within the First International they had served as the
"anonymous spokesmen" of the workers' movement as it
gradually developed its own socialist program. Guiding this
movement with practical advice, Marx had made no attempt
to impose or even expose his Marxism, his theoretical system,
until 1871 and the dispute with Bakunin. Abandoning the
trade socialist movement in 1872, Marx turned his attention
to the formation of national political parties on the German
model.[39] In advising allies on the formation of such parties,
he could not always overcome the legacy of past feuds nor
master the details of national politics, even in his homeland.
During this later period, he was more concerned with
political and theoretical leadership than with trade unions
and workers' experience. Previously, he had recognized the
socialist potential contained in the French trade movement
and Paris Commune. From his later political perspective,
however, the Commune appeared to have been a mere
republican movement and French unions "more colorless

than English trade unions"[40] with Philistine leaders, who were incapable of theoretical insight. Having lost touch with the "real" trade movement, Marx placed his trust in two bourgeois intellectuals to create a party and direct it on a "scientific" course.

Though Guesde and Lafargue represented the rudiments of Marxism in France, they were severely chastised by Marx for their practical errors, for indulging in "revolutionary phraseology," denying the revolutionary value of reformist struggles and ignoring the progressive role of Radicalism. If this was Marxism, Marx told his "Bakuninist" son-in-law, he was not a Marxist. In respect to Radicalism and reformist struggles, Malon and Brousse had a more Marxist attitude than Guesde and Lafargue. Significantly, the left-wing German socialists in Paris sided with the Broussists. Yet, because of the split in the International and his break with the actual trade movement, Marx could not acknowledge Malon and Brousse as authentic socialists.[41]

The Guesdists were finally expelled from the party's Parisian Union Fédérative du Centre for failing to appear at a hearing on the dispute. Denouncing the Broussists as both anarchists and opportunists, they appealed to Parisian groups to join their federation as the legitimate one. Lafargue, who appears to have pushed for the break, believed they would eventually win Brousse and the rest of the party, except Malon, over to their position. Only six out of 100 Parisian groups and unions answered their appeal, including only one actual Parisian club and one dubious union. When these groups sent delegates to the annual regional congress, they were denied admission for their refusal to remove their title as the official federation. While the Guesdists remained a tiny sect, the Parisian Union grew rapidly, adding some sixty groups and unions in 1882 for a total of 102.[42]

By raising the specter of Guesdist dictatorship and Marxist domination, the Broussists won the support of most provincial groups. In opposition, the Guesdists set out to organize workers in previously unorganized industrial centers: Montluçon and Commentry, mining and metallurgical towns in the Allier basin, where Guesde found a disciple in Jean Dormoy; the textile city of Roanne where Guesdists aided a general strike in 1882; the industrial region around Lyons; and the textile, mining, and metal region of the North, especially Lille and Roubaix. As the result of competitive recruitment, the number of groups and unions represented at the third congress of the Parti Ouvrier at Saint-Etienne in 1882 was the largest ever. There were 23 Guesdist delegates representing 31 groups in 11 cities; 6 of the delegates were from Paris, 3 from Lyons, 6 from Roanne, and 4 from the Allier basin. Delegates from the North, Reims, and Rochefort later joined them. The Broussists were supported by a heterogeneous coalition, including both reformists and anarchists, united only in their opposition to Guesde—86 delegates representing 360 groups and unions in 51 cities, especially Paris, Lyons, Saint-Etienne, Rennes, and Marseilles.[43]

Hopelessly outnumbered, the Guesdists used a defeat on a procedural vote as a pretext to walk out and journey to Roanne where they had prepared their own separate congress in advance.[44] Denouncing the Broussists as reformists, they retained the minimum program "exclusively as a means of propaganda, organization and struggle."[45] The only reformist action they approved was the strike, "the preparatory school of the working class," which strengthened its consciousness, organization, and discipline, and which, if properly organized by the party, could reduce working hours and keep wages in line with prices.[46] Instead of a federalist national committee representing regional federations, the Guesdists set up a more centralist national council drawn from local militants at the site of the party congress.[47] In the absence of any intermediary organization between the local group and the national council, the latter, controlled by Guesde and Lafargue, assumed dictatorial authority. While remaining a rather insignificant sect in the 1880s, the Guesdists laid the basis for the first centrally structured political party in France, the Parti Ouvrier Français.

After the Guesdists' departure from Saint-Etienne, Brousse
presented a bill of indictment, accusing them of carrying out
Marx's orders in every detail, even on such minor matters as
the decision to enter *Le Citoyen* or run for office, of using
subterfuge to gain acceptance of the minimum program, and
of seeking to control the party:

> Conciliation is impossible. Water and fire cannot be reconciled.
> Cooperation, federation, is only possible among groups equally
> determined to respect their mutual independence. It dissolves
> through the introduction of a foreign, authoritarian and dominat-
> ing element. By historical tradition the Marxist group must act
> and intrigue until it succeeds in winning control of the party.
> Even if they wanted to, the Marxists could not submit to the
> decisions of the party. How could they at the same time obey the
> votes of the congresses and the will of a man outside of the party,
> living in London beyond reach? They are the *ultra-montains* of
> socialism; one should say the *ultra-marains*. The *ultra-montains*
> cannot obey the law of their country because their leader is in
> Rome. The Marxists cannot obey the decisions of the party and
> its congresses because their real leader is in London.
>   You cannot reconcile the *Parti ouvrier* with the Marxist
> fanaticism any more than in the bourgeois world you can
> reconcile clericalism with the state. There is only one necessary
> solution: the separation of the Marxist Capuchins from the
> socialist workers' State. . . . Let the Marxists go their own way and
> form their own party, and let ours remain as it is: a federation of
> groups respecting decisions of congresses and their mutual
> independence.[48]

Paulard insinuated a more pecuniary motive for Guesde's
"Marxism," contending that he had only turned to London
when his French devotees stopped the subsidies. On his
motion the congress voted overwhelmingly to expel *l'Egalité*
and its allies.[49]

The congress of Saint-Etienne adopted the official title of
Parti Ouvrier Socialiste Révolutionnaire Français and fixed
the party's program along revolutionary lines, not dissimilar
from those of the Guesdists. It too adopted electoral action
"as a means of propaganda to organize the revolutionary

army and hasten the inevitable hour, not to exercise parliamentarism," as Guesde charged, "but on the contrary to deliver continuous ultimatums to the bourgeoisie."[50] This would be assured by the strict surveillance of all elected representatives. The congress also denied the possibility of obtaining significant reforms, calling for constant agitation to provoke the revolution. To replace the minimum program, it approved Brousse's version of Marx's preamble, affirming that "emancipation will only result from the revolutionary action of the exploited classes."[51] It also resolved to assist striking workers in the hopes of recruiting them to the party, eventually using strikes as a revolutionary weapon, and to promote trade congresses where workers could prepare for their future role as the administrators of a socialist economy.[52]

Even in the matter of organization, where the federalist principle was applied, the differences with the Guesdists were minimal. The new statutes guaranteed the autonomy of local groups and unions, granting them the right to draft their own local program and the responsibility for ratifying decisions of the party congress. Yet, though a national committee was set up as a federalist body, it assumed many of the discretionary powers originally proposed by the Guesdists—the arbitration of disputes and the right to receive and offer proposals and to undertake political and economic propaganda.[53]

The Parti Ouvrier that emerged from Saint-Etienne was hardly less revolutionary than the Guesdists.[54] In expelling them, it had not disavowed their revolutionary strategy, but merely condemned their violation of party democracy, their association with Marx, and pretension to dictate the tactics of the party. Despite divergent labels, the split did not involve the basic premises of revolutionary collectivism. Brousse still considered himself an anarchist because he believed in an "administrative" communist state.[55] While considering himself a Marxist, Guesde still bore the imprint of his original collectivism, viewing the dictatorship of the proletariat as a temporary expedient, making way for a federalist socialism administered by trade groups and independent peasants.[56] Rather than basic theory, the division concerned the relationship between theory and practice, with great implications for the future of French socialism.

Having joined a rather rudimentary Marxism to collectivism, Guesde was the first French revolutionary to stress theory as a guide to practice.[57] Marxism led him to break with the trade socialism of urban skilled workers and to create a centralist party with a single national program appealing to the industrial working class, notably in the Allier basin, Rhône valley, Pas-de-Calais, and the North.[58] Among the textile workers of the North, especially, Guesde found recruits whose class condition—low wages, lack of skill, and organizational weakness—confirmed his Lassallean schema.[59] Lacking their own socialist tradition, these workers needed a class theory and organization introduced from above, from "those who 'know more,'" to mobilize them for social change. If such unskilled workers lacked the capacity to emancipate themselves through their own direct efforts, they would be aided by a political apparatus acting on their behalf. Thus, anticipating the revolution as the result of the growth of the industrial working class, Guesde formed a Social Democratic party in opposition to the federalist tradition of the French labor movement.

While Guesde built his party around a small industrial working class, the Parti Ouvrier remained tied to urban skilled workers with their federalist outlook. Arriving at socialism as a result of their experience in trade organization, these workers rejected a theory that condemned job autonomy, trade solidarity, and federalist democracy. Their adhesion to possibilism expressed an ambivalence toward industrialism and its consequences. While accepting industrialism in theory, they refused to follow its practical consequences in terms of political and economic organization. Thus, the Parisian trades in the Parti Ouvrier remained hostile to the abstract theory, organizational centralism, and political authority inherent in Marxist socialism.

Rather than conform to the centralist implications of Marxist theory, whose premises they shared, the possibilists built upon this federalist trade movement, trusting to the experience of class struggle rather than theory to lead workers to socialism. Contrary to the lessons of Marxism, they defended federalist structures and welcomed socialists of all schools, including anarchists, federalists, and coopera-tors, whose strategy and social basis were condemned by industrialization. Thus, building on the past in defiance of the lessons of theory, the possibilists failed to expand into industrial areas and create an enduring political organization.

PARTI OUVRIER: POSSIBILISTS

Growing out of the trade movement, the Parti Ouvrier was unable to unite all factions behind its program. Remaining outside in 1880 were anarchists, who rejected electoral action, cooperators, and Blanquists, who distrusted doctrine. As the first major split, the departure of the Guesdists caused disaffection among militants who were disturbed by inter-necine warfare. Even among the possibilists, temperamental or tactical differences appeared between the more reformist Brousse and Malon and the revolutionary rank and file. The departure of the Guesdists planted the seeds for other splits and divisions.

Whatever the underlying consensus, socialist organization must always contend with the unavoidable tension between organizational and activist temperaments, between those concerned with preparation and organization and those eager for revolutionary action. Because socialists are dedicated to a difficult long-range objective, minor tactical differences may often lead to organizational splits. Other conditions also contributed to a fissiparous socialist history. The geographi-cal dispersion and small-scale of French industry made communication and organization difficult for a workers' party lacking the leisure and material resources to maintain a central national structure. The federalist tradition, with its respect for local autonomy, also militated against unity since local groups were never dependent upon central structures. Nevertheless, one must look for the ideological consensus underlying so many splits and divisions.

Once in control of the national committee, Malon and Brousse tried to shift the party in a more reformist direction, stressing electoral action as a means of propaganda and organization. At Brousse's suggestion the party in 1883 opened its membership to "all workers struggling against their exploiters without distinction of school"[60] and made the revolutionary title voluntary for regional federations. As a "broad class party," it adopted the general title Fédération des Travailleurs Socialistes de France but refused to jettison the obligatory communist preamble. Brousse conformed to the party decision, but Malon and his friends Fournière and Gustave Rouanet decided to abandon the preamble in a Narbonne by-election as a way of attracting more Radical and middle-class votes. Reprimanded by the party, they subsequently resigned. While Brousse continued to urge an opening to Radicalism, he deferred to the revolutionary majority until 1890 when the issue produced a revolt against his reformist leadership.[61]

Brousse justified reformism with his theory of public services. He claimed to have made a discovery, ignored by Marxists, that public services arose naturally under capitalism as an outgrowth of monopoly and the centralized state. Though usually created for the benefit of the bourgeoisie, they could be made to serve the interests of the working class, especially on the local level in municipal industries and stores. Contrary to the view attributed to him by Guesde and subsequent historians, Brousse did not assert that the growth of public services would obviate the need for revolution, which would place all industry under the control of trade federations.[62]

With Brousse's municipal program, the possibilists made rapid progress in Parisian elections. In 1884, they received 7 percent of the vote, doubling their previous total and electing the old militant Chabert in the working class quarter of

Combat. In 1887, they elected nine municipal councillors, Eugène Faillet, Simon Soëns, Brousse, Joffrin, Lavy, Paulard, Chabert, Jean-Baptiste Dumay, and Alexandre Réties, implanting themselves in *arrondissements* with the largest proportion of workers, the 20th, 19th, 11th, and 18th as well as in adjoining quarters like Epinettes, l'Hôpital Saint-Louis, and Enfants-rouges. Because of their refusal to form electoral alliances or present well-known figures, they were less successful in legislative elections. For the list election of 1885, they ran 38 militants, all members of unions and manual workers, the majority of whom had been active in the prewar movement or Commune. Joffrin, the leading candidate, received only 33,452 votes or 8 percent compared to the Radical Edouard Lockroy's 272,650. Benefiting from their alliance with Radicals against Boulanger in 1889, they elected their first deputy Dumay in the 20th and their second Joffrin in the 18th by the default of the General himself.[63]

The possibilists were determined to make the most of republican liberties to build their organization. Stressing electoral action, they avoided any illegal or violent action that might involve arrest or dissolution. They refused to support anarchist demonstrations of the unemployed in 1883, to reconstitute the First International, or join a red flag commemoration of the Commune at Père Lachaise.[64] Facing the industrial crisis that began in 1883, they elaborated an extensive meliorative program for the unemployed in contrast to other socialists who urged revolutionary action. Finally, in opposition to Boulangism, they formed electoral alliances with Radicals. By neglecting opportunities for revolutionary propaganda, they tended to become practically, if not theoretically, reformist. Following the Guesdists, historians have indeed treated them as reformists.[65] Though Brousse and Malon hoped to avoid revolution through gradual reform, even they maintained a revolutionary posture so long as they belonged to the party.

In fact, even during the Boulanger Affair, party militants never renounced their revolutionary perspective, their convic-

tion that "under bourgeois domination the present society is
headed toward a revolution more terrible than that of 1789,
1793, June 1848 and March 1871."[66] Persuaded of the
implacability of the bourgeoisie, experienced so mercilessly
under the Commune, they remained skeptical of achieving
even partial reforms under capitalism. When the national
committee was strengthened in 1883 "as an offensive and
defensive organ," it was with a view toward assuring its
effectiveness as a general staff in the event of a revolutionary
crisis.[67] Campaigns for municipal services were conducted not
as a substitute for revolution, as is often supposed, but as a
method of revolutionary propaganda and organization, dem-
onstrating the ill-will of the bourgeoisie in case of failure,
strengthening workers' organization in the event of success,
in both instances preparing workers for the revolutionary
struggle.[68]

Instead of a state or even communalist socialism, the party
program reflected a trade or syndicalist outlook. The unions
were seen as the administrative organs of reform under
capitalism and main units of production under socialism.
Under capitalism they would administer workshops for
strikers and the unemployed, public works projects, municipal shops, public transport and utilities, technical education,
factory inspection, national unemployment and old-age
insurance, as well as the *Prud'hommes,* for which the party
ran candidates.[69] Other party demands were drawn from the
labor movement—the eight-hour day, abolition of subcontractors and private employment agencies, elimination of
child labor, and so on. Under socialism the unions would be
the source of both political and economic power:

> The present parliamentary system will disappear along with the
> political and economic domination of the class of which it is the
> expression, and the future social form will arise from our workers'
> societies that will have to become the principal wheels of our
> public services, their national and international administration
> being formed simply by the Committee of these societies, which
> are daily perfected in the different congresses of the party.[70]

In contrast to the Guesdists, who emphasized the primacy of the political party, the possibilists wished to act as the agents of the trade unions. Party congresses were open to all unions whatever their tendency. Party members had to belong to their union and recruit it into the party. A majority of the party was composed of trade unions; thus, most members were trade unionists. In 1882, the Parisian Union Fédérative du Centre reached its peak membership of 102 groups—49 *syndicats,* 11 other trade societies, 9 provincial circles, 30 local neighborhood circles, and three cooperatives.[71] Declining after 1882, trade union membership rose again to 41 during the Boulanger Affair. Altogether, 78 out of approximately 210 Parisian unions, generally the largest and best organized, joined the party. Fifty belonged for more than three years and 7—mechanics, tinsmiths, wheelwrights, piano-makers, coopers, painters, and carpenters—for ten. Nearly all types of trades were represented with the largest numbers from metal, wood, leather, and construction and highest percentage from construction, metal, wood, and needle trades. In addition, regional congresses drew between 50 and 100 unions; 135 of the 210 attended at least one such congress where they endorsed the party's revolutionary program.[72]

The party thus included nearly all segments of the skilled working class. They came from both more industrial and more artisanal trades, from the larger-scale mechanics, printers, and copper founders and smaller-scale tailors, jewelers, and saddlers.[73] Only a few luxury and specialized trade unions were recalcitrant—articles of Paris, gunsmiths, scalemakers, phototypers, and so on. There was token representation of unskilled laborers—roadworkers, rag-sorters, sewermen, quarry miners, distillery workers, and the *forts aux Halles*—but industrial workers from the highly concentrated chemical, metallurgical, electrical, and textile industries on the periphery were absent. The organizational rates of member unions ranged from 32 percent for cabinetmakers and 17 percent for tailors to less than 5 percent for joiners and carpenters.[74] The largest member unions were the mechanics' 6,000, bronze workers' 4,000, cabinetmakers' 3,680, tailors' 2,800, upholsterers' 2,000, type-casters' and copper founders' 1,300, iron molders' 1,000, piano-makers' and chair-makers' 700; the average was closer to 200. The total membership of all the unions that joined the party was 30,000 out of approximately 50,000 workers who belonged to Parisian unions in the early 1880s. This did not include workers who were members of local neighborhood circles whose unions did not belong. During the Boulanger Affair, the party claimed an effective following among 50,000 Parisian workers.[75] This was the same number of workers who had actively supported cooperative socialism in 1848 and 1871. Thus, the Parti Ouvrier dominated the organized sector of the Parisian working class, which comprised approximately one-sixth of the total male work force.

From their Parisian base, the possibilists did not sustain regional organization in the rest of France. After its delegates withdrew from Saint-Etienne, the Federation of the North voted to join the Guesdists, with the Lille region becoming their main stronghold. At the regional congress of the Federation of the South in 1881, delegates from Marseilles, Cette, Narbonne, Bézier, and Montpellier reaffirmed their political abstentionism. Affiliating rather indifferently with anarchist, Guesdist, and Radical elements, socialists in the South remained basically autonomous with a common belief in federalism. In Lyons and the East, the possibilists were opposed by a rival anarchist federation as well as by Guesdists, Blanquists, and independents in the region. Since Bordeaux remained in the hands of cooperators until the late 1880s, the possibilists organized a rival federation at Rennes with groups from Poitiers, Angoulême, Limoges, and the Loire valley. Because of its proximity to Paris, the possibilists were able to sustain organization in the West. Outside of scattered groups and contacts in other regions, the only other provincial federation was that of the Ardennes, organized in

1885 by Jean-Baptiste Clément, the *chansonnier* and Communard.[76]

During the 1880s, Radicalism kept its hold on the working class electorate as well as labor leaders in many provincial towns in the West and Southwest. Until the depression and Boulanger detached workers from Radicalism, the possibilists could make little impact without modifying their program, a constant temptation for the party leaders. In a Narbonne by-election in 1883, Rouanet ran without the communist preamble and withdrew on the second round for a Radical. Upon receiving a reprimand, he and his allies Fournière and Malon quit the party and renewed publication of Malon's *Revue socialiste*. With this publication Malon hoped to achieve a broad consensus between socialists and Radicals on a reformist program as well as a theoretical synthesis between Marxism and republican idealism. Malon thus laid the basis for the kind of independent parliamentary socialism that became the hallmark of Jean Jaurès and Alexandre Millerand in the 1890s.[77]

While some socialists were reaching out to the Radicals, many Radicals were becoming more social or socialist. Despite his unequivocal rejection of collectivism, Georges Clemenceau had reacted to the minimum program by borrowing some of its demands for his own campaign: reduction of working hours, abolition of child labor, worker control of mines and railroads, progressive income and inheritance taxes, and so on.[78] Surprised to discover a Parti Ouvrier with a new ideology and set of leaders, most of the returning Communard leaders—Paul Longuet, François Jourde, Ernest Massen, Albert Theisz, Augustin Avrial, Charles Amouroux, and Alphonse Humbert—remained loyal to Radicalism. In 1880, they formed a Socialist Republican Alliance to promote labor reforms and cooperative socialism.[79] During the 1880s, many Radicals began calling themselves Radical-Socialists. In 1886, nineteen Radical deputies formed a "socialist group" seeking the gradual nationalization of

industry. From this group came the socialist supporters of
the Boulangist movement, which rode the wave of working
class protest in the late 1880s, and some of the leading
parliamentary socialists of the 1890s.[80]

Led by the Blanquists, revolutionary socialists outside of
the Parti Ouvrier hoped to profit from the Boulangist
agitation to mount a revolutionary assault on the Republic.
After the death of their leader in 1881, the Blanquists had
formed their own Revolutionary Central Committee to serve
as a vanguard for the popular movement. This committee had
loose ties with several local independent revolutionary clubs.
Blanquism was still an insurrectionary technique rather than
a social doctrine, but several of its new leaders, notably
Edouard Vaillant, had assimilated Marxism while serving on
Marx's general council in London. Together with Guesdists,
anarchists, and independents, the Blanquists tried to promote
a revolutionary alternative to either republicanism or Boulangism during the Affair.[81]

The anarchists had broken with the Parti Ouvrier over
electoral politics. Expelled from the Union Fédérative du
Centre in 1881 for refusing to file their names and statutes,
anarchists from the 5th, 6th, 13th, and 20th *arrondissements*
held their own conclave where they endorsed violent propaganda of the deed. They appealed to artisanal trades with
many small shops and to independent and foreign workers.
With a small following among tailors, shoemakers, and
building joiners, they tried to organize categories of workers
neglected by the possibilists: common laborers, barbers and
cooks, *garçons de café,* and the unemployed. During the
depression they organized street demonstrations of the
unemployed that turned into violence, an equally violent
campaign against private employment agencies, and rent
strikes in working class quarters. During the road-workers'
strike of 1888, the anarchist joiner Joseph Tortelier agitated
for a revolutionary general strike of all workers. At the
Bourse du Travail de Paris, founded in 1887, they propagated
the idea of the general strike and stirred up resistance to the

more moderate possibilist administration. While remaining marginal to the trade unions, they were able to provide leadership for the revolutionary syndicalist movement that emerged in the 1890s.[82]

Acting as a "recruiting and training sergeant" in industrial areas, the Guesdists formed a small band of disciples in the 1880s. Their function was primarily pedagogical. Perceiving in the industrial depression of 1883 the signs of capitalist breakdown, they allied themselves with the activist Blanquists. Under the influence of Lafargue, who saw a socialist revolution rising behind Boulanger, they abandoned the policy of republican defense to promote a revolutionary alternative—"ni Ferry! ni Boulanger!" Through their propaganda activity, they established footholds in several industrial districts where they would reap the electoral rewards that disillusionment with both Boulanger and the Republic would inevitably yield.[83]

As the only organized socialist party in the 1880s, the Parti Ouvrier refused to lend its support to a diffuse protest movement that could only benefit Boulanger. In 1885 it had opposed an alliance of Blanquists, Guesdists, and Radicals, the Union Révolutionnaire, because it was not explicitly socialist and it continued to oppose the opportunistic Blanquist initiatives during the Affair. In Boulanger, the possibilists feared a Napoleonic military dictator who would destroy the republican liberties necessary to build a revolutionary movement. When in 1887 the Boulangist crowd threatened to topple the republican President, the party's national committee vowed to call out Parisian workers in defense of the Republic. In 1888, with the aid of Radicals, Jean Allemane started an anti-Boulangist party daily, *Le Parti ouvrier*. At the height of the crisis, the possibilists joined with Radicals on the anti-Boulangist committee of the rue Cadet, the *Société des Droits de l'Homme,* which campaigned for social reform as the only alternative to Boulangism and dictatorship. During this period they tried to curb the violent agitation of the anarchists at the Bourse du Travail and during

the road-workers' strike. Until the Boulangist peril was
averted in 1890, they practiced both first- and second-round
alliances with Radicals. Yet, even at the height of the Affair,
they reaffirmed their commitment to a violent workers'
revolution. Worried about revolutionary defections, they
quickly left the reformist committee of the rue Cadet. They
defended the Republic not as a reformist but as a revolutionary party.[84]

PARTI OUVRIER: ALLEMANISTS

During the 1880s the Parti Ouvrier had contained the tension
between the reformist hopes of Brousse and the revolutionary skepticism of the working class majority. The majority
had adopted Brousse's program because it was federalist. It
never shared his enthusiasm for municipal elections as a way
of transforming the capitalist system. The election of nine
party councillors in 1887 and the successful Radical alliance
against Boulangism emboldened Brousse. When he negotiated
a permanent alliance with Radicals in 1890, he provoked a
rank and file rebellion. Purging the party of the Broussist
politicians, the Allemanist majority returned to a revolutionary orientation that stressed trade union rather than electoral
activity. In a manner characteristic of the French labor
movement, the more revolutionary working class base reas-
serted its authority over a political leadership that was
becoming more opportunist with its participation in the
political system.

The cause of the rebellion was the Radical alliance. Elected
as a councillor with Radical support in 1887, Brousse had led
the party into a temporary alliance that was sanctioned so
long as the Boulangist peril to liberty existed. Once Boulangism was crushed and the peril averted, the party planned to
return to its uncompromising position. Yet, in 1890, without
consulting the party, Brousse and the other party councillors
negotiated an alliance with Radicals, no longer as a measure
of republican defense, but as a way of increasing votes and
influence for the party. In addition, as vice-president of the

Municipal Council, although Brousse had agreed to welcome a marine battalion that had suppressed the Commune, he refused to join a protest demonstration against the Russian Tsar. Parisian groups were thus alerted to Brousse's opportunistic exercise of political authority.[85]

The leader of the Parisian groups was Jean Allemane, who personified the experience and spirit of the militants. As an adolescent recently arrived from the South, Allemane had been an organizer of the printers' trade union in 1862. During the Commune, he served as an official of the 5th *arrondissement*. Arrested on the barricades, he was deported to New Caledonia. Upon his return in 1880, he parted with the cooperative socialists and joined the Parti Ouvrier. He served the party as orator, journalist, trade unionist, and perpetual candidate in the quarter of Folie-Méricourt. With the grandiloquence and eclecticism that is characteristic of the self-educated, Allemane contributed numerous editorials and orations with a consistently revolutionary message. In 1888, he led the battle against Boulanger, publishing and printing *Le Parti Ouvrier,* the anti-Boulangist socialist daily, which became the party's organ in the battle with Brousse.[86]

The conflict was precipitated in 1890 by the deaths of Chabert and Joffrin, who had served as a bridge between the party and its elected representatives. To replace Chabert, a new revolutionary club backed by the Parisian Union Fédérative du Centre nominated Jean Allemane while the regular club named a Broussist, André Gély, supported by the party's national committee. Sixty of eighty-five groups in the Union backed Allemane. When they demanded a national congress to arbitrate the dispute, the national committee hastily convened one at Châtellerault, which, with proxies from the West, it could expect to control.[87]

The dispute raised the issue of party control over its elected representatives. The Broussists believed that representatives should be responsible to their electors rather than to the party. The Allemanists insisted on party control as a safeguard against electoral opportunism. Holding its own regional congress, the Allemanist Union declared itself the arbiter of all rival candidacies and mandator of all elected officials in the region. In further action against the Broussists, it barred elected officials from the national committee and second-round alliances with other parties. When the Broussists at Châtellerault excluded delegates from the Ardennes, the Allemanists withdrew and called a Parisian assembly, which expelled the Broussists and restored the party's revolutionary orientation.

Without altering the party program, the Allemanists took steps to eliminate the opportunistic and authoritarian tendencies that had developed under Brousse's tutelage. They restored the obligatory revolutionary title of the party, transformed the national committee into a smaller and more federalist secretariat, and altered the preamble to stipulate that electoral action was only a means of revolutionary agitation and that the revolution could "only result from the efforts of the workers themselves."[88] They subjected their representatives to closer supervision, requiring their weekly attendance at party meetings, propaganda services, and the payment of their entire salary to the party, from which they would receive 4,000 francs, a good workers' wage, for living expenses.[89] The revolt of the Allemanists against the Broussists paralleled that of the collectivists against Marx in 1872 and of the possibilists against Guesde in 1882, returning power to a revolutionary federation of workers' circles and trade unions.

As a corrective to the Broussist absorption with elections, the Allemanists stressed direct economic action through the *syndicat* or trade union as the main revolutionary instrument of the present and administrative organ of the future.[90] Borrowing from the anarchists, they became the chief proponents of the revolutionary general strike as the most direct method of abolishing the wage system. Without denying the premises of Marxian socialism, they revived the perspective of a federalist socialism administered by a federation of trades and workers' communes.[91]

Despite its syndicalist orientation, trade union membership in the party declined in the 1890s. Coming on top of other factional quarrels during the Boulanger Affair, the split with Brousse discouraged union membership, especially since several union leaders were Broussists. While leading unions continued to attend regional congresses, only ten retained their active membership—tinsmiths, coopers, lace-makers, artificial florists, carriage-makers, blacksmiths, cabinet-makers, dyers, metal polishers, and wiremakers.[92] Divisions in French socialism made it impossible for any union seeking to unite all members of a trade to join any faction, even the Parti Ouvrier.

Still, the Allemanists provided leadership for the syndicalist movement that emerged in the 1890s: L. Riom, Eugène Guérard, Albert Bourderon, Jean-Baptiste Lavaud, A. Baumé, Lhermite, Hamelin, Joseph Braun, Clément Beausoleil, Pascal Faberot, Arthur Groussier, and others. They were leaders of Parisian unions and such newly formed trade federations as the Fédération du Bâtiment, Fédération Métallurgique, Fédération des Mouleurs en Métaux and the Syndicat National des Chemins de Fer.[93]

They were also leaders of the newly formed Bourses du Travail. In alliance with Blanquists and anarchists, they overthrew the Broussist administration of the Parisian Bourse du Travail in 1891 and initiated the organization of a national federation of bourses as the basis for labor unity. With the tactic of the general strike, they spearheaded the formation of the Confédération Générale du Travail and revolutionary syndicalism. Though a large minority in the CGT, they had to agree to its political neutrality to maintain labor unity. By subordinating the party to the trade unions, the Allemanists became dependent upon the growing syndicalist movement. Losing their capacity to guide this movement, they also lost some of their best militants to it.[94]

Because of their subordination of politics to the trade unions, the Allemanists failed to grow electorally along with the other socialist factions in the 1890s. The possibilists had neglected propaganda in the provinces. Remedying this neglect, the Allemanists sent their best orators to all regions of France and Algeria. Though they formed scattered groups in nearly all regions, especially southeast of Paris, the only large federations were the Seine, Seine-et-Oise and the Ardennes.[95] In Paris they failed to oust the Broussist municipal councillors in the 17th, 18th, and 19th *arrondissements.* In 1893, the year of the great upsurge of parliamentary socialism, the Allemanists reached the peak of their electoral influence with 50,000 out of 132,000 socialist votes and 6 out of 15 socialist seats in the Seine region.[96]

Although the Allemanists fought strongly for immediate reforms on the local level, they used their deputies in the Chamber mostly for revolutionary propaganda. Their deputies were vocal in the defense of striking workers and trade unions. The leader of the Parisian hatters, Faberot, acquired a reputation in the Chamber for his violent outbursts and frequent malapropisms. Acting on party instructions, the Allemanist "five," Faberot and Toussaint of the 11th *arrondissement,* Groussier of the 10th, Victor Dejeante of the 20th, and Alexandre Avez of Saint Denis, were the only socialists who refused to join the Union Socialiste, a loose coalition of fifty deputies dedicated to parliamentary socialism. When in 1896, however, four of the deputies and councillors refused to surrender their salaries, they were expelled, leading to the departure of the Ardennes Federation and other provincial groups and the loss of half of their legislative votes in 1898. By 1900, most Allemanists, in opposition to the centralist Guesdists, had joined Jean Jaurès's new Parti Socialiste Français and had lost most of their former vitality and electoral strength.[97]

In the end, the Allemanists could not combine electoral action with their revolutionary program. As a federation of unions and workers' circles without central political leadership, they were too narrowly based both socially and organizationally to become an effective socialist party. Based narrowly upon skilled workers in Paris and a few scattered other cities, the Allemanists had little appeal for the middle class, peasants, or even industrial workers. Organizationally, they could not muster the national support of the centralist Guesdist party. By subordinating themselves to the trade unions, they lost their capacity to influence the unions' direction. With the strict control of leaders and representatives and *ouvrièriste* ethos, they could hardly compete electorally with those independent socialists, mostly middle class in origin, for whom the legislative victories of 1893 revealed the prospect of impending socialist majorities. In the 1890s, a period of relative prosperity, during which parliamentary assemblies opened their doors to socialism, even the Guesdists relinquished their revolutionary expectation to pursue an exclusively electoral strategy for socialism.[98] In the eyes of revolutionary workers, political socialism, both Guesdist and reformist, became identified with opportunistic politicians who were no longer responsible to their working class base. Rebelling against this parliamentary socialism, most revolutionary workers channeled their energies away from political action into the independent trade union or syndicalist movement.

5

Toward Revolutionary
Syndicalism

Though the nature of the relationship has varied, trade unions have developed in conjunction with socialist parties in nearly all countries. Where political socialism antedated trade unionism, as in Germany, the unions were created and dominated by political socialists. In contrast, English socialism, or at least the Labor Party, was the creature of the trade union movement. The Parti Ouvrier, the first French socialist party, was also a creation of trade unions. Through the party and its offshoots, organized workers acquired a revolutionary ideology. During the 1880s, together with its offshoots, the party served as the political and ideological vehicle of the trade unions. Within the party the working class base acted as a revolutionary check against the reformist temptations of the political leadership, resulting in the formation of a more syndicalist Allemanist party.

The Parti Ouvrier, however, was too small and narrow to contain all the diverse factions of French socialism. As fissures developed among these factions, trade unions were split internally and externally over their loyalties. In the absence of a single revolutionary party articulating their ideology, the unions could only be united outside of political socialism on their own economic ground. Once political socialists started upon the parliamentary road to socialism, the unions were left to pursue the socialist revolution in their own syndicalist movement.

Revolutionary or anarcho-syndicalism is habitually treated as a rather unique movement with a philosophy and outlook all its own. While some historians explained it as the product of new intellectual currents, Proudhonian, Sorelian, even Bergsonian,[1] the syndicalists themselves liked to point to the strictly empirical nontheoretical origins of their movement. Victor Griffuelhes, secretary of the Confédération Générale du Travail, asserted that syndicalism was "not determined by any formulas or theoretical affirmations. . . . It has consisted simply of a series of daily efforts, attached to the efforts of the day before not by rigorous continuity but only by the environment and state of mind of the working class."[2] Indeed, syndicalism was not influenced by its intellectual theories, which came after the fact and were unfamiliar to most syndicalists. Yet, the workers' environment and state of mind to which Griffuelhes referred was not simply empirical, a spontaneous product of daily experience, but ideological, the result of a long experience of trade socialism. Syndicalists first acquired their basic outlook in the Parti Ouvrier as revolutionary socialists. Simply put, syndicalism was nothing but revolutionary socialism or collectivism in a strictly trade unionist setting.

In a nation where trade unions had always been ideological, all efforts to organize them independently of socialist parties were invariably led by revolutionaries. Not so surprisingly then, the first trade union federation was organized by Guesdists and other revolutionaries in opposition to the Parti Ouvrier. Later, the revolt of Allemanists and other revolutionaries against this Guesdist-dominated federation led to the formation of the central labor confederation, the CGT. Finally, in reaction to parliamentary socialism, which revealed its force when the socialist Millerand entered a bourgeois government in 1899, several factions coalesced within the CGT to form the revolutionary syndicalist movement. At each step, the cause of syndicalism was advanced by revolutionary trade unionists in rebellion against more moderate political socialists. In France the trade union rank and file were typically more revolutionary than the political socialist leaders.

The first national federation of trade unions, the Fédération des Syndicats et Groupes Corporatifs de France, was founded at the Lyons congress of 1886. Despite tactical differences a coalition of revolutionary socialists—18 possibilists, 13 independents, 6 Blanquists, 5 anarchists and one Guesdist—joined forces against the Opportunist Union des Chambres Syndicales and won a majority of republican delegates over to their position. By an overwhelming majority, the congress approved the formation of a trade union federation that would pursue the class struggle and socialism independently of the political socialist groups. In such a federation trade unionists would have to bury their tactical differences beneath their common commitment to socialism. Thus, the basic elements of revolutionary syndicalism were already present in the first national federation of trade unions.[3]

Abandoned by the possibilists, who already dominated the Parisian labor movement, the federation fell into the hands of the Guesdists at the second congress held in 1887 at Montluçon, a metallurgical center and Guesdist stronghold. Here the national council of the federation was elected among local Guesdist militants. In contrast to the possibilists, who enrolled trade unions directly in the party, the Guesdists maintained a separation between the ideological party and the economic trade union federation. Embracing all workers in an industry or trade, the unions were primary schools of socialism from which workers would be recruited into the party, which alone could offer "scientific" direction for the movement. Controlling the central organization of the federation, the Guesdists used it to indoctrinate unionists and recruit them into the party. At the third congress in 1888 in Bordeaux, Guesde himself was asked to draft the agenda and some preliminary resolutions. So close was the connection between the party and the federation that, beginning in 1890, their respective congresses were always held successively at the same location.[4]

While nominally independent, the federation became an appendage of the Guesdist party with little organizational substance of its own, a Guesdist head without a trade union body. It connected isolated unions from scattered industrial regions directly to the Guesdist national council without any intermediary local or regional organization. Rarely meeting and offering little in the way of strike assistance, the council served basically as a mouthpiece for Guesdist propaganda. Concentrating on party organization, the Guesdists neglected the trade union movement that began to organize in the 1890s around the local bourses du travail and the myth of the general strike.[5]

During the Boulanger Affair, the Guesdists had worked with Blanquists and anarchists in the trade union federation to mount a revolutionary assault on the regime. Thus, the congresses of 1887 and 1888 had approved an anarchist motion to consider the general strike as an immediate form of revolutionary action.[6] After approving the general strike, the Guesdists quickly turned against it, first in 1890, when they nevertheless recommended a general miners' strike, and then in 1892, when they rejected it as illusory and utopian. If the general strike was the strike of *bras croisés,* the universal work stoppage advocated by Aristide Briand, then it was utopian because the bourgeoisie would never relinquish its privileges without a violent struggle. If, on the other hand, it was the insurrectionary strike, then it was the same as the socialist revolution and should be directed not by the unions but by the party. The Guesdists opposed the idea not so much because they were opposed to violent revolution as because the general strike placed the unions rather than the party in the seat of command. A tactic favored by anarchists and Allemanists, it threatened the primacy of the centralist political party. Despite their leadership of the federation, the Guesdists could not dampen enthusiasm for the general strike at the fourth congress in Calais in 1890 or fifth in Marseilles in 1892 where Briand's resolution passed overwhelmingly. As they became absorbed in electoral activity, the Guesdists quickly lost credibility with a trade union movement galvanized by the myth of the general strike.[7]

The end of the Boulanger Affair and the resumption of economic activity in the early 1890s set the stage for the emergence of an independent revolutionary trade unionism or syndicalism. This movement found its first headquarters in the bourse du travail. The Bourse du Travail de Paris was originally approved by Radicals on the Paris Municipal Council in 1886 to replace the famous Place de Grève, the traditional hiring ground in the construction industry, during inclement weather. While the Municipal Council retained financial control, the administration of the Bourse was confided to a possibilist committee elected by member unions. Besides functioning as a hiring hall, placement center, and bureau of labor statistics, the Bourse immediately became a center for revolutionary activity where the anarchists first proposed the idea of an insurrectionary general strike.[8]

Other Radical municipalities, particularly in the South, followed the Parisian example: Nîmes in 1887, Marseilles in 1888, then Montpellier, Saint-Etienne, Toulouse, Narbonne, Toulon, Lyons, and others. The possibilists controlled the Parisian bourse, but in other areas they had to share the administration with other factions—Blanquists, anarchists, independents, and even Guesdists. In the bourse setting, workers had to bury their factional differences and build upon common ideological ground, their underlying commitment to trade socialism. Thus, the bourses provided an organizational framework outside of the political parties where workers could pursue their revolutionary strategy for socialism.

The Allemanists provided the essential ideological leadership for the emerging syndicalist movement. In reaction to the Broussists' electoralism, the Allemanists stressed the economic class struggle in the trade union. Borrowing from the anarchists, they were the chief proponents of the insurrectionary general strike as the most direct method of abolishing the wage system. The Allemanists first began to advocate the general strike in 1891, a year before Aristide Briand and Fernand Pelloutier, the two middle class journalists who are usually considered its chief propagandists. In contrast to Briand and Pelloutier, who advocated a peaceful universal work stoppage, a strike of *bras croisés,* the Allemanists proposed an insurrectionary strike tantamount to revolution in which military measures would be taken to seize control of the economy and liquidate the class enemy. Despite formal adhesion to Marxist principles, they also revived the vision of a federalist socialism organized around the trade union in a federation of trades and trade communes. Their revolutionary conception of the general strike and federalist socialism came to prevail in the syndicalist movement.[9]

From the outset they accepted the principle of an independent and politically neutral labor movement. While continuing to attend party congresses, most Parisian unions resigned their party membership after the split with the Broussists. The factional disputes among socialist workers, notably among Broussists, Allemanists, and Guesdists, made it impossible for a trade organization, wishing to unite all workers in a trade or locality, to affiliate with any socialist faction. Accepting the principle of political neutrality in order to maintain working class unity, the Allemanists became the leaders of many newly formed trade federations, especially in metal and construction, as well as the new bourses du travail. Combining forces with Blanquists, independents, and anarchists, they overthrew the Broussist administration of the Parisian bourse in June 1891[10] and initiated the formation of the Fédération Nationale des Bourses du Travail at Saint-Etienne in 1892. As a rival to the

Guesdist trade federation, the federation attempted to organize all workers outside of the competing socialist factions.[11]

Through the Fédération Nationale des Bourses du Travail the Allemanists set out to eliminate Guesdist influence and organize all unions into a single independent labor confederation. In 1893, they convoked a general labor congress in Paris open to all unions and placed the general strike on the agenda. For several months they conducted a campaign in favor of the general strike. Frightened by the growing agitation, the government closed the Parisian bourse on May Day and compelled the unions to register in conformity with the Waldeck-Rousseau Law of 1884. When the Allemanists counseled defiance, the government forcibly occupied the bourse, provoking several days of street rioting.[12] In a wave of indignation against the government, nearly all factions sent representatives to Paris. Enthusiasm for the general strike was general with delegates divided only over the advisability of its immediate application. The congress unanimously empowered a committee to prepare its organization.[13] Over Guesdist objections, it also approved an Allemanist proposal to merge the two labor federations the following year at Nantes where the Guesdists had already scheduled their next conclave.[14]

The Nantes bourse accepted the mandate from Paris and conducted a referendum that upheld the merger plan. A majority of French unions, 1,482, were represented at Nantes. With the Guesdists more than ever dedicated to electoral victories, the battle was joined over the general strike. For the Guesdists, the idea was utopian because the workers had neither the consciousness nor the resources to organize the strike effectively. Only political action through the party could prepare workers for the revolution. Its proponents argued that the general strike could be carried out relatively easily once workers in certain key industries—food and transportation—left their jobs. When the delegates voted 63 to 36 to continue preparations for the strike, the

Guesdists quit the proceedings.[15] The congress then established a national labor council to begin the merger of the two
federations into a single confederation.[16]

The following year at Limoges the CGT was founded in
rather inauspicious circumstances. During its early years the
CGT was boycotted both by the Guesdists, who held a rival
congress in 1895, and the Fédération Nationale des Bourses
du Travail, which feared domination by the more moderate
trade federations. While controlled by revolutionaries, the
newly formed federations of trades tended to be more
concerned with trade defense than the bourses. Seventy-five
delegates represented 18 bourses, 126 unions, and 28 trade
federations at Limoges. The leading political force was the
Allemanists whose leaders worked from behind the scenes to
draft the statutes.[17] They were joined by Blanquists as well as
more moderate elements, the Broussist Victor Dalle, the
reformist Guesdist Edouard Treich, and the positivist printer
Auguste Keufer. Drafted by these heterogeneous elements,
the statutes gave a preponderance of votes on the national
labor council to the more moderate trade federations at the
expense of the bourses. Until the CGT was united with the
Fédération Nationale des Bourses du Travail in 1902, it
remained a weak and ineffective organization.

The purpose of the CGT was to unite "on economic
grounds . . . workers in struggle for their complete emancipation."[18] While acknowledging a revolutionary purpose, the
statutes imposed political neutrality on member unions in
order to avoid factional disputes: "The elements of the CGT
must remain outside of all political schools."[19] Yet, far from
being antisocialist, the CGT asked its members to support
those political representatives, presumably socialists, who
defended workers' interests in parliament.[20] Despite moderate opposition, the Limoges congress also decided to make
the committee on the general strike an integral part of the
CGT.[21] The true reformists, those who like Keufer believed
in the preservation of the capitalist system, remained a
marginal element in a labor movement dedicated to a

collectivist objective and united increasingly around the strategy of the general strike.

The role of the Allemanists in the CGT is underscored when we compare the unions that participated in its founding congresses from 1893 to 1896 with those that attended Parisian party congresses.[22] Parisian unions comprised nearly half of those represented at CGT congresses. Nearly all had attended congresses of the Parti Ouvrier, most of them quite recently. Among the Parisian unions in the forefront were many strongly Allemanist unions: hatters, mechanics, iron molders, copper founders, saddlers, printers, piano-makers, plumbers, tinsmiths, and railway workers. In addition to the traditional skilled trades, several industrial categories were represented, namely railroad workers, tobacco and municipal gas workers from Paris, and miners and textile workers from the provinces. It is more difficult to judge Allemanist influence in the provinces. Though their overall numbers were small, they were present in nearly all regions, sharing leadership in the unions with Blanquists, independents, anarchists, and Guesdists. More important than their actual numbers is the fact that their basic strategy and ideology came to prevail in the CGT.

Although the "heroic age" of syndicalism properly begins after 1902 with the merger of the two federations, the basic ideological and organizational framework was already set in the early 1890s. During this period the trade unions emerged from under the tutelage of the socialist parties and developed their own independent organization and program. With the general strike they possessed their own strategy for the collectivization of the means of production in a federation of trades and communes. Within the trade unions workers found a revolutionary socialism purged of the opportunist electoral tendencies that had appeared among the political socialists, namely Broussists, independents, and Guesdists. In this initial process of unification the Allemanists played a decisive role.

While the CGT stagnated as an organization, the Fédération Nationale des Bourses du Travail grew rapidly from thirty-four members in 1895 to eighty-three in 1902 largely under the stewardship of Fernand Pelloutier, a young journalist from Saint-Nazaire. One of the early proponents of the peaceful general strike, Pelloutier had quit the Guesdists in 1892 and drifted into anarchist literary circles in Paris. Collaborating with the Allemanists in the federation, he rose to the position of secretary on the basis of his political neutrality—as an anarchist—and his dedication to the organization. Besides increasing membership, Pelloutier expanded the services of the bourse in the area of trade education, mutual insurance, labor statistics, and the *viaticum* or traveling benefit. In his activity Pelloutier believed he was laying the moral and material basis for the future society where the municipal bourse would serve as a center for exchange and distribution.[23]

The impetus for the unification of the CGT with the Fédération Nationale des Bourses du Travail came in reaction to the Millerand Affair, which revealed the potential force of parliamentary socialism. In this affair Millerand, a Radical turned parliamentary socialist, had entered the bourgeois government of Waldeck-Rousseau as a measure of republican defense along with a hated general who had helped suppress the Commune. The participation of a socialist in a bourgeois government divided reformist from revolutionary elements in both the socialist party and trade unions. With promises of workers' pensions and a law on compulsory arbitration, Millerand exercised an undeniable charm on certain trade union leaders. It was to alert workers to the dangers of reformist socialism that Guesdists, Allemanists, anarchists, and Blanquists came together in a movement of revolutionary syndicalism.[24]

Within the CGT, Millerand's reforms were attacked as snares and illusions designed to destroy the independence of the trade unions: only those reforms won through collective struggle were helpful to the workers' cause; those freely granted by bourgeois governments could only weaken it. To counter the reformist temptation, the CGT in 1900 reaf-

firmed its commitment to the revolutionary general strike
and commissioned a questionnaire on plans for the future
society. Responses received from member unions in 1902
outlined the vision of a federalist socialism in which the local
trade union and national trade federation would manage and
coordinate production, the local bourse and federation would
direct exchange and distribution, and the CGT would serve as
the general regulator and repository of collective property.
The general strike as the means and trade socialism as the
end—this was revolutionary syndicalism.[25]

On the thrust of this movement, the Fédération Nationale
des Bourses du Travail was united with the CGT on an equal
basis in 1902. Within the new CGT, each local union was
required to belong both to its national trade federation and
to the local bourse while the national trade federations and
bourses formed two equal sections of the CGT. General
policy was set at the biennial confederal congresses where
small individual unions, entitled to the same vote as
federations or bourses, had a voting preponderance. The
interim governing body was the confederal committee on
which each bourse and federation had one vote. Because of
their numerical superiority, the more revolutionary bourses
had a greater voice than the federations. Moreover, the
delegates from these bourses were usually proxies chosen
from a list circulated by the revolutionary leadership of the
CGT.[26]

From 1901 until 1909, during the "heroic age of syndicalism," the CGT was directed by a coalition of anarchists and
revolutionary socialists. Most of the leaders and the great
majority of the militants were socialist in background and
outlook. If not actually members of a socialist faction, they
certainly voted for socialists as representatives of the working
class in the political system. Many leaders came from a
Blanquist or Allemanist background: Secretary Griffuelhes,
Léon Martin, J. Majot, Eugène Guerard, Albert Bourderon,
and others. Unlike the anarchists, they viewed the relationship between syndicalism and political socialism as comple-

mentary rather than antagonistic with each movement struggling on its own ground, economic and political, for essentially the same goal.[27]

While few in overall numbers, the anarchists rose during the "heroic age" to positions of influence where they imparted an ultrarevolutionary verve and rhetoric to the movement. Overcoming their dislike for collective action and association, anarchists had originally entered the unions to seek refuge from government prosecution under the 1893 *lois scélérates,* which outlawed their violent propaganda. Within the unions, their antipolitical and insurrectionary attitude merged easily with the developing strategy of the general strike. By virtue of their zeal, rhetorical skill, and political neutrality, former anarchists rose to leading positions: Georges Yvetot, editor of the official newspaper *La Voix du peuple;* Emile Pouget, head of the section of bourses; Paul Delesalle, secretary of the committee on the general strike; and so on. As chief propagandists during this period, they often stressed such anarchist themes as electoral abstention, industrial sabotage, and antipatriotism that were not necessarily shared and were later disavowed by a majority of syndicalists.[28]

During this period, revolutionary action, chiefly strike action, was stressed to the detriment of solid labor organization. While encouraging strikes, the CGT did little to assure their success or to tie workers permanently to their unions. Dues were low and irregularly collected, and only a few unions, notably printers, hatters and mechanics, had any benefit features. Retaining jurisdiction in matters of dues, strikes, and benefits, most local unions remained weak and ineffective with an average membership of 200 in 1912. Few attempts were made to increase membership or organize new categories of workers. To those socialists who chided them for their organizational weakness, the syndicalists replied that it was the "active minorities" not the slow-moving masses who made history. Treating strikes as an exercise of "revolutionary gymnastics" as much as a struggle for concrete reforms, the CGT leaders awaited that fateful strike or incident that would ignite the general revolutionary strike.[29]

Characteristic of the "heroic" approach was the campaign conducted from 1904 to 1906 for the eight-hour day. While the eight-hour day had already been won in America by the American Federation of Labor, it was a radical demand in France where twelve hours were not uncommon. The very impracticality of the demand made it a superb means of agitation. Delesalle, sponsor of the campaign, saw the issue as a "pretext for action and agitation," leading toward the universal work stoppage that would put "the proletariat in a state of war with capitalist society."[30] For eighteen months, the CGT circulated brochures, held meetings, and organized strikes to fan workers' rage into a "white heat." On May Day, it announced that henceforth no one would work more than eight hours, but only 100,000 in Paris and isolated groups in the provinces walked off the job. Though a material and financial failure, the CGT viewed the campaign as a moral success since it had aroused the consciousness of the working class.[31]

The price paid for this campaign, which had given the government and bourgeoisie an unnecessary fright, was a new policy of repression. Drawing the line against revolutionary agitation, Radical governments led by Clemenceau and Briand, the former socialist, took stern measures against the CGT. From 1906 to 1910, they frequently intervened against strikers with troops, conscripted strikers into the army, and arrested leaders of the CGT for conspiracy. The results of Clemenceau's new policy were several bloody clashes, 104 years in prison sentences, 667 wounded workers, 20 dead, and 392 fired from their jobs. Against this relentless attack, the CGT was unable to mount a riposte. The repression demonstrated that revolutionary élan was no substitute for permanent organization.[32]

Under the impact of the repression, the CGT retreated from its ultrarevolutionary posture. The 1908 congress showed its weariness with the inflammatory rhetoric of leaders who had exaggerated the role of the CGT beyond its actual resources. In 1909, Griffuelhes was replaced by Louis Niel, a former anarchist, who promised "action that is more in conformity with the possibilities of the moment, that is less rhetorical and romantic and more rewarding in results."[33] "As inadequate as it may seem," he said, "the struggle for immediate reforms is the most effective one so long as it is inspired by the revolutionary ideal of complete social liberation." Under Niel and his successor, Léon Jouhaux, another former anarchist who was destined to lead the CGT for the next forty years, more attention was paid to trade defense, strike support and coordination, labor legislation and statistics, and the growth and rationalization of union organization. Some balance was thus restored between reformist action and organization and the final revolutionary goal.[34]

The conflict between so-called reformists and revolutionaries in the CGT must not obscure the ideological consensus that united them.[35] Both sides shared a common belief in trade socialism and the general strike. Their differences were tactical and temperamental. Living in the expectancy of an imminent insurrectionary strike, the revolutionaries had neglected the practical work of winning strikes, gaining benefits, and recruiting new members. The new leadership saw this practical work as the only way to organize and prepare workers for the revolution in the long run.[36] The only federation that had an ideologically reformist majority believing in the finality of trade unionism within the capitalist system was the Fédération du Livre.[37] As always, this reformism remained a rather minor current in a labor movement dedicated to the goals of revolutionary syndicalism.[38]

But how representative, one may ask, was this syndicalism of the French working class? Was it, as one writer has recently argued, a cause without rebels, a sectarian current that had practically no influence on the French working class?[39] In 1906, after all, the CGT had about 200,000 members, less than 3 percent of the industrial working class.[40] By 1912, this number had risen at best to 400,000. This was even a minority of all organized workers, most of whom belonged to employer-dominated "yellow" and Christian unions. Syndicalist unions grouped a far larger proportion—perhaps 10 percent—of the urban skilled trades. Still, how could such a tiny minority—even an active and strategically important one—be said to represent the French working class?

Syndicalists represented the working class because they were the leaders of the only independent democratic unions in France. If they were "active minorities" without followers in periods of social peace—periods of complacency, resignation, or despair—they became leaders of masses during moments of social tension and conflict. During mass mobilizations—strikes, professional elections, political crises, and so on—they became the spokesmen for the usually "silent majorities," including many of the normally moderate, apathetic, resigned, and perhaps even conservative workers. As ideological leaders, they gave clarity and consistency to what was at best the episodic class consciousness of the majority.[41] If liberal reformism had been a strong current among this majority, it would have emerged as a viable alternative to syndicalism in the CGT. Since it was not and had never been, the ideological hegemony of syndicalism over the French working class remained unchallenged.

The social composition of the CGT before 1914 has never been thoroughly analyzed,[42] but most accounts point to the predominance of urban skilled workers. The formative role played by Parisian craftsmen under Allemanist influence has already been mentioned. The most active syndicalists appear to have come from the skilled metal and construction trades.[43] Because of the federalist system of voting, the smaller craft unions enjoyed influence in the confederation beyond their actual numbers. With the exception of the printers, most craft federations strongly supported the revolutionary leadership. With their socialist tradition, these craft unions possessed the high degree of ideological commitment upon which the syndicalists, with their reliance on self-directed "active minorities," depended.

Syndicalism thus exhibited the basic ambiguity of trade socialism. Favorable to industrialization and industrial organization in principle, the syndicalists remained tied to professional privilege in practice—job autonomy, craft solidarity, and organizational federalism. Though committed to the emancipation of all workers, they geared their voluntarist strategy to the level of the best organized and most highly conscious workers, neglecting the unskilled and unorganized. Just as the struggle for immediate reforms was tied to the trade so was their vision of socialism structured around a federation of skilled trades. If skilled workers alone had the consciousness to challenge the capitalist system, they were not themselves capable of overthrowing the system. The professional privilege that made skilled workers the vanguard of the working class assured that they would lead the workers corporatively, as a federation of trades, rather than as a unitary working class.[44]

After 1900, skilled workers were increasingly joined in the CGT by new categories from larger-scale mining, industry, and transport: miners and textile, port and maritime, railway, agricultural, chemical, food, and municipal service workers.[45] By 1914, the more industrial federations of miners and textile and railway workers dwarfed the craft federations in membership. In the absence of occupational and union monographs, it is impossible to determine how many workers from these industries were skilled or unskilled, but even if they were from the more elite categories they certainly brought with them more industrial concerns and outlooks.

This influx of new categories was encouraged by a change of policy regarding the occupational basis of national federations. Until 1900 the CGT had favored the national federation of the trade, uniting unions nationally on the basis of narrow craft solidarity. Over the years, such organization had proven far more cohesive and durable than the various experiments with vaster and more nebulous industrial federations in construction, metallurgy, leather, hides, and so on. The federations of mechanics and iron molders, for example, were much stronger and larger than the newly formed metallurgical federation. A report in 1897 concluded that only trade organization was strong enough to ensure strike support, maintain solidarity, and overthrow the capitalist system. By 1900, however, many syndicalists had seen the need for industrial organization. Forseeing the complete destruction of the shoemaking trade through mechanization, Griffuelhes in 1900 asked the CGT to anticipate future forms of struggle through the formation of industrial federations uniting all categories in an industry. In 1906, the CGT altered its statutes to require the formation of federations on an industrial basis and in 1908 began the amalgamation of the remaining trade federations into industrial ones. Many skilled trades like the mechanics resisted amalgamation. Even within the new industrial federations, only a tiny minority of affiliates were themselves organized on an industrial basis. Though the CGT was now theoretically organized on an industrial basis, the basic components of the federations and bourses were still local craft unions.[46]

The effect of the influx of new categories upon the program and policies of the CGT also remains to be studied. One historian of strikes has suggested that the influx of larger numbers of workers after 1906 resulted in the increasing moderation of the CGT and a growing acceptance of collective bargaining.[47] This suggestion seems wrong on a number of counts. First, revolutionary syndicalists never opposed collective bargaining, only such bargaining as a final goal, and after 1900 the CGT definitely encouraged the negotiation of collective contracts where possible.[48] Second, the influx of new workers into the CGT corresponded with the increasing radicalization, not moderation, of its policies, which in fact followed the rising tide of strikes and militancy. The retreat of 1910 came in response to political repression and the failure of the general strike, which resulted in a decline of strikes and organizational growth. While lacking the ideological commitment of skilled militants, the new-comers to the CGT—textile, dock, and metallurgical work-ers—often displayed a considerable degree of militancy in their strike action. Within the CGT they, like the older members, consistently elected revolutionary rather than reformist leadership. This was true not only during the "heroic age," but even after the crisis of syndicalism in 1910, when revolutionary leaders had to abandon their immediate hopes for the general strike. What did accompany the influx of new workers, however, was a growing awareness of the problems of industrialization and the need for greater centralization in the labor movement, which after World War I produced a major reorganization of the confederation and a plan for the nationalization of heavy industry.[49] While reflecting a traditional ideology, the CGT before the war was already in transition to a more industrial form of unionism and ideology.

French trade unions had originally broken from political socialism because of its tendency toward division, electoral opportunism, and the growth of political authority. This raison d'être for syndicalism was thrown into question in 1905 when nearly all socialist factions agreed on a charter of unity based on revolutionary Marxist principles.[50] The newly unified socialist party, the SFIO (Section Française de l'Internationale Ouvrière) was the result of a compromise between Guesdist organizational centralism and Jaurèsian federalism. In conformity with the Marxist principles and practice of the Second International, the Guesdists proposed to establish formal ties between the party of the proletariat and the trade unions. According to the Guesdists, the trade unions were incapable of carrying out the revolution and managing the socialist economy. Their function was limited to obtaining minor reforms within the capitalist system in cooperation with the party, while leaving revolutionary strategy and the conquest of power exclusively to the party. In order to establish this relationship, Victor Renard,

Guesdist secretary of the Textile Federation, introduced a
resolution at the 1906 congress of Amiens calling for joint
consultations between the SFIO and CGT "in order to secure
the triumph of the most important labor reforms." [51]

In response to this Guesdist motion, which was overwhelmingly defeated, the congress endorsed a counterreso-
lution drafted by the leadership that became the most
definitive statement of syndicalist methods and goals, the
Charter of Amiens. [52] Independently of the SFIO, the CGT
announced its pursuit of an essentially socialist goal: "The
CGT unites, outside of all political schools, all workers
conscious of the struggle to be waged for the disappearance
of the wage system and the employer class." [53] It recognized
that the class struggle had both a reformist and revolutionary
dimension:

> In its day-to-day demands, syndicalism seeks the coordination
> of workers' efforts, [and] the enhancement of workers' well-being
> through the achievement of such immediate reforms as the
> shortening of hours, the raising of wages, etc.
>
> This effort, however, is only one aspect of the work of
> syndicalism. It prepares for complete emancipation, which can
> only be achieved by expropriating the capitalist class. It advocates
> the general strike as its means of action to that end and holds
> that the union, which is today an instrument of resistance, will in
> the future be the unit of production and distribution, the basis of
> social reorganization.

While recognizing the right of individual unionists to partici-
pate in political parties, which might also seek the transformation of society, the CGT barred political discussion and
activity within the unions as a source of division. As a labor
organization that united workers in the economic class
struggle, the CGT thus declared its total independence of
political socialism.

In the Charter of Amiens, the CGT declared itself to be an
independent revolutionary labor movement seeking the collectivization of the means of production through direct

economic action and the general strike. In the CGT revolutionary socialists and anarchists had found common ground in a form of trade socialism purged of the divisiveness, opportunism, and oligarchical authority inherent in political socialism. Neither the product of new intellectual theories nor a spontaneous creation, revolutionary syndicalism was the culmination of a long tradition and experience of trade socialism. Writing his history of the First International in 1907, Guillaume put it succinctly when he asked: "What is the CGT if not the continuation of the International? "[54] Despite gradual modifications, the French labor movement would confront the crisis caused by World War I and the Russian Revolution with the revolutionary collectivism of the First International.[55]

6

Conclusion:
Socialism of
Skilled Workers

This study has traced the origins of the French labor movement with a view toward uncovering an underlying ideological tendency or objective. It has defined that tendency as trade socialism, the belief that workers could only end their exploitation through their acquisition of the means of production and that the form or unit of such acquisition should be the organized body of the trade, in other words, a form of socialism that would preserve the autonomy and integrity of the trade. In pursuit of this objective, workers adopted two distinct strategies, a cooperative strategy in alliance with the reformist middle class and then a revolutionary strategy of class struggle. In this latter phase trade unions first tried the instrumentality of the political party but, when this structure proved too confining, they developed their own independent organization and strategy in the CGT and the general strike.

To explain the shift from a cooperative to a revolutionary strategy, this study has largely discounted the structuralist argument of industrialization. Overall, industrialization did not really begin to affect the artisanal character of the organized working class and urban labor movement until after 1900. It was not possible to detect any significant influx of industrial workers or mechanization of skilled trades that might explain the conversion to revolutionary

156

collectivism. There may well have been a growing awareness of the irreversibility of large-scale industrialization manifested in the formal adhesion to Marxist principles, but this psychological awareness is difficult to measure and was not absent during the cooperative phase. In any case, the Parti Ouvrier continued to represent skilled trades and to reflect their concerns and ideological outlook. Though accompanied by a shift to more industrial forms of organization, the influx of some industrial categories into the CGT apparently had only a belated effect on its policies and strategy.

Rather than industrialization, the critical factor in the change was political, the accession of Opportunist republicans to power and workers' disillusionment with the new Republic. The cooperative strategy had always depended upon the active support of republican socialists and the reformist middle class. The accession of the middle class *couches nouvelles* to political power under the stable conditions of the Republic and their reconciliation with the bourgeoisie ended the dream of a social republic that would liberate the working class. By allowing a return of revolutionary activity while disappointing hopes of social reform, the coming of the Republic led labor militants to revise their strategy and adopt a revolutionary program. From a cooperative strategy that assumed class harmony, they shifted to a revolutionary strategy in pursuit of trade socialism.

Further, this study has related trade socialism to its economic and social basis in the semiartisanal mode of production and skilled working class, finding a structural correspondence between the ideology and the social situation of skilled workers. Rather than undertake monographic research on a particular trade or conjuncture, it has sought with the aid of impressionistic evidence, quantitative data, and social theory to identify those long-term social and economic factors common to the activist trades that might explain their enduring commitment to trade socialism. It has analyzed the social situation of skilled workers not in the abstract, but in relation to their ideology, and in the process learned more about both their ideology and social situation.

Since this global approach runs counter to prevailing empiricist and nominalist trends in social history, it requires some final words of explanation. It goes without saying that the schema and generalization presented here must stand the acid test of further empirical investigation. Specifically, they must be tested against monographic studies into the evolution of particular trades and work practices.[1] Yet to begin such monographic work without the benefit of a conceptual framework and historical overview is to run the risk of missing the forest for the trees, mistaking primary for secondary causes, stressing the unique over the general, the short-term result over the long-term, and the conjuncture over the structure and the *longue durée*. In labor history as in other fields, empirical and theoretical work must proceed hand-in-hand with the empirical findings confirming or modifying the concepts and the conceptual work informing the empirical data. This study has attempted to present such a conceptual framework and historical overview.

From a variety of sources, it appeared that common social and economic problems united workers in their adhesion to trade socialism. From the July Monarchy to the Third Republic, there was little change in the types of trades, ranging from the more artisanal clockmakers, tailors, shoemakers, articles of Paris, saddlers, and cabinetmakers to more industrial mechanics, printers, carpenters and iron founders, that participated in the movement. The increase in the number of metal and construction workers and trades in the movement seemed commensurate with their growing importance in the Parisian work force. Along the way the ideological idiosyncrasies of some trade societies were noted—the relative reformism of printers; the revolutionary militancy of mechanics; the anarchism of tailors, shoemakers, and joiners; and the relative timidity of luxury workers—but these were only minor and temporary divergences from the overall ideological pattern. Further, it seemed artificial to isolate any one trade or conjunctural crisis from the general long-term condition of the trades. Nearly all suffered from the gradual erosion of status, security, and relative income that occurred over the course of the century. While varying with each trade, grievances and demands tended to remain the same over time: higher wages, reduction of the work day, public employment, the abolition of private employment agencies, subcontracting, work in prisons and convents, and so on. Impressionistic evidence, monographic studies, quantitative data, and social theory all pointed to a long-term structural crisis that skilled workers encountered in the course of industrialization.

This structural crisis was defined in terms of two opposite features, the proletarianization of skilled workers and the survival of skill. Industrialization in the nineteenth century had advanced far enough in terms of commercial and labor competition to threaten the security, income, and integrity of most crafts, enough to provoke protest and resistance, but not enough in terms of total mechanization to destroy the craft and its organized resistance. The security, income, and integrity of the crafts were threatened by the influx of cheaper labor; standardized production; cyclical unemployment; the introduction of power tools; and increases in the division, speed, and intensity of labor. Yet, while undergoing a relative proletarianization, most activist workers still retained their craft status with its apprenticeship requirement, measure of job control, and trade solidarity. Despite the partial transformation of their crafts, they still possessed the professional and organizational capacity to resist exploitation and offer a transformative ideological response to capitalism.

Complete mechanization with its extreme subdivision of tasks and destruction of job autonomy in the work place did not occur in most trades until the twentieth century.[2] The shift occurred after 1900 with the mechanization of glass-making, shoe and hat manufacture, and the introduction of assembly-line production in automobiles, and in the metallurgical and electrical industries. The great upsurge of strikes over issues of work organization and job control from 1910 to 1914 bears witness to the last-ditch effort of skilled workers to stave off their complete destruction through mechanization. The precise degree and timing of this mechanization must await further monographic research, but on the basis of job descriptions, data on apprenticeship, scale of enterprise and steam power, and economic demands, one can safely conclude that the activist workers in the Parti Ouvrier and the early CGT still came from the skilled trades.

In their adhesion to trade socialism, these workers displayed characteristics of both a trade and a working class consciousness. In seeking collective ownership of the means of production, skilled workers from the very beginning identified themselves as members of a larger class that was separated from such ownership. Yet, insofar as they attempted to preserve their job and organizational autonomy, both in the present and the future, they displayed a more narrow trade consciousness. Just as the defense of their economic position was tied to their craft, so was their vision of the socialist future structured around a federation of skilled trades. Though they identified their project with the emancipation of all workers, they alone possessed the capacity to organize the basis of the new society.

While condemning the Proudhonian utopia of petty production, they also rejected the Marxist utopia of an advanced industrialism that would destroy the job autonomy and organizational solidarity of the craft. If they accepted some features of industrialism—the concentration of capital, the use of power tools, an increased division of labor—they were aiming to stop the process mid-way before it destroyed the remaining privileges of the craft. In this they were fighting a losing battle, for just as job autonomy and trade solidarity would eventually give way before mechanization and the assembly line, so too would the ideology of trade socialism be replaced by a Marxist socialism that was more appropriate for the problems of large-scale industrialism. Thus, the continuing growth of industrial capitalism finally destroyed the socialism of skilled workers, which constituted a transitional phase in the history of socialism and the working class.

Epilogue:
Socialism As
Theory and Process

Since World War II, France has been the only major Western power whose labor movement has been dominated by Marxism. Though the reasons for this Marxist hegemony lie outside the scope of this study, it may be valuable to consider the question in the light of the socialist tradition that has been its main focus. There has been a continuous experience of socialist ideology, uniting new recruits with old militants, one generation with the next, which has set the basic orientation of the labor movement. If the principle of workers' ownership of the means of production has remained constant, the modes and mechanisms of its application have altered with changing conditions and experiences. Socialism began with the utopia of the producers' cooperative as the method and form of workers' emancipation from the wage system. History has witnessed the gradual adaptation and rationalization of this utopia into more general forms as it confronted new historical experiences and conditions.[1]

In general, the direction of this change has been from the cooperative and revolutionary trade socialism of the nineteenth century to the Marxist state socialism of the twentieth. In this change the locus of social action has shifted from the local trade and commune to national industry and the centralized state. Organizationally, federalist structures that were spontaneous and flexible were consolidated into more centralist forms of deliberation, direction, and control. In theoretical terms, the movement broke out of its bourgeois democratic integument to become first a critique of democratic ideology, and finally, as Marxism, a totally new world view. Broadly, this change represented a process of accommodation and adaptation to the growth of the bourgeois democratic state on the one hand and of large-scale industrial production on the other.

If, in the course of this process, socialism became more conscious and theoretical, it was never free from theoretical influences and assumptions. The labor movement dões not develop in an intellectual vacuum but is influenced by ideas in the general culture, especially those introduced by intellectuals who see the movement as an instrument of change. The original cooperative socialism resulted from an interaction between workers protesting their material conditions and idealistic republicans seeking the basis for a harmonious democratic society. Through the republican movement, the idea of the producers' cooperative became part of an overall strategy for the collectivization of the means of production. Socialism, in other words, originated as part of a larger democratic movement and ideology.

Tested over the course of fifty years and three republican regimes, 1848, 1871, and 1880, this socialism eventually yielded disillusionment both with cooperatives as the instrument and republicanism as the lever of emancipation. Professing socialism while in revolutionary opposition, most middle class republicans chose capitalism once in power. Under the Third Republic workers discovered they would have to rely upon their own efforts to overthrow the bourgeois state and establish a regime of associated labor. From a cooperative strategy assuming class harmony, they shifted to a revolutionary strategy based on class struggle.

Formulated in the First International with the help of Marx and Bakunin, this revolutionary collectivism attracted

French leaders before the Commune and most of the exile community afterwards. When Internationalists like Guesde returned to France, they confronted a cooperative labor movement awaiting the coming of a democratic and social republic. By removing juridical barriers to revolutionary activity while disappointing hopes of social transformation, the advent of the Third Republic precipitated organized workers into the revolutionary camp.

Whether in the Parti Ouvrier or the CGT, French socialism preserved the federalist trade character of its origins: the social and organizational basis in local unions and federations of urban skilled workers, the strategy of self-emancipation with its respect for federalist democracy and suspicion of political and theoretical leadership, and the utopia of a federalist socialism administered by local trades and communes. When Guesde after 1880 tried to raise this movement to the level of a more centralist Marxist party, it rejected his "authoritarian" theoretical leadership. As Guesdists and other political socialists became absorbed in parliamentary action, the trade unions continued to pursue the revolution through their own independent syndicalist movement. In the CGT the labor movement remained committed to a federalist form of socialism that was anti-Marxist.

Marxism has a double origin both as a theory of social development and as a historical process. In the theory that Marx expounded in the *Manifesto,* he anticipated the socialist revolution as the result of a historical process involving transformations in the working class and labor movement from a skilled to an industrial working class and from strikes and trade unions to the formation of a workers' and communist party. As a result of this process, workers might develop their own socialist movement but they eventually needed the help of Marxists, who understood "the historical movement as a whole," to raise the movement to the level of theory and organization considered necessary for success.

Marxist theory and historical process were interrelated. The process could not be completed without theory, and theory could not be actualized without the process.

How were Marxists supposed to influence this historical process? Marx's position on the matter, the question of party building, varied in different historical situations.[2] In the *Manifesto* of 1847, he told communists not to form a separate party, but to enter the labor movement, however backward, and to work within to advance it toward higher levels of organization and consciousness. The communist party that was necessary for victory would thus emerge organically out of the trade unions and republican party as the result of a democratic evolutionary process.

At times, however, Marx was tempted to speed up this process, to shorten the birth pangs of the new society, by calling for the immediate formation of a proletarian or communist party. Aiming to skip or combine historical stages in 1849, he recommended the formation of a proletarian party to struggle for the seizure of state power, a policy that was far too advanced for the French labor movement and that failed to make an impact. Returning to political activity in the 1860s, Marx again chose to work within the existing labor movement, helping to guide the International through mutual discussion and united action toward Marxist conclusions. When Bakuninism appeared to threaten the outcome of this process, he decided to use his authority in the International to speed its transformation into a proletarian or communist party. By taking this leap toward a communist party, Marx created the historical distinction between a centralist and authoritarian Marxism and the "real" or existing labor movement, which remained federalist and antiauthoritarian.

As bourgeois intellectuals, who likewise comprehended the movement "as a whole," Guesde and Lafargue were assigned the task of creating the communist party in France. In order to create a more centralist Marxist party, Guesde had to break with the "real" federalist labor movement of skilled workers. Guided by a schematic Marxism, he could only construct a pedagogical party that was unable to combine its teachings with practical activity and provide political leadership for the labor movement. Abandoning the skilled for industrial workers, he cut himself off from the "real" revolutionary forces in the working class, which, consequently, were left without any theoretical or political leadership. Thus, French socialism encountered World War I and the Russian Revolution split between a parliamentary Marxist party and a revolutionary trade union movement.

This bifurcated socialism broke on the shoals of World War I and the Russian Revolution. With the failure first of the electoral revolution and then of the general strike in 1920, syndicalists and socialists reached out for new solutions embodied in the success of the Russian Revolution. By separating reformists from revolutionaries in both the unions and the party, the revolution imposed a greater coordination between political and economic activity, to some degree between the CGT and the Socialist Party and more decisively between the Confédération Générale du Travail Unitaire and the Communist Party.[3] Developed in a nation where the absence of liberty necessitated centralist organization, Leninism represented a set of organizational solutions to the dilemmas of French socialism, a technique for uniting theory with practice—political with economic activity, the political party with trade unions, and central direction with democratic participation.[4] Though many syndicalists were eager to follow the Russian example, their federalist tradition was still too strong in the early 1920s for them to accept the domination of a centralist political party.[5]

In the end, the Communist Party only overcame this federalist tradition through the influx of previously unorganized industrial workers into the labor movement during the Popular Front. Dominated by elite craft and white-collar unions, the CGT after 1920 turned increasingly to collective bargaining and legislative lobbying and lost sight of its revolutionary objective. Blaming the failure of revolution on the reformism of skilled workers, the Communists stressed the organization of industrial workers whom they esteemed to be potentially more revolutionary, disciplined and class-conscious than the skilled. Benefiting from the unification of the CGT and the advent of the Blum government, the Communists led the mass strike and unionization movements among production workers in metallurgical, chemical, electrical, and other industries. In relation to the skilled workers, these industrial workers proved more receptive to the class theory and centralist organization of a party that employed mass struggle to force a global change in the class structure of the state.[6]

The triumph of Marxism in the French labor movement thus resulted from a long process of socialist experience, occurring nearly one hundred years after the publication of the *Manifesto* and fifty years after the formation of the first Marxist party. However much a Marxist leader other than Guesde might have hastened the process, French socialism seemed destined to develop from the ground up on the basis of its own experience, its illusions, disappointments and resulting adaptations, in a long learning process. Just as labor militants abandoned their illusions about republican socialism in the 1880s, so too would they eventually have to admit the inadequacy of the general strike and revolutionary syndicalism to overthrow the capitalist system. Although they had become socialists in a federalist movement, they found that the only way to continue the struggle under new conditions was to adopt more centralist forms of organization. In the same way that the means were adapted to new conditions, so too was there a transformation of the original federalist utopia into the theory of state socialism. Having given the original socialist impetus and orientation to the labor movement, the skilled labor militants were eventually overwhelmed by their own creation in an age of mass production, organization, and ideology, which consigned their original utopia to the annals of history.

Notes

CHAPTER 1: INTRODUCTION

1. See Alain Touraine, *L'Evolution du travail ouvrier aux usines Renault* (Paris, 1955), and his *La Conscience ouvrière* (Paris, 1966); and Robert Blauner, *Alienation and Freedom: The Factory Worker and His Industry* (Chicago, 1964).

2. For a previous synthesis, see Serge Mallet, *La Nouvelle Classe ouvrière* (Paris, 1963).

3. See, for some examples, Marx, Engels, and Lenin, *Anarchism and Anarcho-Syndicalism* (New York, 1972), pp. 49, 55-56, 121, 155, 170, 243.

4. Jules L. Puech, *Le Proudhonisme dans l'Association internationale des travailleurs* (Paris, 1907); Gaëtan Pirou, *Proudhonisme et syndicalisme révolutionnaire* (Paris, 1910); and Maxime Leroy, *La Coutume ouvrière,* 2 vols. (Paris, 1913). Also, see the chapter on "Le Syndicalisme révolutionnaire et Proudhon," in Annie Kriegel, *Le Pain et les roses: jalons pour une histoire des socialismes* (Paris, 1968), pp. 33-50.

5. For a "collectivist" approach, see Daniel Guérin, *Anarchism: From Theory to Practice* (New York, 1970).

6. Pierre-Joseph Proudhon, *Oeuvres complètes,* 8 vols. (Paris, 1924), 7:37-53, 155-76, 275-83, 8:185-205.

7. Tihomir J. Markovitch, "Le Revenu industriel et artisanal sous la Monarchie de Juillet et le Second Empire," *Cahiers de l'I.S.E.A.,* no. 4 (1967), pp. 78-88. Mme. Cahen, "La Concentration des établissements en France de 1896 à 1936," *Etudes et conjoncture; revue mensuelle,* no. 9 (1954), pp. 840-81.

8. François Crouzet, "Essai de construction d'un indice annuel de la production industrielle française au XIX siècle," *Annales; économies, sociétés, civilisations,* 25 (1970): 56-99, derives a dynamic index of 2.97 percent and traditional one of 1.61 percent. Cf. Tihomir Markovitch, "L'Industrie française," *Cahiers de l'I.S.E.A., Série* AF, nos. 4-7 (1965-66), finds averages of 2 percent and 2.8 percent.

9. Louis Chevalier, *La Formation de la population parisienne au XIX siècle* (Paris, 1950), pp. 80, 218-19.

10. Joan Scott, "The Glassworkers of Carmaux, 1850-1900," *Nineteenth-Century Cities: Essays in the New Urban History,* ed. Stephen Thernstrom and Richard Sennett (New Haven, Conn., 1969), pp. 3-48.

11. See biographies of labor candidates in *Le Prolétariat,* Oct. 4, 1885.

12. Census of 1866.

13. Cf. Georges Duveau, *La Vie ouvrière en France sous le Second Empire* (Paris, 1946), pp. 225-30.

14. According to the *Résultats statistiques du recensement des industries et professions de 1896,* these were the only industries employing more than 100 workers per enterprise.

15. Daniel Blumé, "Recherches sur le syndicalisme ouvrier dans le bâtiment à Paris de 1892 à 1906" (Diplôme d'Etudes Supérieures, University of Paris, 1957), hereafter D.E.S.

16. Chevalier, *Formation,* pp. 73-80, 110-15. Cf. George Rudé, "La Population ouvrière parisienne de 1789 à 1791," *Annales historiques de la Révolution française* 39 (1967): 15-35, with Chambre de Commerce de Paris, *Statistique de l'industrie à Paris résultante de l'enqûete faite par la Chambre de commerce pour les années 1847-48* (Paris, 1851), and the *Résultats statistiques de 1896.*

17. See register entitled *Loterie patriotique pour 1832* in the Archives Nationales CC 616. Normal trade distribution was calculated on the basis of deaths in *Recherches statistiques sur la ville de Paris et le département de la Seine* (Paris, 1844). For further details, see Bernard H. Moss, "Parisian Workers and the Origins of Republican Socialism (1830-1833)" in *The Revolution of 1830,* ed. John Merriman (New York: Franklin Watts, forthcoming).

18. See Chap. 2, nn. 49-53.

19. *Le Peuple,* Mar. 23, 1849.

20. Cf. list of trades in Jean Maitron, ed., *Dictionnaire biographique du mouvement ouvrier français,* Four Parts (Paris, 1967), Part Two,

4:71-76, with Chambre de Commerce de Paris, *Enquête sur les conditions de travail en France pendant l'année 1872* (Paris, 1875).

21. See Chap. 4, n. 72.

22. See *Annuaire de la Bourse du Travail, 1890-91* (Paris, 1892).

23. David H. Pinkney, "The Revolutionary Crowd in Paris in the 1830's," *Journal of Social History* 5 (1972) : 521-27; Roger Price, *The French Second Republic: A Social History* (Ithaca, N.Y., 1972), pp. 162-70; Charles Tilly and Lynn Lees, "Le Peuple de Juin 1848," *Annales; E. S. C.* 29 (1974) : 1061-91; and Jacques Rougerie, *Le Procès des communards* (Paris, 1964), pp. 128-32, and his "Belleville," in *Les Elections de 1869,* ed. L. Girard (Paris, 1960), pp. 22-30.

24. Peter Stearns, *Revolutionary Syndicalism and French Labor: A Cause without Rebels* (New Brunswick, N.J., 1971), and Stearns and Harvey Mitchell, *Workers and Protest* (Itaska, Ill., 1971).

25. Percentages calculated from membership figures in the Archives de la Préfecture de Police, B/A 1442, hereafter B/A, for 1882-85, and the Census of 1886. For the 1870s, see Aimée Moutet, "Le Mouvement ouvrier à Paris du lendemain de la Commune au premier congrès syndical en 1876," *Le Mouvement social,* no. 58 (1967), pp. 11-12.

26. Cf. Peter Stearns, *European Society in Upheaval: Social History since 1800* (London, 1967), pp. 138-54; Georges Duveau, "L'Ouvrier de quarante-huit," *Revue socialiste,* nos. 17-18 (1948), pp. 73-79; Price, *French Second Republic,* pp. 5-12, 108-11; Rougerie, *Procès des communards,* esp. pp. 165-208, and his "1871," *Le Mouvement social,* no. 74 (1972), pp. 54-63; and William Sewell, Jr., "Social Change and the Rise of Working Class Politics in Nineteenth-Century Marseille," *Past and Present,* no. 65 (1974), esp. pp. 81-85, 105.

27. For a case study of an artisanal trade completely transformed by mechanization see Joan W. Scott, *The Glassworkers of Carmaux* (Cambridge, Mass., 1974).

28. David Landes, *The Unbound Prometheus: Technological Change and Industrial Development in Western Europe from 1750 to the Present* (Cambridge, Mass., 1969), pp. 293-96. The history of mechanization outside of the factory remains to be written.

29. These generalizations are based upon a variety of occupational sources, especially Jean Vial, *La Coutume chapelière* (Paris, 1941), Henriette Vanier, *La Mode et ses métiers* (Paris, 1960), Joseph Barberet, *Le Travail en France: monographies professionnelles,* 7 vols. (Paris, 1886-90), and Ministère de l'Intérieur, *Enquête de la Commission extra-parlementaire des associations ouvrières,* 3 vols. (Paris, 1883-88).

30. See the Chambre de Commerce de Paris, *Statistique de 1848; its Enquête de 1872*, pp. 37-39; and the *Annuaire de la Bourse du Travail, 1887-1888* (Paris, 1889).

31. Cf. Eric Hobsbawn, "The British Standard of Living, 1790-1850," and "The Labour Aristocracy in Nineteenth Century Britain," in his *Labouring Men: Studies in the History of Labour* (New York, 1964), pp. 75-121, 321-70.

32. Wage inquiry of the Conseil de Prud'hommes, 1830-47, in the Archives de la Seine DM^{12}23. Agricol Perdiguier, *Statistique du salaire des ouvriers en réponse à M. Thiers* (Paris, 1849). Jacques Rougerie, "Remarques sur l'histoire des salaires à Paris au XIX siècle," *Le Mouvement social*, no. 63 (1968), pp. 71-108. Adeline Daumard, "Une Source d'histoire sociale: l'enregistrement des mutations par décès: le XII arrondissement de Paris de 1820 à 1847," *Revue d'histoire économique et sociale* 35 (1957) : 52-75.

33. Rougerie, "Salaires à Paris," pp. 71-108.

34. *Conférence internationale ouvrière tenu à Paris du 23 au 29 août 1886* (Paris, 1887), pp. 44-50, and the *Annuaire de la Bourse du Travail, 1887-88*.

35. Fernand et Maurice Pelloutier, *La Vie ouvrière en France* (Paris, 1900), pp. 183-214. Blumé, "Recherches," pp. 73-76.

36. Cf. with English wage differentials in Hobsbawn, "Labour Aristocracy," pp. 328-35.

37. Regular growth may explain the persistence of labor radicalism more than the pattern of dynamic and sluggish growth suggested by Val R. Lorwin, "Working Class Politics and Economic Development in Western Europe," *American Historical Review* 63 (1958): 338-51.

38. Chambre de Commerce de Paris, *Statistique de 1848*.

39. Chambre de Commerce de Paris, *Enquête de 1872*.

40. Duveau, *Vie ouvrière*, pp. 202-207, 217. Chevalier, *Formation*, pp. 105-106, 120-43, 186-92.

41. See B/A 1442 and B/A 33.

42. According to the 1886 census, workers were a majority in the 3d, 5th, 11th, 12th, 13th, 14th, 15th, 18th, 19th, and 20th *arrondissements*.

43. Duveau, *Vie ouvrière*, pp. 344-49. Chevalier, *Les Parisiens*, pp. 35-41, 49-62, 387-90.

44. Duveau, *Vie ouvrière*, pp. 410-15.

45. Adeline Daumard, "Les Relations sociales à Paris à l'époque de la Monarchie constitutionnelle d'après les registres paroissiaux des mariages," *Population* 12 (1957) : 461.

46. Following are a range of ratios: 54 printers, 29 carpenters, 28 mechanics, 26 founders, 15 piano-makers, 10 jewelers, 9 curriers, 8 joiners, 6 hatters, 5 saddlers and cabinetmakers, 4 tinsmiths and articles of Paris, 3 tailors and shoemakers, 2 clockmakers and 1 carton maker—Chambre de Commerce de Paris, *Statistique de 1848.*

47. For descriptions of Parisian factories see Turgan, *Les Grandes Usines de France,* 9 vols. (Paris, 1860), esp. 2:1-64.

·48. Chevalier, *Formation,* p. 78.

49. Chambre de Commerce de Paris, *Enquête de 1872.* In 1869, the average number of machines per enterprise in France was 1.2 with an average horsepower per machine of 12—Emile Levasseur, *Questions ouvrières et industrielles en France sous la Troisième République* (Paris, 1907), p. 48.

50. Rémi Gossez, "Un Tournant dans nos études," *1848: revue des révolutions contemporaines* 18 (1950) : 183-90. Also, Chevalier, *Formation,* pp. 112-13.

51. See Blauner, *Alienation and Freedom,* esp. pp. 2-23, 35-47, and Touraine, *L'Evolution du travail,* esp. pp. 174-76.

52. Cf. Alain Touraine, "L'Evolution de la conscience ouvrière et l'idée socialiste," *Esprit* 20 (1956) : 693-97.

53. See Philippe Buchez, *L'Européen,* Dec. 17, 1831.

54. Cf. Scott, *Glassworkers of Carmaux,* chaps. 4-5.

55. Edward Shorter and Charles Tilly, *Strikes in France, 1830-1968* (London, 1974), pp. 164-71, 270-83.

56. Leroy, *La Coutume ouvrière,* I, 363-79. Michel Collinet, *Esprit du syndicalisme* (Paris, 1952), pp. 23-35.

57. Leroy, *Coutume ouvrière,* 1:138-71.

58. *Ibid.,* 1:384-90, 412-24.

59. *Ibid.,* 2:835-64.

60. Touraine, "L'Evolution de la conscience ouvrière," pp. 692-705.

61. Cf. Karl Mannheim, *Ideology and Utopia* (New York, 1936), Chap. 4, with Engels's *Socialism: Utopian and Scientific* (New York, 1880).

62. See Chap. 4, n. 4.

63. Cf. Touraine, *Conscience ouvrière,* esp. pp. 305-56; "L'Evolution de la conscience ouvrière," p. 607, who distinguishes between the reformist professional consciousness of skilled workers and proletarian class consciousness.

64. See Epilogue.

65. Touraine, *Conscience ouvrière,* pp. 305-32; "L'Evolution de la conscience ouvrière," pp. 692-705; Collinet, *Esprit du syndicalisme,*

esp. pp. 56-58, 83-85; "Masses et militants: quelques aspects de l'évolution des minorités agissantes au syndicalisme de masse," *Revue d'histoire économique et sociale,* 28 (1950): 200-11. Mallet, *Nouvelle classe ouvrière,* esp. pp. 29-34. Seymour Martin Lipset, *Political Man: The Social Bases of Politics* (New York, 1960), pp. 109-26.

66. *Ibid.* Cf. Shorter and Tilly, *Strikes in France,* pp. 175-84.

67. Peter Stearns, "Patterns of Industrial Strike Activity in France during the July Monarchy," *American Historical Review* 70 (1965): 371-94. Jean-Paul Courtheoux, "Naissance d'une conscience de classe dans le prolétariat textile du Nord, 1830-1870," *Revue économique* 8 (1957): 114-39. Pierre Pierrard, *La Vie ouvrière à Lille sous le Second Empire* (Paris, 1965), pp. 67-75, 150-229, 479-87.

68. Collinet, *Esprit du syndicalisme, passim;* "Masses et militants: quelques aspects"; "Masses et militants: la bureaucratie et la crise actuelle du syndicalisme ouvrier français," *Revue d'histoire économique et sociale* 29 (1951): 65-73. Also, Antoine Prost, *La C.G.T. à l'époque du Front populaire, 1934-39: essai de description numérique* (Paris, 1964), esp. pp. 127-61; and Bertrand Badie, "Les Grèves du Front populaire aux usines Renault," *Le Mouvement social,* no. 81 (1972), pp. 69-109.

69. This model-type is illustrated by Seymour Martin Lipset, Martin Trow, and James Coleman, *Union Democracy: The Internal Politics of the International Typographical Union* (New York, 1962), esp. pp. 13-15, 440-69.

70. Sidney and Beatrice Webb, *Industrial Democracy* (New York, 1920), esp. pp. 3-103, 807-50.

71. See E. P. Thompson, *The Making of the English Working Class* (New York, 1963), Chap. 16; Sidney Pollard, "Nineteenth-Century Cooperation: From Community Building to Shopkeeping," *Essays in Labour History,* ed. Asa Briggs and John Saville (London, 1960), pp. 74-112; John Commons et al., *History of Labour in the United States,* 4 vols. (New York, 1921), 1:57-60, 75-77, 97-100, 506-10, 564-74, 2:41, 53-56, 110-12; P. H. Noyes, *Organization and Revolution: Working Class Associations in the German Revolutions of 1848-49* (Princeton, N.J., 1960), pp. 308-10; and Louis Bertrand, *Histoire de la coopération en Belgique,* 2 vols. (Brussels, 1902).

72. Cf. Jacques Rougerie, "Sur l'histoire de la Première Internationale," *Le Mouvement social,* no. 51 (1965), pp. 23-45.

73. See esp. Rudolf Schlesinger, *Central European Democracy and its Background* (London, 1953), pp. 12-118; Carl Schorske, *German*

Social Democracy, 1905-1917 (Cambridge, Mass., 1955), esp. pp. 8-16, 35; Harry J. Marks, "The Sources of Reformism in the Social Democratic Party of Germany, 1890-1914," *The Journal of Modern History* 11 (1939): esp. 350-55; and Richard Comfort, *Revolutionary Hamburg: Labor Politics in the Early Weimar Republic* (Stanford, Calif., 1966), esp. pp. 25-26, 85-108, 124-29, 142-43, 156, 165-69.

74. Lipset, *Political Man*, pp. 97-130, 220-61. Also, Brian Peterson, "Working Class Communism: A Review of the Literature," *Radical America* 5 (1971): 37-61. Cf. Richard Hamilton, *Affluence and the French Worker in the Fourth Republic* (Princeton, N.J., 1967), Chap. 6, who only apparently denies the connection between lack of skill and radicalism.

75. See Schlesinger, *Central European Democracy*, pp. 77-84, for an excellent discussion of the labor aristocracy thesis. Because of its industrial advance, a labor aristocracy may have arisen earlier in England than elsewhere—see Hobsbawn, "Labour Aristocracy," pp. 321-70.

CHAPTER 2: UTOPIA OF ASSOCIATION

1. Edouard Dolléans and Gérard Dehove, *Histoire du travail en France: mouvement ouvrier et législation sociale,* 2 vols. (Paris, 1953-55), 1:129-35, 155-66. France, Office du travail, *Associations professionnelles ouvrières,* 4 vols. (Paris, 1894-1904), 1:5-19, hereafter *APO.*

2. Dolléans and Dehove, *Histoire du travail,* 1:174-84. Emile Coornaert, *Les Compagnonnages en France du Moyen Age à nos jours* (Paris, 1966), esp. pp. 54-105. Ernest Labrousse, *Le Mouvement ouvrier et les théories sociales en France de 1815 à 1848* (Paris, 1965), pp. 71-78.

3. Labrousse, *Mouvement ouvrier*, pp. 79-82. Octave Festy, "La Société philanthropique de Paris et les sociétés de secours mutuel," *Revue d'histoire moderne* 16 (1911): 170-96.

4. *APO,* 1:27. Labrousse, *Mouvement ouvrier*, pp. 82-87.

5. Edouard Dolléans, *Histoire du mouvement ouvrier,* 2 vols. (Paris, 1947), 1:42-72. Jean-Pierre Aguet, *Les Grèves sous la Monarchie de Juillet (1830-1834)* (Geneva, 1954), pp. 1-25. Octave Festy, *Le Mouvement ouvrier au début de la Monarchie de Juillet, 1830-1834* (Paris, 1908), pp. 34-63. Labrousse, *Mouvement ouvrier*, pp. 81-111.

6. Archives de la Chambre de Commerce de Paris, file entitled "Enquête industrielle pour les années 1831-33." Gabriel Vautier, "La Misère des ouvriers en 1831," *La Révolution de 1848 et les révolutions du XIX siècle* 22 (1923-24): 607-17. Paul Gonnet, "Esquisse de la crise économique en France de 1827 à 1832," *Revue d'histoire économique et sociale* 33 (1955): 284-89.

7. Cited by David Pinkney, "Laissez-Faire or Intervention? Labor Policy in the First Months of the July Monarchy," *French Historical Studies* 3 (1963): 123.

8. Sept. 26-Oct. 17, 1830.

9. Cf. François-André Isambert, "Aux Origines de l'associationnisme buchézien," *Archives internationales de sociologie de la coopération,* no. 6 (1959), pp. 29-66. Also, Bernard H. Moss, "Origins of Republican Socialism."

10. Isambert, "Origines de l'associationnisme buchézien," pp. 29-66; Isambert, *Politique, religion et science de l'homme chez Philippe Buchez* (Paris, 1967), pp. 82-89. Also, *L'Européen,* Dec. 17, 1831; March 31, July 14, 21, 1832. Bibliothèque Historique de la Ville de Paris, Buchez mss. folio 201 (Aug. 30, 1829), folio 202 (Athenée des ouvriers).

11. "Discours de Cavaignac sur le droit d'association," Dec. 15, 1832. *La Tribune,* Jan. 31, Nov. 7, 18, 20, 1833. Fédération de tous les ouvriers en France, *Règlement de la corporation des ouvriers cordon- niers* (Paris, 1833). Jules Leroux, *Aux Ouvriers typographes. De la nécessité de fonder une association ayant pour but de rendre les ouvriers propriétaires des instruments du travail* (Paris, 1833). Aguet, *Les Grèves,* pp. 66-87. Festy, *Mouvement ouvrier,* pp. 202-71.

12. *Procès des citoyens Vignerte et Pagnerre, membres de la Société des droits de l'homme* (Paris, 1834), p. 8.

13. *Gazette des tribunaux,* Dec. 2-3, 1833, Apr. 26-29, 1834. Marc Dufraisse, *Association des travailleurs* (Paris, 1833).

14. Festy, *Mouvement ouvrier,* esp. pp. 148-52, 165-66, 248-59, 280-320; Festy, "Dix Années de l'histoire corporative des ouvriers tailleurs d'habits, 1830-40," *Revue d'histoire des doctrines écono- miques et sociales* 5 (1912): 166-99.

15. Robert J. Bezucha, "The Pre-Industrial Worker Movement: The *Canuts* of Lyons," in *Modern European Social History,* ed. Robert Bezucha (Lexington, Mass., 1972), esp. p. 113. *L'Echo de la Fabrique,* esp. Feb. 12, Nov. 24, 1832; May 26, Aug. 4, Nov. 3, Dec. 1, 1833; Jan. 5, Feb. 23, 1834.

16. Festy, *Mouvement ouvrier,* pp. 345-49. Jean Gaumont, *Histoire*

générale de la coopération en France, 2 vols. (Paris, 1924), 1:119-22, 199-201.

17. It first appeared as an article in the *Revue du progrès* 2 (August 1, 1840): 1-30, and as a book in September. Subsequent editions mistakenly refer to 1839 as the date of its appearance.

18. *Le Journal du peuple,* esp. June 14, July 26, Aug. 2, 9, 23, Sept. 20, 27, Nov. 15, 22, 29, 1840. *Le National,* July 7, May 17, 1840.

19. Armand Cuvillier, *Un Journal d'ouvriers: "L'Atelier,"* *1840-1850* (Paris, 1954), esp. pp. 132-76. *L'Atelier,* esp. Oct. 1840, July, Aug., Dec. 1841, Nov. 1842, Oct. 1843. Also, Auguste Ott, *Les Associations d'ouvriers* (Paris, 1837), p. 10; Ott, *Traité d'économie sociale* (Paris, 1851), p. 314. C. F. Chevé, *Programme démocratique* (Paris, 1840).

20. Gaumont, *Histoire générale,* 1:160-227. *L'Union,* Jan.-Aug. 1844, July-Sept. 1845, July 1846. Christopher H. Johnson, *Utopian Communism in France: Cabet and the Icarians, 1839-1851* (Ithaca, N.Y., 1974), esp. pp. 292-95.

21. Frederick A. de Luna, *The French Republic Under Cavaignac, 1848* (Princeton, N.J., 1969), esp. pp. 23-35, has reminded us that many moderate republicans were also advocates of cooperative association. Also, Georges Weill, *Histoire du parti républicain en France de 1814 à 1870* (Paris, 1900), pp. 185-93. Leo Loubère, "Intellectual Origins of French Jacobin Socialism," *International Review of Social History* 4 (1959): 413-31. *La Réforme,* July 15, 1845.

22. Accounts of differences between moderates and radicals differ. Cf. Louis Garnier-Pagès, *Histoire de la révolution de 1848,* 2 vols. (Paris, n.d.), 1:35-37, 2:294; Daniel Stern, *Histoire de la révolution de 1848,* 2 vols. (Paris, 1862), 2:570-71; Louis Blanc, *L'Organisation du travail,* 5th ed. (Paris, 1848), pp. 270-84; *Almanach des corporations nouvelles* (Paris, 1852), pp. 112-17.

23. Cf. Karl Marx, *The Class Struggles in France (1848-1850)* (New York, 1964), esp. pp. 123-26.

24. See Bernard H. Moss, "Origins of Republican Socialism."

25. *Ibid.* Also, Alain Faure, "Mouvements populaires et mouvement ouvrier à Paris (1830-1834)," *Le Mouvement social,* no. 88 (1974), pp. 51-92.

26. Cf. Donald McKay, *The National Workshops: A Study in the French Revolution of 1848* (Cambridge, Mass., 1933), p. 3. John Plamenatz, *The Revolutionary Movement in France, 1815-1871* (London, 1952), pp. 38-39.

27. De Luna, *Cavaignac,* pp. 15-35, 92. T. Thoré, *La Vérité sur le*

Parti démocratique (Brussels, 1840). *Dictionnaire politique: encyclopédie du langage et de la science politique* (Paris, 1842), pp. 115, 136, 165, 669, 771, 862, 886, 928.

28. See Chapter 1, n. 26.

29. *Ibid.,* n. 32.

30. *Ibid.* Also, Lemann, *De l'industrie des vêtements confectionnées en France* (Paris, 1857), pp. 13-43. Pierre Vinçard, *Les Ouvriers de Paris* (Paris, 1850), *passim.*

31. Peter Stearns, "Patterns of Industrial Strike Activity," pp. 371-94. Aguet, *Les Grèves,* esp. pp. 366-93.

32. *Le Journal des travailleurs,* June 4, 1848.

33. The major work is Rémi Gossez, *Les Ouvriers de Paris; l'organisation, 1848-1851* (Paris, 1967), pp. 10-26, 45-79, 100-224, 314-21. Gossez' insistence that the association movement represented a line of retreat that only got underway after the June repression is inconsistent with the numerous examples of earlier projects he cites. Cf. his article, "Pré-syndicalisme ou pré-coopération? l'organisation ouvrière unitaire et ses phases dans le département de la Seine de 1834 à 1851," *Archives internationales de sociologie de la coopération,* no. 6 (1959), pp. 67-89.

34. *Ibid.*

35. Consult also Price, *French Second Republic,* de Luna, *Cavaignac,* Gaumont, *Histoire générale,* Dolléans, *Histoire du mouvement ouvrier,* Georges Renard, *La République de 1848* (1848-1852), vol. 9 of *Histoire socialiste,* ed. Jean Jaurès (Paris, 1904), and Georges Cahen, "Louis Blanc et la Commission du Luxembourg, 1848," *Annales de l'Ecole libre des sciences politiques* 12 (1897): 187-225, 362-80, 459-81.

36. *Le Journal des travailleurs,* June 8-25, 1848.

37. Gossez, *Ouvriers,* pp. 314-19. Emile Heftler, *Les Associations coopératives de production sous la Deuxième République* (Paris, 1899). Octave Festy, *Les Associations ouvrières encouragées par la Deuxième République* (Paris, 1915), esp. pp. 1-10; Festy, ed., *Procès-verbaux du Conseil d'encouragement pour les associations ouvrières, juillet 1848-24 octobre 1849* (Paris, 1917), pp. 123-25, 180-86, 407-42. Also, Bernard Schnapper, "Les Sociétés ouvrières de production pendant la Seconde République: l'exemple girondin," *Revue d'histoire économique et sociale* 43 (1965): 163-68, and de Luna, *Cavaignac,* pp. 294-99.

38. P. J. Proudhon, *Banque du peuple suivi du rapport de la commission des délégués du Luxembourg* (Paris, 1849), pp. 36-39.

39. The trades of 8,694 members found in *Le Peuple,* Mar. 23, 1849, were compared to the general distribution in the Chambre de Commerce, *Statistique de 1848.*

40. *Le Peuple,* Sept. 1848-June 1849, *passim. Le Travail affranchi,* esp. Jan. 17,21, Mar. 21, 1849. Gossez, *Ouvriers,* pp. 327-45.

41. Gossez, *Ouvriers,* pp. 345-51. *La République,* Nov. 13-15, 1850. *Le Nouveau Monde,* July 15, 1849-Sept. 15, 1850, *passim.* Jeanne Deroin, *Lettre aux associations sur l'organisation du crédit* (Paris, 1851).

42. Gossez, *Ouvriers,* pp. 351-64. *Almanach des corporations nouvelles.* Gaumont, *Histoire générale,* 1:237-311.

43. Gaumont, *Histoire générale,* 1:382-421.

44. A compilation of 284 Parisian associations was obtained from *ibid.,* 1:256, 279-80, *Le Nouveau Monde,* Sept. 1849, Aug. 15-Sept. 15, 1850, and Gossez, *Ouvriers,* pp. 319-22. Also, *Almanach du Nouveau Monde pour 1851* (Paris, 1851), pp. 151-54.

45. *Association des ouvriers bijoutiers* (Paris, 1850), p. 5. *Pacte fondamentale de l'association fraternelle des ouvrières chemisières et couturières* (n.p., n.d.).

46. *Projet d'association destiné à l'industrie du bronze* (Paris, 1850), p. 3.

47. For a bibliography of statutes studied see Gossez, *Ouvriers,* pp. 411-23. See also, André Cochut, *Les Associations ouvrières* (Paris, 1851), J.-P. Gilland, *Revue anécdotique des associations ouvrières* (Paris, 1850), and Antonym Romand, *Manuel des associations ouvrières* (Paris, 1849).

48. Festy, *Associations,* esp. pp. 7-9, 158-63. Also, above, n. 44.

49. Sixty-five of 120 associated trades were located in the Chambre de Commerce, *Statistique de 1848.*

50. Five percent of Parisian workers earned more than five francs daily. Forty-four trades had a lower percentage of their workers earning more than five francs and another seventeen had a higher percentage. Fourteen percent of all workers earned less than three francs. Forty-two trades had a lower percentage and twenty-two a higher percentage.

51. Thirty trades had a higher and thirty a lower rate.

52. Fifty percent of Parisian businesses were owned by individual artisans with or without an aide. Forty-seven trades had a lower percentage and sixteen a higher percentage than 50 percent. Fifteen percent of all workers were employed at home. Forty-six trades had a

lower percentage and sixteen a higher percentage than 15 percent. Five percent were apprentices. Thirty-three trades had a lower percentage and twenty-two a higher percentage. Only 10 percent of Parisian enterprises employed more than ten workers. Thirty-nine trades had a higher percentage and twenty a lower percentage than this average.

53. Twenty-one percent lived in *garnis* or lodging houses. Forty-four trades had fewer workers in *garnis* and fifteen had more than 21 percent in *garnis*. According to employers 87 percent could read and write. Nineteen trades had a lower literacy rate and forty-three had a higher rate, including many with total literacy.

54. See Chapter 1, n. 7.

55. Karl Marx, *Class Struggles in France,* esp. pp. 123-26. His views in spring 1850 were conditioned by the expectation of a new revolutionary upsurge that would lead directly to proletarian revolution.

56. This alliance has never been studied, but see *ibid.* and Price, *French Second Republic,* chaps. 5-7.

57. See Peter H. Amann, *Revolution and Mass Democracy: The Paris Club Movement in 1848* (Princeton, N.J., 1975), esp. pp. 43-44. I. Tchernoff, *Associations et sociétés secrètes sous la Deuxième République* (Paris, 1905).

58. Georges Weill, *Histoire du mouvement social en France, 1852-1902* (Paris, 1904), pp. 49-51. Gaumont, *Histoire générale,* 1:430-36. Albert Thomas, *Le Second Empire* (1852-1870), vol. 10 of *Histoire socialiste,* ed. Jean Jaurès (Paris, 1904), pp. 91, 187, 410-12. France, Office du travail, *Les Associations ouvrières de production* (Paris, 1897), pp. 27-29, hereafter, *AOP.*

59. E. Véron, *Les Associations ouvrières de consommation, de crédit, et de production* (Paris, 1865), p. 233.

60. *APO,* 4:203-23.

61. Jeanne Gaillard, "Les Associations de production et la pensée politique en France," *Le Mouvement social,* no. 52 (1965), pp. 63-73. Gaumont, *Histoire générale,* 1:466-68, 496. Also, Vicomte Lemercier, *Etudes sur les associations ouvrières* (Paris, 1857), and Casimir Périer, *Les Sociétés de coopération* (Paris, 1864).

62. *L'Association,* 1864-65, esp. pp. 3-7, 10-11, 41-45, 67-70, 99-103, 135-39, 154-58, 163-75. Jean-Pierre Beluze, *Les Associations, conséquences du progrès. Crédit au travail* (Paris, 1863), pp. 11-18, 72. Gaumont, *Histoire générale,* 1:484-91. On Lyons, see Sveten Maritch, *Histoire du mouvement social sous le Second Empire à Lyon* (Paris, 1930), esp. pp. 120-41.

63. Thomas, *Second Empire,* pp. 193-207. Weill, *Histoire du mouvement social,* pp. 53-65. *APO,* 1:224-25, 2:613, 3:98. Also, David I. Kulstein, *Napoléon III and the Working Class: A Study of Government Propaganda under the Second Empire* (Los Angeles, 1969).

64. Thomas, *Second Empire,* pp. 208-34.

65. Cited in *ibid.,* pp. 216-24.

66. *Ibid.,* pp. 225-26, 243-46. Proudhon, *Oeuvres complètes,* 8 vols. (Paris, 1924), 8:Introduction, Prologue, and Part I. Rather than seeing a return to the "inherited formulas" of 1848 in the Manifesto, as does Thomas, we have stressed the modification of these formulas to suit new conditions.

67. See G. M. Stekloff, *History of the First International* (New York, 1928), pp. 34-50. Julius Braunthal, *History of the International,* 2 vols. (New York, 1967), 1:85-94. Henry Collins and Chimen Abramsky, *Karl Marx and the British Labour Movement: Years of the First International* (London, 1965), pp. 14-51. Jules L. Puech, *Le Proudhonisme,* pp. 37-42. Thomas, *Second Empire,* pp. 236-43.

68. E. E. Fribourg, *L'Association internationale des travailleurs* (Paris, 1871), pp. 12-96.

69. Puech, *Le Proudhonisme,* pp. 98-185. Jacques Freymond, ed., *La Première Internationale: receuil de documents,* 2 vols. (Geneva, 1962), 1:18, 47, 73, 85-107.

70. Proudhon, *Oeuvres complètes,* 7:37-53, 155-76, 275-83, 8:185-205.

71. *APO,* esp. 1:41-49; 2:491-92 (hatters), 617-20 (tailors), 679-80 (cabinetmakers), 788 (coopers); 3:25-26 (jewelers), 99-101 (bronze-workers); 4:104 (joiners), 224 (masons), 324-32 (painters).

72. Cited in *APO,* 3:107.

73. Fribourg, *L'Association internationale,* pp. 35, 40.

74. The term *syndicat* will generally be translated as union.

75. Commission ouvrière de 1867, *2ème Recueil des procès-verbaux des assemblées générales des délégués et des membres des bureaux électoraux,* 2 vols. (Paris, 1869), 1:28-33, 2:150-80, 228-80. *APO,* 1:45-47; 2:23-24 (shoemakers), 204 (curriers), 497-99 (hatters), 620-22 (tailors); 3:191-93 (tinsmiths), 258 (mechanics); 4:30-32 (carpenters), 113 (joiners), 227-29 (masons).

76. *L'Association,* 1865, p. 341, *La Coopération,* Apr. 21, May 19, 1867. *Almanach de la Coopération pour 1868* (Paris, 1869), pp. 316-19. *APO,* 2:613-22.

77. Cited by Gaillard, *Les Associations de production,* pp. 80-81.

78. Commission ouvrière de 1867, *2ème Recueil,* 1:160.

79. Cited by Geneviève Proisy, "Recherches sur les chambres syndicales ouvrières," *Revue d'histoire moderne* 12 (1938): 56.

80. *Ibid.,* pp. 46-66; *APO,* 2:132-34. Jean Maitron, ed., *Dictionnaire,* 4:12-16, apparently confounds the membership of these trade federations with that of the International. On Lyons, see Jacques Rougerie, "La Première Internationale à Lyon (1865-70)," *Annali dell'Istituto Giangiacomo Feltrinelli* 4 (1961): 126-61.

81. Freymond, ed., *Première Internationale,* 1:131, 209-10. Fribourg, *L'Association internationale,* pp. 35, 100-101, 115-18. Thomas, *Second Empire,* pp. 313-16.

82. Freymond, ed., *Première Internationale,* 1:126-30, 134-38, 190-93, 200-205, 209-210, 297-300, 347-78, 388, 392-402; 407-12; 2:61-92, 108-15. Fribourg, *L'Association internationale,* pp. 88-89, 95. James Guillaume, *L'Internationale: documents et souvenirs (1864-1878),* 4 vols. (Paris, 1905), 1:65-66, 196-200, 204-206.

83. *Procès de l'Association des travailleurs, première et deuxième Commissions du Bureau de Paris* (Paris, 1870).

84. Thomas, *Second Empire,* pp. 322-31, 389-43. Benoît Malon, *Histoire du socialisme depuis ses origines jusqu à nos jours* (Lugano, 1879), pp. 354-55. Also, G. de Molinari, *Le Mouvement socialiste et les réunions publiques avant la révolution du 4 septembre 1870* (Paris, 1872).

85. Thomas, *Second Empire,* pp. 316-20, 337-38. Albert Richard, "Les Propagateurs de l'Internationale en France," *La Revue socialiste,* 2d series, 1 (1896): 642-45, 650-53, 663-65. Also, *La Marseillaise,* Jan. 1, 1870.

86. Jacques Kayser, *Les Grandes Batailles du radicalisme* (Paris, 1962), pp. 36-42, 318-20. Jacques Rougerie, "Belleville," in *Les Elections de 1869,* ed. L. Girard (Paris, 1960), pp. 3-36. Also, Robert Wolfe, "The Parisian *Club de la Revolution* of the 18th *arrondissement,* 1870-1871," *Past and Present,* no. 39 (1968), esp. pp. 83-88. Most writers ignore the social dimension of Radicalism, which is often merely implicit in its program and labor alliance.

87. Gaumont, *Histoire générale,* 1:58-68.

88. See, for example, P. Malardier, *La Coopération et la politique* (Paris, 1867).

89. Thomas, *Second Empire,* pp. 337, 342-48, 358-61, 366-67, 374-77. Richard, "Propagateurs," pp. 464, 655-61. Rougerie, "Première Internationale à Lyon," pp. 139-48 Guillaume, *L'Internationale,*

1:241-42, 257-79. "Lettres d'Eugène Varlin à Albert Richard," *International Review of Social History* 2 (1937): 181-87.

90. Membership figures range from 433,785 claimed by the prosecutor in June 1870 to 120,000 acknowledged by Albert Richard in "Les Débuts du Partı socialiste français," *Revue politique et parlementaire* 11 (1897): 85. These figures probably included all members of trade societies who were expected to follow the lead of the International. Cf. Rougerie, "Sur l'histoire de la Première Internationale," p. 31, with Maitron, ed., *Dictionnaire*, 4:12-16.

91. Thomas, *Second Empire*, pp. 348-53, 362-64, 382-91. *Troisième Procès de l'Association internationale des travailleurs* (Paris, 1870). "Lettres de Varlin à Richard," pp. 181-83. Guillaume, *L'Internationale*, 1:258.

92. Jean Dautry and Lucien Scheler, *Le Comité central républicain des vingt arrondissements de Paris* (Paris, 1960), esp. pp. 11-47, 118-20, 146-47, 154-55, 159-76. Jacques Rougerie, "L'A. I. T. et le mouvement ouvrier à Paris pendant les événements de 1870-1871," *International Review of Social History* 17 (1972): 3-102. P. O. Lissagaray, *Histoire de la Commune*, 3 vols. (Paris, 1967), 1:50-78. Edward S. Mason, *The Paris Commune: An Episode in the History of the Socialist Movement* (New York, 1930), pp. 63-78, 81-84, 93-98.

93. *Les Murailles politiques françaises*, 2 vols. (Paris, 1874), 1:866.

94. Lissagaray, *Histoire de la Commune*, 1:80-81, 109-17. Mason, *Paris Commune*, pp. 100-15, 120-38, 156-58. Frank Jellinek, *The Paris Commune of 1871* (London, 1937), pp. 86-101, 109-35. Dautry and Scheler, *Le Comité central*, pp. 178-79, 194-200. Also, Eugene W. Schulkind, "The Activity of Popular Organizations under the Paris Commune," *French Historical Studies* 1 (1960): 396-98.

95. *Murailles politiques*, 2:52-53. Also, Georges Bourgin, *La Guerre de 1870 et la Commune* (Paris, 1934), pp. 194-96, and France, Assemblée Nationale, *Enquête parlementaire sur l'insurrection du 18 mars 1871* (Paris, 1872), pp. 523-33, for minutes of the International Federation.

96. Schulkind, "Activity of Popular Organizations," pp. 394-415. Mason, *Paris Commune*, pp. 182-86, 256-66. Charles Rihs, *La Commune de Paris: sa structure et ses doctrines* (Geneva, 1955), pp. 65-94.

97. Cited by Rougerie, *Procès des communards*, p. 150.

98. Cited in *ibid.*, p. 153.

99. Jacques Rougerie, "La Commune de 1871: problème d'histoire sociale," *Archives internationales de sociologie de la coopération*, no. 8

(1960), pp. 52-57. Rihs, *Commune de Paris*, pp. 172-78, 212. Schulkind, "Activity of Popular Organizations," pp. 412-15.

100. Jacques Rougerie, *Paris libre, 1871* (Paris, 1971), pp. 77-78, 128-30, 136-47, 153-57, 179-87; Rougerie, *Procès des communards*, pp. 209-29; Rougerie, "La Commune de 1871," pp. 59-65.

101. Cited by A. Molok, "Les Ouvriers de Paris pendant la Commune," *Cahiers du communisme* 27 (1951): 619.

102. Cited by Rougerie, *Procès des communards*, p. 227.

103. Cited in *ibid.*, pp. 217-19. Also, Rougerie, "Commune de 1871," pp. 62-63. Molok, "Ouvriers de Paris," p. 620.

104. Karl Max and Friedrich Engels, *Writings on the Paris Commune*, ed. Hal Draper (New York, 1971), esp. pp. 30-32, 76-77. Also, T. Lowit, "Marx et le mouvement coopératif," *Cahiers de l'I. S. E. A.*, no. 129 (1962), pp. 89, 100-101.

105. Cf. Marx and Engels, *Writings on the Paris Commune*, p. 34; Monty Johnstone, "The Paris Commune and Marx's Conception of the Dictatorship of the Proletariat," in *Revolution and Reaction: The Paris Commune 1871*, ed. John Hicks and Robert Tucker (Amherst, Mass., 1973), esp. p. 83; and Jacques Rougerie, "Karl Marx, l'Etat et la Commune," *Preuves*, nos. 212-13 (1968), pp. 34-44, 45-56.

106. Rougerie, *Procès des communards*, pp. 17-21, 126-29. Lissagaray, *Histoire de la Commune*, 3:21-25. Report of General Appert cited by Alexandre Zévaès, *De la Semaine sanglante au Congrès de Marseille* (Paris, 1911), p. 3. Joseph Barberet, *Le Travail en France*, 1:15.

107. Irene Collins, *Government and Newspaper Press in France, 1814-1881* (London, 1959), pp. 169-77. Lissagaray, *Histoire de la Commune*, 3:80.

108. Cited by Weill, *Histoire du mouvement social*, p. 160, n. 1. See also, France, Assemblée Nationale, *Enquête parlementaire*, pp. 52, 57-58, Oscar Testut, *L'Internationale et le jacobinisme au ban de l'Europe*, 2 vols. (Paris, 1872), esp. 2:170-72, and Georges Bourgin, "La Lutte du Gouvernement français contre la Première Internationale," *International Review of Social History* 4 (1939): 54.

109. Joseph Barberet, *Les Grèves et la loi sur les coalitions* (Paris, 1873), pp. 112-44; Barberet, *Le Mouvement ouvrier à Paris de 1870 à 1874* (Paris, 1874), pp. 24-115; *APO*, esp. 2:135-37, 625-30; 3:27-35, 109-13, 199-200, 262-64, 393-97; 4:230-31, 421-34.

110. Gaumont, *Histoire générale*, 2:31-37, 44-45. See also, *Bulletin du mouvement social*, 1872-73.

111. Jan. 7, 1873.

112. See Maitron, ed., *Dictionnaire*, 4:183-84, *Gazette des tribunaux*, May 7-8, 1880, and Joseph Barberet, *Bataille des intérêts* (Paris, 1879), pp. 327-30. Also, Bernard H. Moss, "Police Spies and Labor Militants after the Commune," *European Labor History Newsletter*, no. 5 (1974), pp. 16-19.

113. Maitron, ed., *Dictionnaire*, 5. Also, *La Revue socialiste*, 2d series, 48 (1908): 502. See Dupire's reports in B/A 199, *inter alia*, under the code named *Pamphile*.

114. Maitron, *Dictionnaire*, 5. Also, B/A 1005. Where evidence is cumulative, reference to specific reports is omitted.

115. Barberet, *Mouvement ouvrier*, pp. 84-115. *Le Rappel*, Jan. 7, 12, Apr. 1, 8, 9, 1873; Sept. 21, Oct. 23, 28, Dec. 31, 1874. Weill, *Histoire du mouvement social*, pp. 187-88. B/A 199, 1442.

116. *Le Rappel*, Oct. 29, 1875; Jan. 2, 15, 23, 28, Feb. 10-22, Apr. 8, 15-18, May 1, 2, 1876. B/A 1005.

117. Moutet, "Mouvement ouvrier," pp. 9-15, 32-33, 36-38.

118. Weill, *Histoire du mouvement social*, pp. 187-88. Samuel Bernstein, *The Beginnings of Marxian Socialism in France* (New York, 1965), pp. 68-73.

119. *Séances du Congrès ouvrier de France, session de 1876* (Paris, 1877), p. 3.

120. *Séances, 1876*, pp. 4-50. Also, B/A 33, 34, 36. *La Tribune*, June-Sept. 1876. Archives nationales, F7 12 488, hereafter F7. Few delegates had police records. Only two Parisian delegates can be identified from the prewar movement.

121. *Séances, 1876*, esp. pp. 315-415.

122. *Ibid.*, pp. 521-22.

123. *Ibid.*, p. 522.

124. *Ibid.*, pp. 280-81.

125. *Ibid.*, p. 518.

126. *Séances du Congrès ouvrier de France, deuxième session* (Lyons, 1878), p. 594.

127. *Ibid.*, pp. 600-601.

128. *APO*, 2:625-30.

129. List of associations in B/A 1440. Also, *APO*, 1-4, *passim*. On the economic cycle see Jean Bouvier, *Crédit lyonnais de 1863 à 1882*, 2 vols. (Paris, 1961), 1:241-44, 250-53, 266.

130. On the triumph of Radicalism, see Sanford Elwitt, *The Making of the Third Republic: Class and Politics in France, 1868-1884* (Baton Rouge, La., 1975), which appeared too late for consultation.

CHAPTER 3: FROM COOPERATION TO REVOLUTION

1. Cf. Maxwell Kelso, "The Inception of the Modern French Labor Movement, 1871-1879," *The Journal of Modern History* 8 (1936): 188-89.

2. Cf. Paul Louis, *Histoire du mouvement syndical en France,* 2 vols. (Paris, 1947), 1:113-14.

3. Jeanne Gaillard, "Les Usines Cail et les Ouvriers métallurgistes de Grenelle," *Le Mouvement social,* nos. 33-34 (1960-61), pp. 35-53.

4. François Crouzet, "Essai de construction d'un indice annuel de la production française au XIX siècle," *Annales; E. S. C.* 25 (1970): 56-91, shows that many industrial sectors surpassed their prewar level only after 1880.

5. See Chap. 1, esp. nn. 14-20, and Chap. 4, n. 72.

6. Guillaume, *L'Internationale,* 1:15.

7. Collins and Abramsky, *Karl Marx,* pp. 30-55. Braunthal, *History of the International,* pp. 94-99. Maximilien Rubel, "La Charte de l'Internationale," *Le Mouvement social,* no. 51 (1965), pp. 3-22.

8. E. H. Carr, *Michael Bakunin* (London, 1937), pp. 327-50, 422. Guillaume, *L'Internationale,* 1:74-75, 132-33.

9. Guillaume, *L'Internationale,* 1:283-85.

10. See Eugène Varlin, "Les Sociétés ouvrières," *La Marseillaise,* March 11, 1870.

11. *Ibid.* "Lettres de Varlin à Hins," *La Vie ouvrière,* 6 (1914): 500-03. Maitron, ed., *Dictionnaire,* 9:276-79.

12. Guillaume, *L'Internationale,* 2:152, 166-73, 177-86. Freymond, ed., *Première Internationale,* 2:266-67. Marc Vuilleumier, "Les Proscrits de la Commune en Suisse," *La Revue suisse d'histoire* 12 (1962): 522-28. G. Lefrançais, *Etude sur le mouvement communaliste à Paris en 1871* (Neuchâtel, 1871), pp. 390-92. Benoît Malon, *La Troisième Défaite du prolétariat français* (Neuchâtel, 1871), pp. 529-31. A. Claris, *La Proscription française en suisse, 1871-72* (Geneva, 1872), pp. 49-59.

13. Rubel, "La Charte de l'Internationale," pp. 3-22.

14. See Guillaume, *L'Internationale,* Carr, *Bakunin,* and Miklos Molnar, *Le Déclin de la Première Internationale: La Conférence de Londres de 1871* (Geneva, 1963).

15. Cited by Molnar, *Déclin,* pp. 95-97. Also, *ibid.,* pp. 45-47, 107-109, 129-40. Freymond, ed., *Première Internationale,* 2:191-205.

16. Guillaume, *L'Internationale,* 2:11-21. Cf. Rubel, "La Charte," pp. 17-20.

17. Guillaume, *L'Internationale*, 2:216-19, 222-27, 247-48. Vuilleumier, "Les Proscrits," pp. 531-33. Also, Benoît Malon, *L'Internationale: son histoire et ses principes* (n. p., 1872).

18. Guillaume, *L'Internationale*, 2:240.

19. *Ibid.*, 2:249-310. Molnar, *Déclin*, pp. 147-86. Richard Hostetter, *The Italian Socialist Movement I: Origins (1860-1882)* (Princeton, N.J., 1958), pp. 186-290. Freymond, ed., *Première Internationale*, 2:266-307.

20. Guillaume, *L'Internationale*, 2:319-51; 3:2-10, 108-34, 224-25. Freymond, ed., *Première Internationale*, 2:326-80. Jean Maitron, *Histoire du mouvement anarchiste en France (1880-1914)* (Paris, 1955), p. 85.

21. Rougerie, "Sur l'histoire de la Première Internationale," pp. 30-35.

22. Guillaume, *L'Internationale*, 3:75, 220, 229-33; 4:99-100, 154-55; Guillaume, *Idées sur l'organisation sociale* (Chaux-de-Fonds, 1876), p. 54.

23. Hostetter, *Italian Socialist Movement*, pp. 312-68.

24. Cited in *ibid.*, p. 368.

25. Freymond, ed., *Première Internationale*, 2:79-88, 102-108. Guillaume, *L'Internationale*, 3:219-24; 4:97-98, 103-106, 269. "Lettres de César de Paepe à Benoît Malon," *Revue socialiste* 57 (1913): esp. 290-94, 298-99, 393-97.

26. Guillaume, *L'Internationale*, 4:276.

27. *Ibid.*, 4:261-79, 304-305, 322-25. Hostetter, *Italian Socialist Movement*, pp. 397-98, 412 ff. "Lettres de de Paepe," pp. 393-403. Maitron, *Mouvement anarchiste*, pp. 78-79.

28. David Stafford, *From Anarchism to Reformism: A Study of the Political Activities of Paul Brousse within the First International and French Socialist Movement, 1870-90* (Toronto, 1971), pp. 23-150. Also, Marc Vuilleumier, "Paul Brousse et son passage de l'anarchie au socialisme," *Cahiers Vilfredo Pareto* 7-8 (1965): 63-69; and B/A 985.

29. Guillaume, *L'Internationale*, 3:106, 196-97, 221; 4:86, 202-203.

30. *Ibid.*, 2:313-15; 3:167; 4:10-14. Hostetter, *Italian Socialist Movement*, pp. 306-309, 352-54.

31. "Correspondance de Benoît Malon à César de Paepe," *La Revue socialiste*, 2d series, 48 (1908): esp. 318-24, 501-508. Benoît Malon, "Le Collectivisme en France de 1875 à 1879," *La Revue socialiste*, no. 23 (1886), pp. 1001-1003.

32. Guillaume, *L'Internationale,* 2:244; 3:40, 62-63, 91. Hostetter, *Italian Socialist Movement,* pp. 271, 309-310. I. D. Belkin, *Jules Guesde and the Struggle for a Workers' Party in France* [in Russian] (Moscow, 1952), pp. 78-98. Claude Willard, ed., *Jules Guesde: Textes choisis* (Paris, 1959), pp. 7-16, 41-60.

33. (Paris, 1912.)

34. Jules Guesde and Paul Lafargue, *Le Programme du Parti ouvrier, son histoire, ses considérants, ses articles (Paris, 1883), pp.* 6-7; *Alexandre Zévaès, inter alia, Histoire du socialisme et du communisme en France de 1871 à 1947* (Paris, 1947); Zévaès, *Jules Guesde* (Paris, 1929); and Zévaès, *De l'Introduction du marxisme en France* (Paris, 1947); Adéodat Compère-Morel, *Jules Guesde, le socialisme fait homme, 1845-1922* (Paris, 1937); Belkin, *Jules Guesde;* Bernstein, *Beginnings;* and most recently, Claude Willard, *Les Guesdistes: le mouvement socialiste en France (1893-1905)* (Paris, 1965). Non-Marxist historians have followed suit, for example, Mermeix [Gabriel Terrail], *La France socialiste* (Paris, 1886), and Léon Seilhac, *Les Congrès ouvriers de France de 1876 à 1897* (Paris, 1899).

35. June 2, 1878.

36. *L'Egalité,* Nov. 12, 1877. Cf. Malon, "Collectivisme," pp. 997-98, 1001.

37. See Malon, "Collectivisme," pp. 997-98; Malon, *Histoire du socialisme,* 2d ed. (Lugano, 1879), pp. 569-70.

38. *L'Egalité,* Jan. 13, 27, 1878. Also, Jules Guesde, *La Loi des salaires et ses conséquences* (Paris, 1878).

39. Jules Guesde, *Cà et là* (Paris, 1914), pp. 110-51. Guillaume, *L'Internationale,* 4:185-86, 282-83, 296-97.

40. Jules Guesde, *Collectivisme et révolution* (Paris, 1879), pp. 26-28.

41. *L'Egalité,* Jan. 13, July 14, 1878.

42. *Ibid.,* Feb. 10, 1878.

43. Guesde, *Cà et là,* pp. 110-12. *L'Egalité,* Apr. 14, 1878.

44. Maurice Dommanget, *L'Introduction du marxisme en France* (Lausanne, 1969), pp. 115-58. Also, Mermeix, *France socialiste,* pp. 50-68, and Belkin, *Jules Guesde,* pp. 134-36.

45. Belkin, *Jules Guesde,* pp. 143-45. Malon, "Collectivisme," pp. 997-98. *Gazette des tribunaux,* Oct. 25, 1878.

46. Letter of 1879 cited by Zévaès, *De l'Introduction du marxisme,* pp. 91-96.

47. *L'Egalité,* Feb. 10, 1878.

48. *Ibid.,* Dec. 30, 1877; Jan. 13, Mar. 17, 24, 1878.

49. Cf. Michelle Perrot, "Le Premier Journal marxiste français: *L'Egalité,*" *L'Actualité de l'histoire,* no. 28 (1959), pp. 7-12.

50. *L'Egalité,* June 16, 1878.

51. *Gazette des tribunaux,* Mar. 27, May 4-5, Oct. 25, 1878. *L'Egalité,* Jan. 20, May 12, 1878. Guillaume, *L'Internationale,* 4:321-22. Also, Gianni Bosio and Franco Della Peruta, "La 'svolto' di A. Costa con documenti sul soggiorno in Francia," *Movimento operaio* 2 (1952): 287-313. Peter Kropotkin, *Memoirs of a Revolutionist* (New York, 1930), p. 406. B/A 199.

52. B/A 34. Also, *Bulletin de la Fédération jurassienne,* Dec. 9, 1877.

53. *La Philosophie de l'avenir,* 1877-78, 3:347, 409-410, 474, 523-24, 570-83.

54. *L'Avant-garde,* Dec. 1, 1877; Feb. 23, Mar. 1, 1878. *Séances du Congrès ouvrier de France, deuxième session* (Lyons, 1878), pp. 251-54, 333-50, 431-43, 506-510.

55. *Séances, deuxième session,* p. 441. Dupire's speech bears the imprint of his thought and style, not that of Guesde, as suggested by Willard, ed., *Jules Guesde,* p. 21.

56. *Séances, deuxième session,* pp. 211, 399, 422-29, 475-77, 525-32, 595, 613, 616-18. *La Philosophie de l'avenir,* 1877-78, pp. 574-77. F7 12 488, Feb. 5-6, 1878.

57. *Séances, deuxième session,* pp. 144, 587, 610. *L'Egalité,* Dec. 16, 1877. *L'Avant-garde,* Dec. 29, 1877. Guillaume, *L'Internationale,* 4:278-79.

58. B/A 28, 29. *Gazette des tribunaux,* Oct. 23-25, 1878.

59. *Ibid.*

60. Brochure reprinted in Guesde, *Cà et là,* pp. 155-83.

61. *Ibid.,* p. 169.

62. *Gazette des tribunaux,* Oct. 23-26, 1878.

63. B/A 1439, Oct. 24, Nov. 22, 25, Dec. 25, 1878. B/A 29, May 10, 1878.

64. Gabriel Hanotaux, *Contemporary France,* 4 vols. (New York, 1907), 4:411-44, 460, 505. Daniel Halévy, *La République des ducs* (Paris, 1937), chaps. 8-9.

65. *Le Prolétaire,* Dec. 11, 28, 1878; Feb. 1, 8, Mar. 1, 8, 18, 24, 1879.

66. *Ibid.,* Nov. 23, 1878; Aug. 23, 1879. *L'Egalité,* May 26, 1878.

67. *Le Prolétaire,* Dec. 7, 21, 25, 1878; Jan. 1, 18, Feb. 8, May 11, Aug. 23, 30, 1879.

68. *Ibid.,* Nov. 22, 1879.

69. Jean Joughin, *The Paris Commune in French Politics, 1871-1880,* 2 vols. (Baltimore, 1955), 2:245-85.

70. *Le Prolétaire,* June 28, Aug. 2, 20, 1879. On strikes see Emile Levasseur, *Questions ouvrières et industrielles en France sous la Troisième République* (Paris, 1907), pp. 649-50.

71. *L'Egalité,* Jan. 21, 1880.

72. *Ibid.*

73. B/A 37. *Le Prolétaire,* Apr. 19, May 31, June 21, Aug. 2, 9, 23, 30, Sept. 6, 13, Oct. 4, 11, Nov. 8, 1879. *APO,* 3:268-73.

74. Chap. 1, esp. nn. 14-20.

75. Cf. Mermeix, *France socialiste,* p. 108; Seilhac, *Congrès ouvriers,* p. 29; and Zévaès, *Histoire du socialisme,* p. 88.

76. *Séances du Congrès ouvrier socialiste de France, troisième session* (Marseilles, 1879). For a further breakdown of the delegates, see Bernard H. Moss, "Origins of the French Labor Movement: The Socialism of Skilled Workers" (Ph.D. diss., Columbia University, 1972), pp. 260-75.

77. Malon, "Collectivisme," pp. 1001-1003, 1016, 1065-79. Jean Lombard, *Au Berceau du socialisme français* (Paris, 1932), pp. 41-53. *Séances, troisième session,* pp. ii-xiv, 19-20, 33-45.

78. *Séances, troisième session,* esp. pp. 224-25, 275-76, 300-32, 407-11, 489-512, 521-25, 550-58, 602-605, 607-12, 621-40, 652, 725-41.

79. *Ibid.,* p. 808. Also, pp. 296-376.

80. *Ibid.,* pp. 809-14. Mermeix, *France socialiste,* p. 99, cites a vote of 73 to 27 for collective property. Also, F[7] 12 488, Nov. 1, 1879.

81. *Séances, troisième session,* pp. 226, 249, 316, 332, 357, 441, 514, 520, 605, 700, 716-17, 746, 749, 771. Also, I. Dauthier, *Congrès socialiste ouvrier de Marseille* (Paris, 1880), pp. 65, 97. B/A 1084, Oct. 30, Nov. 6, 1879.

82. *Le Petit Lyonnais,* Nov. 5, 1879. Also, *Séances, troisième session,* pp. 254-66, 543-47, 614-21.

83. *Séances, troisième session,* pp. 557, 813-14, 816-19.

84. B/A 1477, esp. Apr. 20, June 15, 1880. *Le Prolétaire,* esp. Jan. 31, Feb. 17, 1880.

85. *Le Citoyen,* July 31, 1880.

86. B/A 32, 39. F[7] 12 489. *L'Egalité,* July 21, Aug. 4, 1880.

87. See below, nn. 95-96.

88. *Le Prolétaire,* 1880-81, *passim. L'Egalité,* esp. Aug. 18, 1880.

Indications of financial aid are scattered in B/A 38, 1442, 1477-78. For proof of Ministerial payments to the leader of the Union at Bordeaux see F^7 13966 July 28, Aug. 10, 1882.

89. *AOP*, pp. 29-41, 46-55, 74-77. Gaumont, *Histoire générale*, 2:82-87, 544. Also, Pierre Sorlin, *Waldeck-Rousseau* (Paris, 1966), pp. 236-98.

90. *AOP*, pp. 7-8, 36-37, 547 ff. France, Ministère de l'intérieur, *Enquête de la commission extra-parlementaire*, esp. 1:169-70, 241-43, 293-95, 357; 2:359, 422, 456. *APO*, 2:690-703, 736-39, 789-95; 3:37-43, 120-29; 4:36-38, 120-36, 233-39, 347-62, 422-31, 816-30.

91. Sorlin, *Waldeck-Rousseau*, pp. 254-55, 260, 270, 293-96.

92. *Ibid.*, p. 269.

93. *AOP*, pp. 547-66. See also, Albert Meister, "La Démographie des groupes coopératifs de production en France depuis 1884," *Etudes sur la tradition française de l'association ouvrière*, ed. Henri Desroches (Paris, 1950), pp. 71-75.

94. *Le Prolétaire*, Aug.-Nov. 1880. B/A 1477. F^7 12 489.

95. "Congrès ouvrier du Havre, 1880" (ms. Musée social, Paris).

96. *Le Petit Havre*, Nov. 23, 1880. Also, *L'Emancipation*, Nov. 18-24, 1880.

97. *APO*, 2:30-31, 138, 630-35, 736-39, 789-95, 816-30; 3:120-29, 199-204, 269-90; 4:347-62, 422-31.

98. B/A 39. F^7 12 489.

99. See Chap. 4, n. 72.

100. F^7 12 491. *APO*, 2:285-324.

101. *Congrès national des syndicats ouvriers, tenu à Lyon en octobre 1886* (Lyons, 1887), esp. pp. 220-338, 347-75.

102. Jacques Néré, "La Crise industrielle de 1882 et le mouvement boulangiste," 2 vols. (diss., University of Paris, 1959), esp. 2:203-207.

103. *AOP*, pp. 577-80.

104. *L'Association ouvrière*, Mar. 15, May 25, Nov. 25, 1907. *Les Associations de production: Compte-rendus des congrès national et international, tenus le 8-10 et 11-13 juillet 1900* (Paris, 1900), pp. 146, 185-89, 215. Also, Ch. Clerc, *Les Syndicats professionels dans leurs rapports avec les sociétés coopératives* (Paris, 1910), pp. 118, 135-36; Edmond Coutard, *La Production coopérative par les associations ouvrières* (Paris, 1900), pp. 104-107; Firmin Verdier, *Le Mouvement coopératif et le socialisme* (Toulouse, 1903), pp. 50-61, 117; Meister, "Démographie," pp. 71-75.

CHAPTER 4: FORMATION OF THE PARTI OUVRIER

1. Cited by Bernstein, *Beginnings*, pp. xviii-xix.
2. Cited by Zévaès, *De l'Introduction du marxisme*, pp. 91-96.
3. Willard, *Les Guesdistes*, pp. 128-32. *Le Prolétaire*, Mar. 3, 1883.
4. Jules Guesde, "La Propriété collective et le Congrès de Marseille," *La Revue socialiste*, no. 1 (1880), pp. 19-25. *L'Egalité*, Jan. 21, 1880. Cf. Guesde, *Essai de catéchisme socialiste* (Paris, 1912), pp. 40-45; Guesde, *Cà et là* (Paris, 1914), pp. 83-101.
5. *L'Egalité*, Feb. 18, 25, Mar. 2, 9, 18, 1880.
6. *Ibid.*, Mar. 31, Apr. 14, 21, July 21, 1880.
7. Benoît Malon, "Le Programme de 1880," *La Revue socialiste*, no. 25 (1887), pp. 41-43. Guesde Papers, Institut français d'histoire sociale, Letters of Malon to Guesde, Apr. 3, 8, 27, 1880. *Le Prolétaire*, May 29, 1880. Neil McInnes, ed., "Les Partis socialistes français (1880-1885). Lettres et extraits de lettres d'Engels à Bernstein. Trad. de Bracke," *Cahiers de l'I. S. E. A.*, no. 109 (1961), pp. 49-54. Also, *Selected Correspondence of Marx and Engels* (Moscow, 1939), pp. 403-405.
8. *L'Egalité*, June 30, 1880.
9. Stekloff, *History of the First International*, pp. 240-41.
10. *L'Egalité*, June 30, 1880.
11. Malon's letters to Guesde, Apr. 4, May 21, June 7, and June 1880, Guesde Papers, contradict Malon's account in "Programme de 1880," pp. 47-48, written to justify his subsequent repudiation of the program.
12. Jean Grave, *Le Mouvement libertaire sous la Troisième République* (Paris, 1930), pp. 7, 11-14. *L'Egalité*, July 28, 1880. *Le Citoyen*, July 20-21, 1880.
13. *Le Prolétaire*, June 12, 19, July 10, 14-17, 24, 1880.
14. Letters of Malon to Guesde, Apr. 3, 8, 27, 1880; May 6, June 15, 29, Nov. 21, 1879, Guesde Papers.
15. Benoît Malon, "Un Premier Mot," *La Revue socialiste*, no. 10 *(1880)*, pp. 420-23.
16. McInnes, ed., "Lettres d'Engels à Bernstein," pp. 54-56.
17. Malon's letters to Guesde, June 14, July 3, Aug. 25, 1880, Guesde Papers.
18. *L'Emancipation*, Nov. 20, 1880. See also, *Le Prolétaire*, Mar. 3, 1883; *L'Egalité*, Jan. 22, 1882; McInnes, ed., "Lettres d'Engels à Bernstein," pp. 49-50; B/A 1170; and *Compte-rendu de la Séance de nuit, septembre 25, question de discipline* (Paris, 1882), p. 26.

19. B/A 985; Vuilleumier, "Paul Brousse," pp. 69-79; Stafford, *From Anarchism to Reformism,* chaps. 4-5.

20. *Le Prolétaire,* Jan. 1, 1881.

21. Election results in the *Compte-rendu de la Conférence nationale de 1895, tenu à Paris les 29 et 30 septembre 1895* (Paris, 1895), pp. 50-54. Benoît Malon, *Le Nouveau Parti: Le Parti ouvrier et sa politique* (Paris, 1882), pp. 4-8, 73.

22. *Le Prolétaire,* Feb. 26, 1881.

23. *Compte-rendu, septembre 25,* p. 13. Also, letter of June 9 in Adéodat Compère-Morel, *Jules Guesde: le socialisme fait homme, 1845-1922* (Paris, 1937), pp. 202-204.

24. *Le Prolétaire,* May 21, July 16, 23, 1881, Mar. 3, 1883; *Compte-rendu, septembre 25,* pp. 17-19, 30-32; *L'Egalité,* Jan. 22, 1882; and *Le Citoyen,* Aug. 1881.

25. *Le Citoyen,* Aug. 24, 25, 1881. *Compte-rendu, Conférence nationale, 1895,* pp. 63-65.

26. *Le Citoyen,* Aug. 25, 28, 1881; *Le Prolétaire,* Aug. 27, Sept. 3, 10, 17, 24, Oct. 22, 1881.

27. *Le Prolétaire,* Oct. 8, 1881; B/A 985, June 9, 17, Sept. 15, Oct. 5, 1881.

28. Malon, *Nouveau Parti,* pp. 79-84, 94-95.

29. *Cinquième Congrès national tenu à Reims du 30 octobre au 6 novembre 1881,* publié par le Comité national (Paris, 1882). Also, *Le Prolétaire,* Nov. 19, 26, 1881. *Le Citoyen,* Nov. 10-13, 1880.

30. *Le Prolétaire,* Sept. 3, Oct. 22, Dec. 2, 10, 1881. Malon, *Nouveau Parti,* pp. 73-98.

31. *Le Prolétaire,* Nov. 19, 1881.

32. *Ibid.,* Dec. 24, 1881. *Le Citoyen,* Dec. 1, 8, 11, 1881. B/A 1126.

33. *L'Egalité,* Dec. 11-Feb. 4, 1882.

34. *Ibid.,* May 21, June 18, 1882. *Le Citoyen,* June 9, 16, 27, 1882. *Compte-rendu, septembre 25,* pp. 22-23, 28-29. Jean Dormoy, *Rapports et résolutions des congrès ouvriers de 1876 à 1883* (Paris, 1883), pp. 46-55.

35. *Le Prolétaire,* Dec. 31, 1881, Jan. 18, 1882.

36. Maximilien Rubel, "La Charte de l'Internationale," *Mouvement social,* no. 51 (1965), p. 5.

37. Paul Brousse, *Le Marxisme dans l'Internationale* (Paris, 1882), p. 7.

38. *Ibid.,* p. 31.

39. See Franz Mehring, *Karl Marx: The Story of His Life* (London, 1936), Chap. 15.

40. McInnes, ed., "Lettres d'Engels à Bernstein," pp. 49-50, 72.

41. *Ibid.,* pp. 51-54, 63-65, 67. Also, Engels to Bebel cited by Belkin, *Jules Guesde,* pp. 265-67; Mehring, *Karl Marx,* p. 530.

42. Compère-Morel, *Jules Guesde,* pp. 230-34. *Compte-rendu, septembre 25,* pp. 10-11, 14-15, 58-59. *Le Prolétaire,* Dec. 31, 1881-Jan. 28, 1882. B/A 1478.

43. Willard, *Les Guesdistes,* pp. 22-25; Compère-Morel, *Jules Guesde,* pp. 235, 240, 244; *Compte-rendu du 6e Congrès national tenu à Saint-Étienne du 25 au 31 septembre, 1882* (Paris, 1883), pp. 9-15.

44. Willard, *Les Guesdistes,* pp. 23-25. *Compte-rendu, 6e Congrès, 1882,* pp. 21-28. *Compte-rendu, septembre 25,* pp. 3-4.

45. Cited in Dormoy, *Rapports et résolutions,* pp. 28-32.

46. *Ibid.,* pp. 38-43.

47. *Ibid.,* pp. 16-22.

48. *Compte-rendu, 6e Congrès, 1882,* pp. 88-89.

49. *Ibid.,* pp. 91-95.

50. *Ibid.,* pp. 174-75.

51. *Ibid.,* p. 166.

52. *Ibid.,* pp. 172-73.

53. *Ibid.,* pp. 167-71. For membership of the federations see *ibid.,* pp. 184-209.

54. Cf. Willard, *Les Guesdistes,* pp. 20-21; Alexandre Zévaès, *Les Guesdistes* (Paris, 1911); and Sylvain Humbert, *Les Possibilistes* (Paris, 1912).

55. *Le Prolétaire,* Nov. 12, 19, 1882; July 10, Oct. 13, 1883. Also, Vuilleumier, *Paul Brousse,* p. 79.

56. Guesde and Lafargue, *Le Programme du Parti ouvrier, son histoire, ses considérants, ses articles* (Paris, 1883), esp. pp. 112-27. Willard, *Les Guesdistes,* pp. 16-17, 28, 78-80, 196-97, does not see these federalist traits as part of Guesde's "collectivist" heritage.

57. Willard, *Les Guesdistes,* pp. 28-31, 90-91, 159-67, 171-78, 213-14.

58. *Ibid.,* pp. 112-35, 153-55, 171-78, 345-46, 382-83.

59. *Ibid.,* pp. 229-35, 316-20. Also, Robert P. Baker, "Socialism in the *Nord,* 1880-1914: A Regional View of the French Socialist Movement," *International Review of Social History* 12 (1967): 362-69.

60. *Compte-rendu du 7e Congrès national à Paris, 1883* (Paris, 1883), p. 20.

61. *Ibid.*, pp. 19-22. *Le Prolétaire*, May 19, June 2, Oct. 4-6, 1883; Nov. 8, Dec. 21,1884; Aug. 1, 1885; Apr. 24, July 17, 1886; Aug. 11, 1888. Also, Letter of Fournière to Allemane, Aug. 3, 1883, Institut français d'histoire sociale, Paris.

62. Paul Brousse, *La Propriété collective et les services publics* (Paris, 1883). Cf. Jules Guesde, *Services publics et socialisme* (Paris, 1883).

63. *Compte-rendu, Conférence national, 1895*, pp. 50-73. *Le Prolétaire*, Oct. 4, 1885. Archives de la Seine, D_2M_2, 1885.

64. *Compte-rendu, 7e Congrès, 1883*, pp. 14, 16-18. *Le Prolétaire*, June 2, 1883; B/A 32.

65. Cf. Humbert, *Les Possibilistes*, pp. 15-17, 67-71; Stafford, *From Anarchism to Reformism*, Chap. 6; and Carl Landauer, "The Origin of Socialist Reformism in France," *International Review of Social History* 12 (1967): 81-107.

66. *Compte-rendu, 7e Congrès, 1883*, p. 17.

67. *Ibid.*, pp. 19-22; *Le Prolétaire*, May 19, June 2, 1883; B/A 32, Oct. 3, 6, 1883.

68. *Le Prolétaire*, esp. May 20, 1882; March 31, May 5, 23, June 2, Oct. 6-20, 1883. *Le Prolétariat*, esp. Dec. 13, 1884; Aug. 10, Oct. 22, 1887; June 30-July 14, 1888. Malon, *Nouveau Parti*, pp. 79-84, 94-95. Aimé Lavy, *Le Parti ouvrier à l'Hôtel de Ville* (Paris, 1887), pp. 8-14.

69. *Compte-rendu, 7e Congrès, 1883*, pp. 13-14, 16. *Compte-rendu du 8e Congrès national à Rennes, 1884* (Paris, 1885), pp. 13-22. *Compte-rendu du 9e Congrès national à Charleville, 1887* (Paris, 1888), pp. 31-41. *Compte-rendu du 10e Congrès national à Châtellerault, 1890* (Poitiers, 1891), pp. 72-83. *Compte-rendu du 9e Congrès régional ouvrier de l'Union fédérative du Centre* (Paris, 1888), pp. 140-76.

70. *Compte-rendu, 7e Congrès, 1883*, p. 15. See also, *Cinquième Congrès national, 1881*, pp. 18-73, and F^7 12 489.

71. *Compte-rendu, 6e Congrès, 1882*, p. 184.

72. Active party members were taken from attendance records in *Le Prolétaire, Le Prolétariat*, and *Le Parti ouvrier*, and from B/A 1477-78 and the *Compte-rendu, 6e Congrès, 1882*, pp. 184-88; congress attendance from the *compte-rendus*, B/A 32 and F^7 12 489; union memberships from the police inventories of 1882 and 1885 in B/A 1442 and P. Coupat, "L'Union des ouvriers mécaniciens de la Seine," *Le Mouvement socialiste*, no. 48 (1900), pp. 736-50. See tables in Moss, "Origins of the French Labor Movement: The Socialism of Skilled Workers" (Ph.D. diss., Columbia University, 1972), pp. 403-21.

73. For trend of scale see Chap. 1, n. 16.

74. Total workers in each trade from the 1886 census.

75. *Le Prolétariat*, Nov. 26, 1887.

76. *Compte-rendu, 6e Congrès, 1882,* pp. 184-209. *Le Parti ouvrier,* Sept. 12, 1890. B/A 32.

77. Landauer, "Origins of Socialist Reformism," pp. 101-102. Willard, *Les Guesdistes,* pp. 401-402. Benoît Malon, *Le Socialisme réformiste* (Paris, 1886). Malon apparently quit the party in August 1883—B/A 1170.

78. Georges Clemenceau, *Discours prononcé à Marseille le 28 octobre 1880* (Paris, 1880).

79. Albert Orry, *Les Socialistes indépendents* (Paris, 1911), pp. 4-7. Malon, *Nouveau Parti,* pp. 55-57, 124-26.

80. Néré, "Crise industrielle," 2: esp. Chap. 4. Also, Frederick Seager, *The Boulanger Affair: Political Crossroads of France* (Ithaca, N.Y., 1969), esp. pp. 135-40, 191-97.

81. B/A 1480. See also Patrick H. Hutton, "The Role of the Blanquist Party in Left-wing Politics in France, 1879-90," *The Journal of Modern History* 46 (1974): 277-95. Néré, "Crise industrielle," 2:165-67, 317-22, 412-35, 508-33, 627. Also, Maurice Dommanget, *Edouard Vaillant: un grand socialiste, 1840-1915* (Paris, 1956). Jolyn Haworth, "La Propagande socialiste d'Edouard Vaillant," *Le Mouvement social,* no. 72 (1970), pp. 83-119.

82. Néré, "Crise industrielle," 2: esp. pp. 47-78, 132-33, 221-36, 362-84. Maitron, *Mouvement anarchiste,* pp. 107-73. B/A 1611.

83. Willard, *Les Guesdistes,* Chap. 2. Néré, "Crise industrielle," 2: esp. 43, 321-26. Also, Jean Dautry, "Lafargue et l'unité ouvrière," *La Pensée,* no. 120 (1965), pp. 25-56.

84. Néré, "Crise industrielle," 2: esp. 41, 61, 196, 241, 314-15, 338-49, 407-11, 627. *Le Parti ouvrier,* esp. Apr. 8, May 25, 1888. *Le Prolétaire,* June 14, 1884, *Le Prolétariat,* Nov. 19, 26, 1887; Feb. 18, 25, Mar. 24, 31, May 26, July 14, Aug. 4, 11, Sept. 8, 1888.

85. Michel Winock, "La Scission de Châtellerault et la naissance du parti 'allemaniste' (1890-91)," *Le Mouvement social,* no. 75 (1971), pp. 33-62. Also, *Le Parti ouvrier,* 1890. *Le Prolétariat, 1890.* B/A 31.

86. Maitron, ed., *Dictionnaire,* 4:103-107.

87. Winock, "La Scission," pp. 33-62. *Le Parti ouvrier,* 1890. *Le Prolétariat,* 1890. Also, Maurice Poujade, "Les Allemanistes à Paris de 1890 à 1905" (D.E.S., Paris, 1960), pp. 7-14. M. Charnay, *Les Allemanistes* (Paris, 1912), pp. 6-7, 29-30. Humbert, *Possibilistes* pp. 69-71.

88. *Compte-rendu du 10ᵉ Congrès régional tenu à Paris, 1890 et 1891* (Paris, 1892), pp. i-vii, 100-107.

89. Poujade, "Allemanistes," pp. 25-29, 48-52. Charnay, *Allemanistes*, pp. 38-47.

90. *Compte-rendu, 10ᵉ Congrès régional, 1890, 1891*, pp. 100-101. *Compte-rendu de l'11ᵉ Congrès régional à Paris, 1892* (Paris, 1893), pp. 87-90. *Compte-rendu de l'11ᵉ Congrès national à Saint-Quentin, 1892* (Paris, 1893), pp. 39-41, 53.

91. *Compte-rendu du 12ᵉ Congrès régional à Paris, 1894* (Paris, 1895), pp. 21-36. *Compte-rendu du 12ᵉ Congrès national à Dijon, 1894* (Paris, 1895), pp. 15-16. *Compte-rendu du 13ᵉ Congrès national à Paris, 1896* (Paris, 1897), pp. 87-101. J. Allemane, *Notre Programme développé et commenté* (Paris, 1895), p. 3.

92. *Le Parti ouvrier*, 1890-1895.

93. James Butler, "Fernand Pelloutier and the Emergence of the French Syndicalist Movement, 1880-1906" (Ph.D. diss., Ohio State University, 1960), p. 233.

94. Poujade, "Allemanistes," pp. 54-66, 71-75, Charnay, *Allemanistes*, pp. 74-75. See also Chap. 5.

95. Poujade, "Allemanistes," pp. 20, 29, 53; Willard, *Les Guesdistes*, pp. 397-98.

96. *Le Temps*, Aug. 20, 1893.

97. Poujade, "Allemanistes," pp. 31, 68-70, 75-90. Charnay, *Allemanistes*, pp. 74-80.

98. Willard, *Les Guesdistes*, pp. 75, 187-94.

CHAPTER 5: TOWARD REVOLUTIONARY SYNDICALISM

1. See most recently Annie Kriegel, "Le Syndicalisme révolutionnaire et Proudhon," *Le Pain et les roses: jalons pour une histoire des socialismes* (Paris, 1968), pp. 33-50, and F. F. Ridley, *Revolutionary Syndicalism in France: The Direct Action of its Time* (Cambridge, England, 1970).

2. Victor Griffuelhes, *L'Action syndicaliste* (Paris, 1908), p. 7.

3. See Chap. 3, nn. 100-101.

4. Willard, *Les Guesdistes*, p. 35. Seilhac, *Congrès ouvriers*, p. 204. *2ᵉ Congrès national des syndicats ouvriers de France, tenu à Montluçon en octobre 1887* (Montluçon, 1888), pp. 12-17, 82-84.

5. Mermeix [Gabriel Terrail], *Le Syndicalisme contre le Socialisme* (Paris, 1907), p. 97. Seilhac, *Congrès ouvriers*, pp. 204-15, 229-30.

Fernand Pelloutier, *Histoire des bourses du travail* (Paris, 1902), pp. 107-11.

6. *2e Congrès national, 1887*, pp. 88-89. *3e Congrès national de la Fédération des syndicats et groupes ouvriers de France, tenu à Bordeaux, 1888* (Bordeaux, 1888), pp. 17-18. Also, Jacques Néré, "Crise industrielle," 2:416-22.

7. Willard, *Les Guesdistes*, pp. 187-96, 355-60. "Congrès corporatif national des syndicats ouvriers, Calais, 13-18 octobre 1890" (Ms., Musée social, Paris), pp. 48-56. *5e Congrès national des syndicats et groupes corporatifs de France, 1892* (Paris, 1909), pp. 46-53. Also, F7 12 491.

8. Louis Le Theuff, *Histoire de la Bourse du Travail de Paris* (Paris, 1902). B/A 1611.

9. *Compte-rendu du 10e Congrès régional, 1890* (Paris, 1892), pp. 71-72, 100-101. *Compte-rendu du 11e Congrès régional à Paris, 1892* (Paris, 1893), pp. 87-90. *Compte-rendu du 11e Congrès national à Saint Quentin, 1892* (Paris, 1893), pp. 39-53. *Compte-rendu du 12e Congrès régional à Paris, 1894* (Paris, 1895), pp. 21-36. *Compte-rendu du 12e Congrès national à Dijon, 1894* (Paris, 1895), pp. 15-16, 24-47.

10. *Annuaire de la Bourse du Travail, 1890-91* (Paris, 1892). *Bulletin officiel de la Bourse du Travail de Paris*, 1890-93, *passim*.

11. *Congrès de Saint-Etienne, février 1892. Rapport du citoyen Branque* (Toulouse, 1893), *passim*. Pelloutier, *Histoire des bourses*, pp. 233-36.

12. B/A 1068. Le Theuff, *Histoire de la Bourse*, pp. 59-65.

13. *Compte-rendu du Congrès national des chambres syndicales et groupes corporatifs ouvriers, tenu à Paris en juillet 1893* (Paris, 1893), esp. pp. 38-43.

14. *Ibid.*, p. 45.

15. *6e Congrès national des syndicats de France, tenu à Nantes, du 17 au 22 septembre, 1894* (Nantes, 1894), pp. 16-41, 65.

16. Leroy, *Coutume ouvrière*, 2:450-51.

17. *7e Congrès national corporatif, tenu à Limoges, 23-28 septembre, 1895* (Limoges, 1896), pp. 6, 51-57, 86-89. F7 12 493, esp. Sept. 25-27, 1895.

18. *7e Congrès national corporatif, 1895*, p. 86.

19. *Ibid.*

20. *Ibid.*, pp. 77-81.

21. *Ibid.*, pp. 67-71.

22. See Chap. 4, n. 72.

23. See Butler, "Fernand Pelloutier," chaps. 3-4; Jacques Julliard, *Fernand Pelloutier et les origines du syndicalisme d'action directe* (Paris, 1971), Chap. 4; and Louis Levine, *Syndicalism in France* (New York, 1914), pp. 73-89.

24. Levine, *Syndicalism,* pp. 112-20; Butler, "Fernand Pelloutier," pp. 325-58.

25. Butler, "Fernand Pelloutier," pp. 325-58; Levine, *Syndicalism,* ·pp. 121-35.

26. See Leroy, *Coutume ouvrière,* 2:481-575.

27. Butler, "Fernand Pelloutier," esp. pp. 361-63, 366-68.

28. *Ibid.,* pp. 363-66. Also, Maitron, *Mouvement anarchiste,* pp. 249-310.

29. Levine, *Syndicalism,* pp. 210-14. Val Lorwin, *The French Labor Movement* (Cambridge, Mass., 1954), pp. 23-27, 42-44. Cf. Stearns, *Revolutionary Syndicalism, passim,* and Jacques Julliard, "Théorie syndicaliste révolutionnaire et pratique gréviste," *Le Mouvement social,* no. 65 (1968), pp. 55-69.

30. Maitron, *Mouvement anarchiste,* pp. 294-95.

31. Weill, *Histoire du mouvement social,* rev. ed. (Paris, 1924), pp. 374-75.

32. Dolléans, *Mouvement ouvrier,* 2:145-55. Also, Jacques Julliard, *Clemenceau, briseur de grèves* (Paris, 1965).

33. Cited by Bernard Georges *et al, Léon Jouhaux: cinquante ans de syndicalisme* (Paris, 1962), p. 22.

34. *Ibid.,* pp. 20-26. Levine, *Syndicalism,* pp. 185-194.

35. Cf. Peter Stearns and Harvey Mitchell, *Workers and Protest* (Itaska, Ill., 1971), pp. 106, 199; Levine, *Syndicalism,* pp. 206-209, 216-17; and Christian Gras, "La Fédération des métaux en 1913-14; l'évolution du syndicalisme révolutionnaire français," *Le Mouvement social,* no. 77 (1971), pp. 85-111.

36. Gras, "Fédération des métaux," pp. 101-102.

37. See Hubert Sales, *Les Relations industrielles dans l'imprimerie française* (Paris, 1967).

38. Annie Kriegel, *Aux Origines du communisme français,* 2 vols. (Paris, 1964), 1:529-42.

39. Stearns, *Revolutionary Syndicalism,* chaps. 3-4.

40. Levine, *Syndicalism,* p. 194. Jacques Julliard, *Fernand Pelloutier,* pp. 257-59.

41. For an opinion survey that demonstrates this process in contemporary France, see G. Adam *et al, L'Ouvrier français en 1970* (Paris, 1970), esp. Chap. 6.

42. Jacques Julliard is preparing a doctoral dissertation on the subject at the University of Paris.

43. Levine, *Syndicalism,* pp. 100, 185, 207-210. Lorwin, *French Labor Movement,* pp. 43-44.

44. See similar analysis in James Hinton, *The First Shop Stewards' Movement* (London, 1973), Chap. 2.

45. See tables in Annie Kriegel and Jean-Jacques Becker, *1914: La Guerre et le mouvement ouvrier* (Paris, 1964), pp. 280-85. Also, Shorter and Tilly, *Strikes in France,* pp. 150-70.

46. Collinet, *Esprit du syndicalisme,* pp. 23-35. Leroy, *Coutume ouvrière,* 1:363-79. Gras, "Fédération des métaux," pp. 104, 107, 110.

47. Cf. Stearns, *Revolutionary Syndicalism,* esp. pp. 92-93.

48. Julliard, "Théorie syndicaliste," pp. 60-63.

49. Kriegel, *Origines du communisme,* 1:316-18. Stearns and Mitchell, *Workers and Protest,* p. 74.

50. See Aaron Noland, *The Founding of the French Socialist Party* (Cambridge, Mass., 1956), esp. Chap. 7.

51. *Confédération générale du travail, 15e Congrès national corporatif, tenu à Amiens du 8 au 16 octobre, 1906* (Amiens, 1906), p. 136.

52. Georges Lefranc, "La Charte d'Amiens," *Information historique,* no. 5 (1956), pp. 176-77. Maitron, *Mouvement anarchiste,* pp. 297-300. *CGT, Congrès national corporatif, 1906,* pp. 166-67.

53. *CGT, Congrès national corporatif, 1906,* pp. 169-71.

54. Guillaume, *L'Internationale,* 4:vii.

55. See Kriegel, *Origines du communisme,* 1:529-42, 2:724-30.

CHAPTER 6: CONCLUSION: SOCIALISM OF SKILLED WORKERS

1. Scott has given us a model in *Glassworkers of Carmaux,* whose experience, however, does not seem typical of the urban crafts considered here.

2. Shorter and Tilly, *Strikes in France,* pp. 67, 149-55, 202-27.

EPILOGUE: SOCIALISM AS THEORY AND PROCESS

1. See Karl Mannheim, "Utopia," *Encyclopedia of the Social Sciences,* ed. Edwin Seligman, 15 vols. (London, 1935), 15:200-203.

2. Cf. Monty Johnstone, "Marx and Engels and the Concept of the Party," in *The Socialist Register 1967,* ed. Ralph Miliband and John Saville (New York, 1967), pp. 121-58.

3. Kriegel, *Origines du communisme,* esp. 1:316-18, 2:729-30, 752-54.

4. See Solomon Schwartz, *Lenine et le mouvement syndical* (Paris, 1955).

5. See Robert Wohl, *French Communism in the Making, 1914-1924* (Stanford, Calif., 1966), chaps. 9-12.

6. See Chap. 1, n. 68. Also, Lorwin, *French Labor Movement,* pp. 60-79.

Bibliographical Essay

General surveys of the French labor movement in the nineteenth century suffer from weakness of interpretation and analysis, which often has its source in the artificial distinctions drawn among labor, cooperative, republican, and socialist movements. The semistandard survey by the Proudhonian Edouard Dolléans, *Histoire du mouvement ouvrier,* 2 vols. (Paris: Armand Colin, 1947-48), stresses the "heroic" struggle of a militant elite for a vaguely defined social justice. See also Dolléans and Gérard Dehove, *Histoire du travail en France: mouvement ouvrier et législation sociale,* 2 vols. (Paris: Domat-Montchrestian, 1953-55). Georges Lefranc, a reformist socialist, tends to highlight ideological divisions in Jean Montreuil [pseud.], *Histoire du mouvement ouvrier en France des origines à nos jours* (Paris: Aubier, 1947), and his more recent *Le Mouvement syndical sous la Troisième République* (Paris: Payot, 1967). The Marxist Paul Louis relates the development of union organization rather schematically to the growth of industry in his *Histoire du mouvement syndical en France,* 2 vols. (Paris: Valois, 1947). In a sensitive *Essais sur le mouvement ouvrier en France* (Paris: 1901), the liberal Daniel Halévy was critical of cooperation and socialism for diverting workers from reformist trade unionism. Despite its narrow focus, Jean Gaumont's *Histoire générale de la coopération en France,* 2 vols. (Paris: Fédération Nationale des Coopératives de Consommation, 1924), is a veritable encyclopedia of information on the labor movement. Equally comprehensive, though lacking in interpretive analysis, is Georges Weill's *Histoire du mouvement social en France, 1852-1902* (Paris: 1904).

The standard treatments of French socialism by Alexandre Zévaès, *Histoire du socialisme et du communisme en France de 1871 à 1947* (Paris: France-Empire, 1947), Aaron Noland, *The Founding of the French Socialist Party, 1893-1905* (Cambridge, Mass.: Harvard University Press, 1956), Daniel Ligou, *Histoire du socialisme en France, 1871-1961* (Paris: Presses Universitaires de France, 1962), and Georges Lefranc, *Le Mouvement socialiste sous la Troisième République* (Paris: Payot, 1963), all begin with party organization under the Third Republic. "Histoire des Partis socialistes en France," a series of factional histories edited for the SFIO by Zévaès in 1911, conveys a misleading impression of ideological division and confusion. For an interesting survey of earlier socialist doctrine as it relates to the labor movement see Benoît Malon, *Histoire du socialisme depuis ses origines jusqu'à nos jours* (Lugano: 1879). Several volumes in the *Histoire socialiste,* a socialist history of modern France edited by Jean Jaurès (Paris: Rouff, 1902) are excellent for their periods.

The richest primary source on the labor movement is *Associations professionnelles ouvrières,* 4 vols. (Paris, 1894-1904), published by France, Office du Travail under the direction of the positivist labor leader Isidore Finance, which contains the organizational records of leading trades in Paris and other major cities. Official surveys of producers' associations may be found in Office du Travail, *Les Associations ouvrières de production* (Paris: 1897), and Ministère de l'Intérieur, *Enquête de la commission extra-parlementaire des associations ouvrières,* 3 vols. (Paris: 1883-88). A major research tool is Jean Maitron, ed., *Dictionnaire biographique du mouvement ouvrier français* 4 Parts (Paris: Les Editions ouvrières, 1964-), which is currently being completed for the period 1871-1914. For an excellent guide to labor congresses, see Robert Brécy, *Le Mouvement syndical en France: essai bibliographique, 1871-1921* (Paris: Mouton, 1963).

My analysis of the socialism of skilled workers combines a Marxist approach with the industrial sociology presented in three publications of Alain Touraine: *L'Evolution du travail ouvrier aux usines Renault* (Paris: Centre National des Recherches Scientifiques, 1955), "L'Evolution de la conscience ouvrière et l'idée socialiste," *Esprit* 20 (1956): 692-705, and *La Conscience ouvrière* (Paris: Seuil, 1966); as well as Robert Blauner's *Alienation and Freedom: The Factory Worker and his Industry* (Chicago: University of Chicago Press, 1964). It has also benefited from the sociological formulations of Serge Mallet, *La Nouvelle Classe ouvrière* (Paris: Seuil, 1963), Michel Collinet, *Esprit du syndicalisme* (Paris: Les Editions Ouvrières, 1952), and Seymour Martin Lipset, *Political Man: The Social Bases of Politics* (New York: Doubleday, 1960), and S. M. Lipset et al, *Union Democracy: The Internal Politics of the International Typographical Union* (New York: Doubleday, 1962). Edward Shorter and Charles Tilly have applied a similar model to the study of *Strikes in France, 1830-1968* (London: Cambridge University Press, 1974).

Two classic studies of artisans or skilled workers are Norman Ware, *The Industrial Worker, 1840-1860* (Boston: Houghton Mifflin, 1924), and E. P. Thompson, *The Making of the English Working Class* (London: Gollancz, 1963). Eric Hobsbawn gives a Marxist analysis in "The Labour Aristocracy in Nineteenth Century Britain," in his *Labouring Men: Studies in the History of Labour* (New York: Basic Books, 1964), pp. 321-70. For a more refined view see James Hinton, *The First Shop Stewards' Movement* (London: George Allen & Unwin, 1973). Joan Scott has written a model occupational case study, *The Glassworkers of Carmaux* (Cambridge, Mass.: Harvard University Press, 1974). Two intriguing articles by William Sewell, Jr. relate radicalism to trade mobility: "La Classe ouvrière de Marseille sous la Seconde République: structure sociale et comportement politique," *Le Mouvement social,* no. 76 (1971), pp. 27-65, and "Social Change and the Rise of Working Class Politics in Nineteenth-Century Marseille," *Past and Present,* no. 65 (1974), pp. 75-109.

Despite appearances to the contrary, there is a paucity of reliable information on Parisian workers. Based on impressionistic evidence, the standard Georges Duveau, *La Vie ouvrière en France sous le Second Empire* (Paris: Gallimard, 1946), tends to exaggerate the degree of Parisian industrialization during this period. Equally impressionistic, Louis Chevalier, *Les Parisiens* (Paris: Hachette, 1967), still contains valuable insights. Utilizing literary sources that reflected middle class fears, Chevalier presumed a fusion of *Classes laborieuses et classes dangereuses à Paris pendant la première moitié du XIX siècle* (Paris: Plon, 1958), which appears highly problematical as far as most active workers were concerned. Far more trustworthy is his statistical essay, *La Formation de la population parisienne au XIX siècle* (Paris: Presses Universitaires de France, 1950). The most comprehensive data on Parisian industry was collected in three studies by the Chambre de Commerce de Paris, *Statistique de l'industrie à Paris, 1847-48* (Paris: 1851), a second book by the same title for the year 1860 (Paris: 1864), and *Enquête sur les conditions de travail en France, 1872* (Paris: 1875).

The best account of the wage question is Jacques Rougerie, "Remarques sur l'histoire des salaires à Paris au XIX siècle," *Le Mouvement social,* no. 63 (1968), pp. 71-108.

The occupational monographs on Parisian trades are few and sketchy: Jean Vial, *La Coutume chapelière: histoire du mouvement ouvrier dans la chapellerie* (Paris: Domat-Montchrestien, 1941), Henriette Vanier, *La Mode et ses métiers: frivolités et luttes des classes, 1830-1870* (Paris: Armand Colin, 1960), Paul Chauvet, *Les Ouvriers du Livre en France de 1789 à la constitution de la Fédération du Livre* (Paris: Rivière, 1956), and the uncompleted Joseph Barberet, *Le Travail en France: monographies professionnelles,* 7 vols. (Paris: 1886-90). For definitions and descriptions of skilled crafts consult Ministère du travail, *Répertoire technologique des noms d'industries et de professions* (Paris: Berger-Levrault, 1909).

Several first-hand accounts offer interesting impressions of working class life, notably, Pierre Vinçard, *Les Ouvriers de Paris* (Paris: 1850); Agricol Perdiguier, *Mémoires d'un compagnon* (Paris: Denoël, 1943); Martin Nadaud, *Mémoires de Léonard, ancien garçon maçon* (Paris: 1912); A. Corbon, *Le Secret du peuple de Paris* (Paris: 1863); Denis Poulot, *Le Sublime* (Paris: 1870); and Henry Steele, *The Working Classes in France* (London: 1904). Jacques Valdour, *De la Popinqu'à Menilmuch* (Paris: Editions Spes, 1924), gives a fascinating view of the social psychology of bronze workers.

For the origins of republican socialism see Georges Weill, *Histoire du parti républicain en France de 1814 à 1870* (Paris: 1900); J. Tchernoff, *Le Parti républicain sous la Monarchie de Juillet: formation et évolution de la doctrine républicaine* (Paris: 1901); and Gabriel Perreux, *Au temps des sociétés secrètes: la propagande républicaine au début de la Monarchie de Juillet (1830-1835)* (Paris: Hachette, 1931). For a Marxist view see Roger Garaudy, *Les Sources françaises du socialisme scientifique* (Paris: Editions Hier et Aujourd'hui, 1948). Three important articles are V. Volgin, "Levelling and Socialist Tendencies in French Secret Societies, 1830-1834" [in Russian], *Historical Questions,* no. 6 (1947), pp. 26-49, Leo Loubère, "Intellectual Origins of French Jacobin Socialism," *International Review of Social History IV* (1959): 413-31, and Bernard H. Moss, "Parisian Workers and the Origins of Republican Socialism, 1830-33," in *The Revolution of 1830,* ed. John Merriman (New York: Franklin Watts, forthcoming). An extensive collection of pamphlet literature has been published by the Editions d'histoire sociale as "Les Révolutions du XIXe siècle, 1830-34." On

Buchezian socialism, see Armand Cuvillier, *Hommes et idéologies de 1840* (Paris: Rivière, 1956), and François-André Isambert, *Politique, religion et science de l'homme chez Philippe Buchez* (Paris: Cujas, 1967); on Icarian socialism, Christopher Johnson, *Utopian Communism in France: Cabet and the Icarians, 1839-1851* (Ithaca: Cornell University Press, 1974).

The pioneer labor historian for the July Monarchy was Octave Festy, *Le Mouvement ouvrier au début de la Monarchie de Juillet, 1830-34* (Paris: 1908); "Dix Années de l'histoire corporative des ouvriers tailleurs d'habits, 1830-40," *Revue d'histoire des doctrines économiques et sociales* 5 (1912): 166-99; "Le Mouvement ouvrier à Paris en 1840," *Revue des sciences politiques* 30 (1913): 67-79, 226-40, 333-61. He treated cooperative association as a middle class idea. In his course at the Sorbonne, *Le Mouvement ouvrier et les théories sociales en France de 1815 à 1848* (Paris: Presses Universitaires de France, 1965), Ernest Labrousse has placed developments in an economic context. On strikes in this period, see Jean-Pierre Aguet, *Les Grèves sous la Monarchie de Juillet (1830-1847)* (Geneva: Droz, 1954), and Peter Stearns, "Patterns of Industrial Strike Activity in France during the July Monarchy," *The American Historical Review* 70 (1965): 371-94. Three recent local studies are Robert Bezucha, *The Lyon Uprising of 1834: Social and Political Conflict in the Early July Monarchy* (Cambridge, Mass.: Harvard University Press, 1974), Alain Faure, "Mouvements populaires et mouvement ouvrier à Paris (1830-1834)," *Le Mouvement social,* no. 88 (1974), pp. 51-92, and Maurice Agulhon, *Une Ville ouvrière au temps du socialisme utopique: Toulon de 1800 à 1851* (Paris: Mouton, 1970).

The best recent synthesis on the Second Republic is Roger Price, *The French Second Republic: A Social History* (Ithaca, N.Y.: Cornell University Press, 1972). Good accounts of labor may also be found in Frederick de Luna, *The French Republic under Cavaignac, 1848* (Princeton, N.J.: Princeton University Press, 1969); Georges Renard, *La République de 1848 (1848-1852),* vol. 9 of *Histoire socialiste,* ed. Jean Jaurès (Paris: 1904); and the titles by Edouard Dolléans and Jean Gaumont cited above. The major work is Rémi Gossez, *Les Ouvriers de Paris; l'organisation, 1848-1851* (Paris: Société de l'Histoire de la Révolution de 1848, 1967), and his interpretive article, "Pré-syndicalisme ou pré-coopération? l'organisation ouvrière unitaire et ses phases dans le département de la Seine de 1834 à 1851," *Archives internationales de sociologie de la coopération,* no. 6 (1959), pp. 67-89.

By remaining on the level of labor organization and structure, Gossez tends to neglect the more general political and ideological dimension of the movement. On associations, see Emile Heftler, *Les Associations coopératives de production sous la Deuxième République* (Paris: 1899), and Octave Festy, *Les Associations ouvrières encouragées par la Deuxième République* (Paris: 1915). The best analysis of the June insurrection is Charles Tilly and Lynn Lees, "Le Peuple de Juin 1848," *Annales; économies, sociétés, civilisations* 29 (1974): 1061-91. On provincial workers, see John Merriman, "Social Conflict in France and the Limoges Revolution of April 27, 1848," *Societas* 4 (1974): 21-38, and George Fasel, "Urban Workers in Provincial France, February-June 1848," *International Review of Social History* 17 (1972): 661-74. Recent work in social history has tended to confirm the substance of Marx's analysis in *The Class Struggles in France* and *The Eighteenth Brumaire of Louis Napoléon,* despite his errors of political judgment.

The best accounts of labor under the Second Empire may be found in Georges Weill, *Histoire du mouvement social,* and Albert Thomas, *Le Second Empire (1852-1870),* vol. 10 of *Histoire socialiste,* ed. Jean Jaurès (Paris: Rouff, 1904). Thomas rather uniquely stresses continuity rather than change. On Bonapartist socialism, see David Kulstein, *Napoléon III and the Working Class: A Study of Government Propaganda under the Second Empire* (Los Angeles: Ward Ritchie, 1969). Maxwell Kelso, "The French Labor Movement during the Last Years of the Second Empire," *Essays in the History of Modern Europe,* ed. Donald McKay (New York: Harper, 1936), and Fernand L'Huillier, *Lutte ouvrière à la fin du Second Empire* (Paris: Armand Colin, 1957), highlight trade unionism. Both Sveten Maritch, *Histoire du mouvement social sous le Second Empire à Lyon* (Paris: Rousseau, 1930), and Maurice Moissonnier, *La Première Internationale et la Commune à Lyon* (Paris: Editions sociales, 1972), view cooperation as a petty bourgeois movement. Only Jeanne Gaillard, "Les Associations de production et la pensée politique en France, 1852-1870," *Le Mouvement social,* no. 52 (1965), pp. 59-84, and Jacques Rougerie, "La Première Internationale à Lyon (1865-70): problème d'histoire du mouvement ouvrier français," *Annali dell Istituto Giangiacomo Feltrinelli* 4 (1961): 126-61, see its socialist thrust.

On the question of Proudhonism see Jules L. Puech, *Le Proudhonisme dans l'Association internationale des travailleurs* (Paris: 1907). The best biography is George Woodcock, *Pierre-Joseph Proudhon* (London: Macmillan, 1956). For a recent "collectivist" view, see Jean

Bancal, *Proudhon: pluralisme et autogestion,* 2 vols. (Paris: Aubier-Montaigne, 1970). Pierre Ansart, *Naissance de l'anarchisme: esquisse d'une explication sociologique de proudhonisme* (Paris: Presses Universitaires de France, 1970), is able to relate Proudhonism to the social situation of Lyons silk workers only because he exaggerates the collectivism of Proudhon and the individualism of the *canuts.* For a neoliberal rendering that seems more faithful to the original, see Alan Ritter, *The Political Thought of Pierre-Joseph Proudhon* (Princeton, N.J.: Princeton University Press, 1969).

The standard histories of the First International, written by socialists, tend to overclassify and overintellectualize its ideological currents. The so-called Proudhonian, Bakuninist, and Marxist delegates had more in common than is suggested by Julius Braunthal, *History of the International,* 2 vols. (New York: Praeger, 1967); G. M. Stekloff, *History of the First International* (New York: Eden and Cedar Paul, 1928); G. D. H. Cole, *Socialist Thought: Marxism and Anarchism, 1850-1890* (New York: St. Martin's Press, 1967); and Henry Collins and Chimen Abramsky, *Karl Marx and the British Labor Movement: Years of the First International* (London: St. Martin's Press, 1965). The major primary sources, including the minutes of all congresses, are available in *La Première Internationale: recueil de documents,* publié sous la direction de Jacques Freymond, 4 vols. (Geneva: Droz, 1962-71), and the classic James Guillaume, *L'Internationale: documents et souvenirs (1864-1878),* 4 vols. (Paris: 1905).

Discussions of the split between Marx and Bakunin have not completely outgrown the polemical stage. The fairest accounts are perhaps E. H. Carr, *Michael Bakunin* (London: Macmillan, 1937), and Miklos Molnar, *Le Déclin de la Première Internationale: La Conférence de Londres de 1871* (Geneva: Droz, 1963). For the Bakuninist view, see Arthur Lehning, ed., *Bakounine et les conflits dans l'Internationale, 1872* (Leiden: E. J. Brill, 1965). On the Jurassian period, see Leo Valiani, "Dalla I alla II Internationale," *Questioni di Storia del Socialismo* (Turin: Einaudi, 1958); Jean Maitron, *Histoire du mouvement anarchiste en France (1880-1914)* (Paris: Société Universitaire d'Editions et de Librairie, 1955); and M. Vuilleumier, "Les Proscrits de la Commune en Suisse, 1871," *Revue suisse d'histoire* 12 (1962): 488-537, who is preparing a full-length study of the Swiss exiles. A key article is Jacques Rougerie, "Sur l'histoire de la Première Internationale," *Le Mouvement social,* no. 51 (1965), pp. 21-45, who perhaps reacts too much against ideological history.

The work of Rougerie represents an important breakthrough in discussions of the Commune. Until the completion of his dissertation, the best introductions are his *Procès des Communards* (Paris: Julliard, 1964) and *Paris-libre, 1871* (Paris: Seuil, 1971). Despite his demurrer in, "Karl Marx, l'Etat et la Commune," *Preuves,* nos. 212-13 (1968), pp. 34-44, 45-56, his work tends to confirm Marx's analysis in *The Civil War in France.* Past historians, both liberal and Marxist, failed to appreciate the socialist dimension of the Commune because they were looking for the wrong kind of socialism, Marxism, rather than the cooperative socialism of the period. The best contemporary account is P. O. Lissagaray, *Histoire de la Commune de 1871,* 3 vols. (Paris: François Maspero, 1967); the best liberal account is Edward Mason, *The Paris Commune: An Episode in the History of the Socialist Movement* (New York: Macmillan, 1930); the best socialist one is Frank Jellinek, *The Paris Commune of 1871* (London: Gollancz, 1937). On ideology see Charles Rihs, *La Commune de Paris: sa structure et ses doctrines* (Geneva: Droz, 1955). The official Marxist view is given in Jean Bruhat, Jean Dautry, and Emile Tersen, *La Commune de 1871* (Paris: Editions sociales, 1960). Two important articles are Eugene Schulkind, "The Activity of Popular Organizations under the Paris Commune," *French Historical Studies* 1 (1960): 394-415, and A. Molok, "Les Ouvriers de Paris pendant la Commune," *Cahiers du communisme* 28 (1951): 608-22, 728-51.

On the post-Commune period, the major works are Jean Joughin, *The Paris Commune in French Politics, 1871-1880,* 2 vols. (Baltimore, Md.: Johns Hopkins University Press, 1955), Samuel Bernstein, *The Beginnings of Marxian Socialism in France* (New York: Russell & Russell, 1965), Maxwell Kelso, "The Inception of the Modern French Labor Movement (1871-79)," *The Journal of Modern History* 8 (1936): 173-93, and Aimée Moutet, "Le Mouvement ouvrier à Paris du lendemain de la Commune au premier congrès syndical en 1876," *Le Mouvement social,* no. 58 (1967), pp. 3-39.

Beginning with the post-Commune period, extensive research was undertaken in the Archives Nationales and the Archives de la Préfecture de Police de Paris. The series F^7 12 488-493 of the former contains police reports on all national and labor congresses from 1876 to 1900. Far more comprehensive and probing for this period are the reports of the Paris Prefecture in the B/A series. Following the repression of the Commune, it was able to recruit insiders, including leading labor militants, into its intelligence network, which covered all labor, Radical, and socialist activities. The reliability of these reports is enhanced by the knowledge of their authors. For details, see Bernard H. Moss, "French Archival Note: Police Spies and Labor Militants after the Commune," *European Labor History Newsletter*, no. 5 (1974), pp. 16-19.

Socialist historians have usually stressed the role of Marxist intellectuals who brought theory to the labor movement. The Guesdists originally established the orthodoxy that they had converted a moderate reformist or Proudhonian labor movement to Marxism. The first accounts of their triumph were written by liberal journalists, Mermeix [Gabriel Terrail], *La France socialiste* (Paris: 1886); and Léon de Seilhac, *Les Congrès ouvriers de France de 1876 à 1897* (Paris: 1899); and his *Le Monde socialiste; groupes et programmes* (Paris, 1896). Later, Alexandre Zévaès wrote several accounts from a Guesdist perspective, notably *De la Semaine sanglante au Congrès de Marseille (1871-1879)* (Paris: 1911), *De l'Introduction du marxisme en France* (Paris: Rivière, 1947), and a biography, *Jules Guesde* (Paris: Rivière, 1929). The best narrative is Samuel Bernstein, *The Beginnings of Marxian Socialism in France,* cited above. The Soviet historian I. D. Belkin draws upon unpublished letters at the Marxist-Leninist Institute and a Leninist critique in *Jules Guesde and the Struggle for a Workers' Party in France* [in Russian] (Moscow: 1962). The recent exhaustive study by Claude Willard, *Les Guesdistes: le mouvement socialiste en France (1893-1905)* (Paris: Editions Sociales, 1965), investigates the Guesdist social base, but tends to be overly schematic and uncritical of the Guesdist orthodoxy.

The first writer who perceived the continuity between cooperative and revolutionary socialism was Léon Blum, *Les Congrès ouvriers et socialistes,* 2 vols. (Paris: 1901). In his *Syndicalism in France* (New York: 1914), Louis Levine also touched upon the underlying continuity. In "The Inception of the Modern French Labor Movement," Maxwell Kelso was the first to challenge directly the Guesdist orthodoxy, but his reappraisal did not extend to the period before 1876. Most general accounts continue to follow the Guesdist orthodoxy.

The major work on the possibilist *Parti ouvrier* is David Stafford, *From Anarchism to Reformism: The Political Activities of Paul Brousse within the First International and the French Socialist Movement, 1870-90* (Toronto: University of Toronto Press, 1971), whose scholarly thoroughness is marred only by an overdrawn reformist interpretation.

A key article is Marc Vuilleumier, "Paul Brousse et son passage de l'anarchie au socialisme," *Cahiers Vilfredo Pareto* 7-8 (1965): 63-80. Carl Landauer correctly distinguishes between possibilism and reformism in "The Origin of Socialist Reformism in France," *International Review of Social History* 12 (1967): 81-107. The contemporary account by Sylvain Humbert, *Les Possibilistes* (Paris: 1912), is sketchy. For the activities of the different socialist factions during the Boulanger Affair, see Jacques Néré, "La Crise industrielle de 1882 et le mouvement boulangiste," 2 vols. (diss., University of Paris, 1959).

The literature on the Allemanists is even more sketchy, including the contemporary account by M. Charnay, *Les Allemanistes* (Paris: 1912); an excellent article by Michel Winock, "La Scission de Châtellerault et la naissance du parti 'allemaniste' (1890-91)," *Le Mouvement social,* no. 75 (1971), pp. 33-62; and a diplôme by Maurice Poujade, "Les Allemanistes à Paris de 1890 à 1905" (Diplôme d'Etudes Supérieures, University of Paris, 1958). The major primary sources for the study of the possibilists and Allemanists are the party newspapers, *Le Prolétaire,* 1878-1884, *Le Prolétariat,* 1884-90, *Le Parti ouvrier,* 1888-1914, and *Le Prolétaire,* 1891-94, and the party congresses, which are available at the Musée Social in Paris.

The best introduction to revolutionary syndicalism is still Louis Levine, *Syndicalism in France,* who stresses continuity with the past. Other good treatments are J. A. Estey, *Revolutionary Syndicalism: An Exposition and a Criticism* (London: 1913), James Butler, "Fernand Pelloutier and the Emergence of the French Syndicalist Movement, 1880-1906" (Ph.D. dissertation, Ohio State University, 1960), and Edouard Dolléans. Jacques Julliard is preparing a Sorbonne dissertation on the subject of which only small parts have appeared, *Clemenceau; briseur de grèves* (Paris: Julliard, 1965), and *Fernand Pelloutier et les origines du syndicalisme d'action directe* (Paris: Seuil, 1971). Minutes of the congresses of the CGT and Fédération Nationale des Bourses du Travail are available at the Musée Social. For a juristic account of syndicalist organization, see Maxime Leroy, *La Coutume ouvrière,* 2 vols. (Paris: 1913). Peter Stearns, *Revolutionary Syndicalism and French Labor: A Cause without Rebels* (New Brunswick, N.J.: Rutgers University Press, 1971), focuses on strike activity. On the syndicalist legacy see Val Lorwin, *The French Labor Movement* (Cambridge, Mass.: Harvard University Press, 1954), Annie Kriegel, *Aux Origines du communisme français,* 2 vols. (Paris: Mouton, 1964), and Robert Wohl, *French Communism in the Making, 1914-1924* (Stanford, Calif.: Stanford University Press, 1966).

Index

211